☞ **CARP'S WASHINGTON**

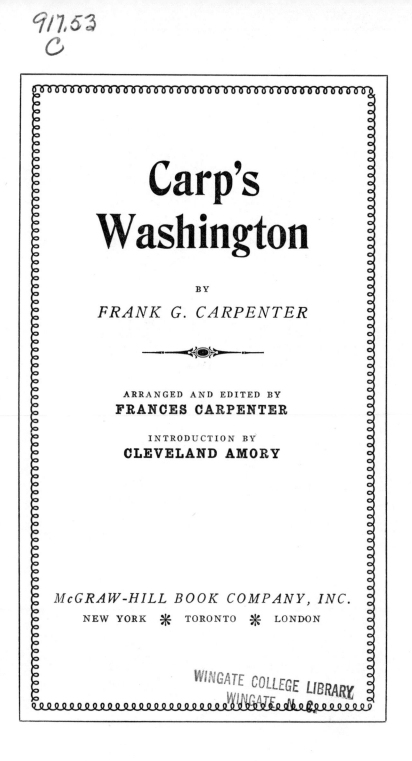

Carp's Washington

BY

FRANK G. CARPENTER

ARRANGED AND EDITED BY
FRANCES CARPENTER

INTRODUCTION BY
CLEVELAND AMORY

McGRAW-HILL BOOK COMPANY, INC.
NEW YORK ✳ TORONTO ✳ LONDON

CARP'S WASHINGTON

First Edition
10080

to

Carp's bride of the eighties

Joanna Condict Carpenter

who lovingly preserved his columns

in her scrapbooks

CONTENTS

FOREWORD

BY

FRANCES CARPENTER

The place is the United States; the period, the high old times of the eighties. As you sit in your antimacassared armchair of an evening, no radio or television interferes with your leisurely reading of your newspaper. No telephone rings, for you have not yet felt a personal need for this newfangled invention.

As you stretch your toes toward the blaze of your Franklin stove, you search your paper for its Washington news. You are interested above all else in what goes on in your country's capital, for history is being made there every day.

It is now nearly twenty years since the end of the Civil War. The trying period of the Reconstruction is only just over. The nation is sobering up after its postwar orgy of spending and extravagance, and is once more getting down to work. Industry is growing by leaps and bounds. Railroads are being consolidated. Financial giants—some say financial pirates—are abroad in the land.

In Washington the Republican powers-that-be are trembling before the displeasure of the voters. The Democrats are rejoicing in their sure hope of victory in the next election and the chance to try out their low tariffs. Civil Service Reform is a burning question, while the low moral tone of many government officials is an open scandal. The Senators and Representatives from your state are acting their parts in the colorful drama being played in the capital, and you are vitally interested in their performance.

On your parlor table there are copies of current magazines, but these are few and thin. You get your most vivid pictures of the contemporary scene from your newspaper, and of all its articles about Washington, you find the most lively are those signed with the pen name "Carp."

"Who's Carp?" you ask. Your question is answered by a certain syndicated article written in 1883 by another correspondent who signs himself "The Idler":

A good many persons have inquired of The Idler about the personality of "Carp," the correspondent of the *Cleveland Leader* whose stories are being copied more widely than those of any other writer in Washington. I can tell you that the gentleman is Frank G. Carpenter, whose father is a prominent banker in Mansfield, Ohio.

Carp is a slender young man, not more than five feet, eight inches tall, with a thin face, twinkling gray eyes, a small sandy mustache and unmanageable red hair. He is popular, overflowing with kindness and good humor, always anxious to do you a favor, or at least to say a kind word. Retiring and seeming slightly embarrassed, you would never take him for the brilliant journalist he is. Carp is a human dragnet. Everything is fish that comes in his direction, to be written of now or stored away for use later on.

As you read your paper you may think Carp's columns just a bit shocking with their gossipy anecdotes and their intimate personal descriptions of men and women in Washington. You will not find in them scholarly interpretations of Congressional legislation or profound analyses of the foreign policy of the United States. These matters, Carp believes, belong in the province of the editorial and political writers.

He writes, however, of everything else: of the Capitol and Congress, of horsecars and herdic cabs, of salons and saloons, and of the boardinghouse life so common in the days before the coming of the apartment house. In his search for news and human interest, Carp meets everybody, goes everywhere, sees everything. He pens for the average reader of the eighties a clearer picture than he has yet had of Washington.

In less than two years Carp's spectacular success as a correspondent places him on the top rung of the journalistic ladder. A few years more and he decides to leave the capital and try his luck as a correspondent roaming the entire world.

But it is with the young writer at the beginning of his career that we are concerned here. It is from his earliest columns, preserved by his young wife in scrapbooks now fast crumbling to bits, that this book has been put together by his daughter.

This is Carp's book. It is with him that you, dear reader, turn back your clock to visit his Washington of the eighties. You make your journey with a keen observer, who saw with his own eyes, and who wrote on the spot of what he saw.

Carp was there. And as you step into the past with Carp as your guide, you are there, too.

INTRODUCTION

BY

CLEVELAND AMORY

Out of materials that other reporters found too trifling, Frank G. Carpenter, in one of those ironies of history, wrought this most enduring and endearing portrait of his time. Between the wild seventies and the gay nineties came those good gold days of the eighties—complex, changing, seldom written about. But Carp wrote about them, with warmth, depth, and perception. Whether considering President Cleveland's love-life, the low-cut evening gowns of Washington hostesses, the Congressmen's spittoons, or women "enameling" themselves, Carp does so with a contemporary, present-tense style that brilliantly brings his era to life. His relaxed and discursive reporting reminds us of the late Ernie Pyle, although the only war involved is the Civil War, and that in retrospect. Yet here, too, Carp seems oddly contemporary, for the Civil War was the same number of years removed from Carp's Washington that World War II is removed from the Washington correspondents of today.

"Washington is like no other city in the world," Carp writes early in his book. "It is a living curiosity, made up of the strangest and most incongruous elements." And these very "incongruous elements"—the little asides as well as the Big News, the demimonde as well as the *haut monde*—are what makes this book, as Carp capsuled his city, a "living curiosity."

For thirty pages or so Carp discusses, as he calls it, "the little city on Capitol Hill" and its not always so capital Senators and Congressmen. At one moment he is concerned about an eight-dollar-a-yard velvet carpet, the next he comes within an ace of dropping a black blob of ink from his pen down from the press gallery onto the bald pate of the Senator from Texas, directly below him. He did not do it, but the point is, we feel he could have. For Carp was second to no reporter of his time when it came to taking his weapon in hand and pen-pointing a pretension.

From this informal, diary-like beginning we move on into a more orderly discussion of Grover Cleveland—how he got to the White House to begin with, and, once there, how he conducted himself. "What a big man President Cleveland is!" Carp gasps at the opening of one chapter. "He must weigh nearly three hundred pounds, and a line drawn through the center of his stomach to the small of his back would measure at least two feet." Again, Carp did not actually draw the line and measure it, but the important thing is we feel he could have. And since he is a reporter who dearly loves a good story, he then proceeds to tell one about the man who had "voted for lots of Presidents in my time" but "ain't never seen one before." We will not spoil the story by telling it here, but suffice it to say that no small part of Carp's reportorial technique is that he has as sensitive an ear for anecdote as he has eye for detail.

President Cleveland's marriage with twenty-two-year-old Frances Folsom, youngest First Lady of the land in White House history, is next on the bill of fare. Standing beside Carp in his front-row seat, we watch this fair lady from her first public reception when she produces "five thousand new smiles and no two alike" to her final days in the White House, when she retains to the end "her simplicity and her charm, her good sense and her dignity." From President and Mrs. Cleveland, we move on to the Supreme Court and, later, to the foreign legations in a day when the United States was considered only a second-class mission and foreign diplomats infinitely preferred the higher society hubs of Europe—Paris, London, Berlin, and Vienna. But Washington, too, has what passes muster in this regard, and Carp does not neglect what he calls the "only real cosmopolitan society in the United States." And cosmopolitan it must be, for Carp, one of whose chief charms is that he is never overcritical, says, in another place, "Lucifer himself will be welcomed if he will dress well, keep his hoofs hidden in patent leather, and his tail out of sight."

Carp's curiosity knows no bounds and seems to be almost equally infectious—whether he is writing on such ordinarily mundane subjects as Civil Service or the Washington Monument (a particularly enthralling chapter) or is exploring such byways as the literati, houses with pasts, or the odd types he presents in the chapter entitled "Curiosities and Cranks." For the book's dramatis personae are not only the Ulysses Grants, the Jay Goulds, the Ben Butlers, the Leland Stanfords, and the Susan B. Anthonys, they are also Indians, inventors, lobbyists, swindlers, actors, hermits, and even a curious character who lives in a tree. With all of them Carp is a prober. He goes himself to his story and, once there, writes it without personal intrusion and at the same time with his own personal slant. Besides his uncriticalness, he is also gently philosophical and often alarmingly accurate in his predictions. Indeed his harsh prophecy concerning the future of the "Jersey Lily"—Miss Lily Langtry—is remarkable because it is (a) one of the few extremely critical comments and (b) it turned out to be so wrong. On the other hand, one of the most touching paragraphs in the book, and the one which perhaps best illustrates Carp's ever-present concern with the passage of time, is the story of his call on the only surviving granddaughter of Thomas Jefferson —a lady to whom Congress had just refused a pension.

At the end of the book President Harrison has come to town, and a new and more sophisticated era has dawned. Mrs. Harrison has come too, and Carp says, a little wryly, "No dusty corner in the big mansion escapes her eyes." Neither, we feel, did it escape Carp's.

It remains only to note that we owe a debt to Carp's daughter for her part in bringing this long-forgotten material to light. Frances Carpenter has not only fashioned her father's reporting into a book that will beguile and astonish any reader, she has raised the pleasing possibility that, as a writer on Washington, Carp may once again become a household word.

CHAPTER I

The Season Opens

WITHIN the past two days the season of 1882-1883 has opened. The hotels are filling up, and scores of strangers are wearing out the soles of their shoes looking up comfortable quarters for the winter. Washington is a city of boarding-houses, and of all cities which charge extraordinary prices for very ordinary board, it bears the palm. Every man, woman, and company holding property here expects to feast off the newcomers. The city plans to make, during the few months of a session of Congress, enough to keep itself alive during all the rest of the year.

The coming season promises to be one of the liveliest, both socially and politically. Nearly every desirable house in the fashionable localities has been rented. New buildings are going up rapidly but the demand is far in excess of the supply. The rent for furnished rooms is fully one hundred per cent higher

1

than in Cleveland. The two in which I live are of moderate size, on the second floor of a three-story brick on F Street, near the Ebbitt House. They are fairly well furnished, and some Congressman or politician would gladly pay one hundred dollars a month for them. In my search for living quarters I saw others at forty and fifty dollars, shabbily furnished, and a full mile from the Capitol. These were without board, and so dreary that their occupants would be in danger of suicide from the blues.

The hotels are being refitted and repainted. The hotel men say they never saw a brighter outlook at this period of the year. They have received enough letters inquiring for rooms to have disposed of their whole space, and they predict that more people will be in Washington this winter than ever before.

There is little doubt that this is true. It is a new session of Congress with a change of party power. The Democrats have the House and it will be a long session. The lobbyists have already arrived in swarms. It is a session preceding a national election, and the politicians will be busy keeping their pots boiling.

The prices at the Washington hotels are much higher than those for private board. It would take the best part of a Congressman's salary to pay his board and whisky bills, if he did not take a room high up under the roof and leave his family at home. One New York Congressman paid last year six hundred dollars a week for his rooms at one of the hotels here, and his extras made his monthly bills run into the thousands.

The hotel scenes of the capital present many strange features. These are different at the different houses. The Arlington, on Fifteenth Street near the White House, is staid and quiet, high priced and eminently respectable. The Ebbitt, the Riggs, and the Willard are the homes of the politicians and the centers of gossip. Their lobbies and reading rooms are large, and filled every night from five o'clock until eleven with a crowd of politicians, statesmen, and strangers, all jabbering away about the Government, society, and public men. All classes, and all sorts of characters meet in the Washington hotel of an evening. Now a newspaper correspondent, his whole frame an interrogation point, comes in, looks over the crowd, glances at the register, and either stops to interview some statesman or rushes away to some other source of news.

The Westerners stay more at the National, the Metropolitan, and the other hotels near the Capitol. These houses have an atmosphere all their own, and their billiard rooms especially are worth a visit. I have seen fifteen tables going at one time in one hotel, and a hundred men, many of them Congressmen, sitting in a line on the chairs along the wall, watching the play as though they were Monte Carlo gamblers and had money to win on each stroke of the cue.

They use plenty of tobacco at these Washington hotels. The floor of an office is often made a general spittoon, where if one dropped a coin, he would want to put on a glove before picking it up. Our national habit of tobacco-spitting reigns supreme in these hotels filled with the Westerners. Their marble floors often look as though walnuts had been hulled on them and the stains left wet on their bright, polished surfaces.

In respect to the social relation, Washington is one of the wickedest cities of its size in the country. It is natural it should be so for the bulk of the population here are transients. They are away from home; most are far from their families; many have but few friends and acquaintances.

There are thousands of young unmarried people in the government departments whose work ends at four o'clock and does not begin again until nine the next morning. Time hangs heavy on their hands, and associations, not of the best, are often contracted to make it pass. The large number of unmarried men, or married men away from their wives—together with the fact that most of them have money in their pockets— make the capital a great resort for the demimonde. Many a female clerk, losing her position, devoid of family and friends, drifts into their number in order to keep body and soul together.

In no other city are such affairs carried on more openly. The following advertisements, which I clip from a half dozen issues of the *Star* newspaper, show that here no bones are made about them.

WANTED—A FURNISHED ROOM in a quiet family, for gentleman and lady; board for lady only; no questions. Address "Prompt," Star Office.

WANTED—ROOM BY A GENTLEMAN of elegant habits, stranger in the city, but located here for a year; would like room or rooms and board in home of a discreet young widow, where he can enjoy all the comforts of a home. Address, in entire confidence, G. R., Star Office.

WANTED—A PLEASANT FURNISHED ROOM, heated, to be used occasionally, where no questions will be asked. Address E. H., Star Office.

WANTED—By two sisters, two large unfurnished rooms, where no questions will be asked. Address E. H., Star Office.

PERSONAL—A widow lady desires a gentleman to assist her financially. Mrs. B. C., Star Office.

PERSONAL—A widow of culture desires the acquaintance of a liberal gentleman between 45 and 50. Address Mrs. L. Meredith, Star Office.

PERSONAL—A young widow desires position as housekeeper for a widower of means. Mrs. M. Smith, Star Office.

I might repeat a hundred such advertisements, for they appear daily in the Washington papers. Here, as in all big cities, the advertising sheets of the press are full of stories for those who read between the lines.

Washington is like no other city in the world. It is a living curiosity, made up of the strangest and most incongruous elements. There is a fairy-tale sense of instability about it. As with the palace of Aladdin which flew away in the night, one feels that this city could easily vanish and that he could wake up some morning to find himself stranded on the empty Potomac Flats. The city looks as if it had sprung up in a morning, or rather as if a whirlwind had picked up some great town, mixed the big houses up with the little ones, then cast the whole together in one miscellaneous mass, keeping intact only the city streets.

These Washington streets are the finest in the country. Broad and smooth, made of black asphaltum as hard as stone, they are kept as clean as your parlor floor. The street cleaner is a character whom you will seldom find out of Washington. He rides a great machine whose roller is covered with hundreds of stiff little twigs, arranged in a spiral. As the horses pull the machine along, the roller turns, and the broomlike twigs sweep the dust and dirt off to the side where they are gathered up and carted away.

I never saw such a machine before, and it could not well be used on other than asphalt streets. It makes a whirring noise as it goes along, raising a great dust, which is kept out of the air by the covering frame. Several such machines move daily over the streets here, with the result that Washington is the cleanest city in the Union.

But Washington houses are all jumbled together. A five-story palace that cost originally a million dollars rubs elbows with a shanty costing a few hundreds, just as the owner of the one crowds the owner of the other on the Washington sidewalks. The shanty says to the palace, "This is a free country. We are equals. You are nothing but a house. And all your fine trimmings make you no better than me; I am a house too. My master may be bigger than yours during the next administration; then perhaps I shall be built up, and you'll be sold for that mortgage which you know very well is now on your roof."

The small houses and the big ones are all equal here. So are the men. Fine clothes have little to do with making the man here in Washington, and the rugged Westerner, clad in his homespun, can get as good credit at the hotels as the New York dandy with his broadcloth coat and his diamond stud. The most simply clad are often the richest and the most powerful.

Editor Battelle, of Toledo, told me the other day that this city reminds him of one vast boardinghouse. Most of its people do not really live in it; they merely stay for a time. So it is that only a few own property, and that the renting class is so large. Thousands make their homes in suites of rooms, taking their meals in restaurants, or having them sent in by caterers.

The Washington caterer is a curious character. He is usually a colored gentleman, who supplies families and single boarders with meals at so much a month. Twenty dollars per person is the average price. For that he will bring your breakfast and dinner in a square tin box to your rooms, every morning and evening for thirty days.

The caterer's box is about two feet square. Fitted inside it are shelves of grated iron like those of the oven of a cooking stove. The box opens at one end and the victuals are placed hot on its shelves. The box then is closed tight for carrying, but although his horse trots fast, the caterer may have to come a long way, and the soup will often need reheating on your own little stove.

The dinner my caterer brought me last night was hardly up to the usual standard, but I had soup, roast beef and roast mutton, fresh lettuce and asparagus, macaroni, white potatoes and sweets, warm apple sauce, sliced oranges and lemon pie.

To my mind, this is not the most pleasant way in which to eat. Sometimes the coffee spills upon the beefsteak; the salt and the pepper get into the preserves or the sugar. Often a knife is forgotten, or a napkin fails to put in appearance. After trying a caterer for a week or so, the roomer often becomes disgusted. Then he goes back to the boardinghouse table of gossip, or takes refuge in one of the numerous restaurants which are found in every quarter of the city. Many a Congressman eats nowhere else.

Washington has the most reasonable streetcar system in the United States. There are two-cent, three-cent, and five-cent fares. I know of no other place where you can get about more easily. There are hundreds of horsecars, and the transfer system is such that you can go all over the city for one fare, or at the farthest for two.

Some of the streetcar scenes in Washington are as amusing as those in the theaters of another city. The greatest of the great ride in streetcars here. It is not unusual to find yourself wedged in between a Senator whose oratory brings thousands out to hear him, and a General whose deeds will live in history as long as time lasts. Today your companion may be a noted lawyer, tomorrow you may hobnob and chat, if you will, with a member of the President's Cabinet.

I rode home from the Capitol last night in a car in which there were half a dozen Justices of the Supreme Court. Off the bench, they are as jolly a lot of fellows as you could meet anywhere. They had left their gowns in the disrobing room, and they came into the car in overcoats and mufflers. Stanley Matthews, who led the procession, took his seat up near the fare box, and during the trip he bobbed up and down putting in fares and getting their change for the people behind him.

In addition to the streetcars, there is a line of herdic cabs in operation which charge the same fares and which carry great numbers of passengers. The first of these were small affairs with seats for six or eight. Large ones, longer than the biggest omnibus, have been more lately put into service, and they are both comfortable and elegant.

These herdics are boxlike compartments with glass windows and doors at the back, mounted on wheels. They are comfortably cushioned and handsomely finished in rich olive green. The driver sits up in front and handles his horses with skilled hands and a loud voice. To pay the fare each passenger walks to the front of the compartment and drops his nickel into a slot.

One of these herdic lines which runs from the Capitol into the fashionable Northwest section of the city, is more patronized by noted men than are the higher-priced private vehicles. The herdics, in all, carried 1,300,000 passengers last year. They are proving so profitable that a new line is to be put on within a few weeks. The smooth streets of Washington are especially adapted to such vehicles, which have surely come to stay.

The more expensive two-wheeled hansom cabs also roll over the Washington streets in great numbers. They accommodate two persons and their charges are seventy-five cents an hour, or twenty-five cents a trip. The driver sits on a small seat, high at the back, and looks over the roof of the cab. His reins stretch well above his passengers' heads to the horse's bit. The glass doors in the front of the cab may be opened wide so that nothing impedes the view of the thoroughfare.

There is a bill now in Congress which may give Washington a cable-car line. Such cable street railroads, I predict, will be largely used here some day. The climate is right for them. The magnificent distances of the capital call for them. When they come, they will bring suburban property in great demand, increasing many times the values of the outlying territories.

Last week I spent a few days in New York, in order to take myself out of the ruts of Washington do-less-ness, and to find out what the people of other sections of the country are thinking. Washington City is the poorest place in the United States from which to judge the temper of the nation. Its citizens have a different outlook on life than those of the individual states, and its atmosphere is artificial and enervating.

In New York everything throbs with the chase for the almighty dollar; you catch the spirit of intense energy which pervades every corner of the metropolis. In Washington often pleasure takes precedence over work. The surroundings tend to deaden, rather than quicken you into activity.

On Broadway a streetcar will not wait for you if you are not just at its stopping point. It goes on and you must stand there until the next car comes along. In Washington people a block away signal the cars by waving their hands or their umbrellas. Then they walk to the car at a leisurely pace, while the drivers wait patiently and the horses rest. I have seen herdics as well as cars stop for as much as two minutes, and no passenger objected.

In New York, if an eighty-cent legal-tender dollar of the past was rolled along the sidewalk, everyone on the street would make a rush for it. In Washington it would be watched with interest; the people would wonder why it was rolling and where it came from before they would make the effort to pick it up. In New York the chief talk is of money; in Washington gossip and great men are the leading subjects. In New York a fall in stocks sets all tongues buzzing; in Washington, if a bureau chief loses his job, the same result is accomplished.

New York is a city of things, as well as of money. Washington is a city of persons. A friend said to me today, "In New York you can see almost any *thing* you want to see, while in Washington you can see almost any great man."

Yet, on the whole, Washington is the pleasanter place in which to live. With all its great men, there is more opportunity for a nobody to become somebody than in the great whirlpool of New York, which seethes and boils, which keeps the poor and the moderately well-to-do at the bottom, and which allows to be seen in the foreground only those who have already made their millions or their fame.

CHAPTER II

The Little City on Capitol Hill

THE OPENING of Congress yesterday* presented the usual scenes of the first day of the session. The House came to order at eleven o'clock, and showed about one hundred of the chairs vacant. Upon many desks there were bouquets of flowers, gifts of admirers of the various lawmakers. The Chamber has been put into new clothing, and thirteen hundred yards of red Brussels carpet, ornamented with blue flowers, covers the floor.

The desks have been rearranged, and the three hundred and twenty-five members of the House now sit in a crescent made of two wedge-shaped rows of desks, running back from the Speaker's stand as a center. At their rear is a barrier of navy-blue cloth, hung on a brass railing. The little great men rise tier above tier, posing in their seats in various attitudes until, in

* December 4, 1882.

the back row, they can lean their august heads against the blue curtains.

Many of the Congressmen, especially the new ones, wear an air of great importance as they cast an eye now and then at the crowds in the galleries. They remind me of the Congressman who said "On my first day in the House I looked around on that magnificent body of men, and wondered how in the dickens I got there. But after I had been here a few months, I looked around again. Then I wondered how in the dickens those other fellows got there."

The galleries of both House and Senate were filled today, but they thinned rapidly during the droning of the clerks who waded through the reading of the President's message. Arthur's message is variously received here. His recommendation to remove all revenue taxes except those on whisky, is meeting objections, especially from the Western members. The people may be ready, they say, to have the tax removed from tobacco, but they will hardly consent to take it off beers and wines. Other members go further and favor a total abolition of the revenue tax system.

One thing is certain: No effort will be spared by the Republicans to reduce the internal revenue taxes, and to cut down the tariff list. But the Democrats will filibuster on any such bills, and only the Lord Himself can tell what will be done in the end.

The Capitol is a little city in itself, with a population of the busiest, wittiest, and brainiest men of all parts of the nation. Some of its citizens are aristocrats, some are plebeians. Some are millionaires, others paupers. Some are masters, some servants. The same differences in station to be found in every city are in this miniature city on Capitol Hill.

The chief street of this Congressional city is the main corridor of the Capitol, leading from the House of Representatives to the Senate Chamber. It is a long street, perhaps twenty feet wide, through which hurrying throngs of anxious people continually pass and repass. Little shops for the sale of photographs, candies, and newspapers are found here and there along this Main Street. A telegraph office upon it, midway between Senate and House, daily clicks out hundreds of business messages and tens of thousands of words of newspaper dispatches.

At the ends of the capital's Main Street there are always crowds of lobbyists, politicians, and strangers. The jostling, hurrying throng is a strange one. Now a newsboy darts in front of a Justice of the Supreme Court, a department clerk brushes against the wife of a prominent Senator, or a gawking sight-seer runs full tilt into the capacious stomach of some noted statesman.

The House of Representatives is the busiest and most important end of the street. Here, during the sessions, a dozen men of all classes may be seen, each with an anxious look in his eyes, and an I-want-something-which-I-am-afraid-I-can't-get expression on his face. Now and then one will send his card in to some member of Congress. Perhaps the Congressman will come out and speak to him. More likely he won't. I have often seen such cards torn to bits and thrown down on the floor of the House or the Senate.

One of these anxious men standing by a door looks like an Indian. He wears his black hair long, has prominent cheekbones and a complexion the color of fresh apple butter. I am told he is a professional lobbyist and that he has been here for years.

The House of Representatives could hardly be called a dignified body. As I make my notes, I see a dozen men reading newspapers with their feet on their desks. Of two Congressmen standing talking in the aisle, one has his hands in his pockets, and his head bobs to emphasize his words. Amos Townsend is sitting with his arms folded, looking into the future. And "Pig-Iron" Kelley, of Pennsylvania, has dropped his newspaper and is paring his fingernails.

Do Congressmen smoke during the session? Why, bless you, yes! I have seen ladies grow sick in the galleries from the vile odor of the tobacco that rises from the two-for-five-cents cigars in the mouths of the so-called gentlemen below. The Congressmen smoke in their very seats, and peer through wreaths of smoke to catch the eyes of members behind them.

They chew, too! Every desk has a spittoon of pink and gold china beside it to catch the filth from the statesman's mouth. It costs at least four hundred dollars a year to care for the spittoons of the House, even though your average Congressman often disregards his spittoon and spits on the floor.

The gallery floor is reached by marble stairs, supported by columns as fine as those of Hadrian's villa in Rome. But your admiration, inspired by their symmetry, changes to disgust when on each landing your eyes fall on a big rubber spittoon, surrounded by a yellow-brown ring of tobacco juice made by unscientific spitters. In every part of the Capitol, spittoons are to be found. If they were not emptied often, they would soon overflow.

The United States Treasury has the biggest spittoon on record. An oblong wooden box, as big as a bed, it is filled with sawdust. It lies at the foot of the four-floor spiral staircase, and the Treasury employes delight in squirting their juice over the marble banisters, down the stair well. Such target practice, they think, is a good game.

Ex-Senator Allen G. Thurman, of Ohio, told me the other day that he learned to take snuff from his old French teacher in the period when taking snuff was more common than it is now. Mr. Thurman, who has been a presidential candidate for years, always uses a red silk handkerchief, both for blowing his nose and for a polisher. From this has come his title "The Knight of the Red Bandana." At the Chicago convention this year his friends wore as their colors a red bandana handkerchief around their hats. They made the Palmer House a bedlam with their cheers for "Old Snuff," as they affectionately call him.

In earlier times there was hardly a man in the Senate who was not addicted to snuff. Henry Clay was an inveterate snuffer. There is a story that he once stopped in the midst of an argument before the Supreme Court and asked Chief Justice Marshall for a pinch of the sneezing powder.

Captain Bassett, the venerable doorkeeper of the Senate, tells me there used to be a snuffbox on the desk of the President of the Senate. One of the duties of the pages of the past was carrying pinches of snuff from that box to the different Senators. Bassett says he himself learned to snuff just by smelling his fingers after he had taken so many pinches to Henry Clay. Pages today still have trouble to keep from acquiring the same habit.

When Fillmore was Vice-President, he became disgusted with Senators running to his desk in the midst of a debate to get pinches from the snuffbox on the rostrum. So he instructed Captain Bassett to buy two snuffboxes and put them in recesses in the walls on each side of his desk. Full boxes are kept there to this day and in the incidental expenses of the Senate, you may see the item of the cost of the snuff which still is consumed. It is a small item now compared with that of the past, for there are only a few Senators who sniff the titillating powder today.

Only about half the Senators are now in their seats. Some are talking in the lobby, some are in the cloakrooms, some in their committee rooms. I doubt not that a number are eating fried oysters and drinking Bass ale or champagne in the restaurant. There used to be a bar in the Capitol, midway between the House and the Senate. It was known as "The Hole in the Wall" and in it drinking was done openly. Now, when a Senator wants a drink, he has to go down into the restaurant and ask for "cold tea." If he winks at the waiter, the teacup will be brought to him half filled with whisky. And the good temperance lobbyists never know the difference.

The bathrooms of the Capitol are well patronized this season. Fifty members of the lower House take a bath every day, so the bath superintendent tells me, and nearly every Congressman has a bath now and then at the expense of Uncle Sam.

There are nine bathtubs in the basement under the House, in rooms each as big as the ordinary hotel bedroom. The tubs are immense, too, so that the fattest man in Congress can roll about in them without grazing his elbows or bumping his knees. Some of these tubs, the ones made of marble, were installed at a cost of $175 apiece. In one a certain member of Congress was bathing one day when there was a roll call on an important bill. His vote was badly needed, so a page came to fetch him. Holding a blanket tightly around his dripping form, the Congressman made his way to the floor of the House, where his vote was counted just as though he had been clothed in the more conventional manner.

Senators and Supreme Court Justices are reported to use these Capitol baths as often as the Representatives. In the basement under the Supreme Court Chamber there is a new kind of electric bath. This, it is said, will make a dead man think. It is resorted to by such men as are very tired indeed, from overwork or over-drink, and want to put themselves into immediate trim for a debate or a speech.

A special police force guards the Capitol. In addition to the army of messengers and doorkeepers, there are a captain, three lieutenants, and twenty-one other officers in blue coats and brass buttons who march through this Capitol city and keep order among its inhabitants.

The officers tell me they have many strange experiences. Now and then they find a pickpocket at work, and they keep constant watch for the half-crazy cranks who drift in and out of the lobbies. Not long ago one of these lunatics caused a commotion by rushing into the Rotunda without a stitch of clothes on. He had slipped into the stairway leading up into the dome, and there disrobed. He came to the very center of the crowded Rotunda and posed, evidently imagining himself to be a Capitol statue. A coat was quickly thrown round him and he was taken away by the police.

At night the Capitol's interior is full of curious sights, and the weirdness of some parts is in sharp contrast with the glitter and brilliance of others. Descend into the crypt, or the basement, by the main corridor, and you look down a long arcade in which the gas globes which blaze at your end fade into stars at the other. The ceilings are low, the walls are massive, and the view is as ancient as the Serapeum at Memphis, which was built, as you know, long before the Congress at Rome criticized Antony's playing with that chief of woman lobbyists, Cleopatra.

A thousand gas globes light the brighter passages of this city on Capitol Hill. Their mellow light bathes the polished marble with a warm glow. The statues are vivified with it, and one can easily imagine these old statesmen opening their stony eyes and scowling at the hurrying, undignified throngs.

The paintings seem brighter and as the stranger goes up the Senate stairs, the bloody scene of Perry's battle on Lake Erie has a wonderful vitality. The Rotunda paintings are lighted with rows of globes across the top of each one. In the gaslight, Pocahontas loses her coarseness and George Washington his stiffness. The Rotunda itself seems larger, and the beauty of the dome in the soft light is impressive. The Pantheon at Rome is the only building in the world that will compare with our Capitol, and both are supremely beautiful.

A question often asked in the Senate Chamber, is, by day as well as by night, "Where does the light come from?" The room is perfectly illuminated with a mellow, soft light. Yet no gas jets, no lamps, no electricity are to be seen. Soon the eye reaches the glass roof of the Chamber, and then it is evident that gas light streams down through its frosted panes, brightening the coats of arms done in stained glass, and making the bald heads of the older Senators shine like rosy apples.

The light falls softly on the rosewood desks, shows every stain of tobacco juice on the eight-dollars-a-yard velvet carpet, and plays on the maroon leather of the empty chairs. Many of the Senators are out of their seats, and the light shows such piles of rubbish and torn paper under them as would make a Western Reserve housekeeper wild. The average Senator is by no means as cleanly as John Bunyan, and his habits of neatness will not bring him near to godliness—at least not during this session.

Outside, the Capitol at night is a magnificent sight. From its perch on Capitol Hill it is visible for miles, looking like some great illuminated temple or banqueting hall. Its hundreds of windows blaze with light, and a spiral flame of burning gas jets runs about its dome.

The view over the city from the Capitol also is impressive. Stand just above the fountain and look up at the great inverted bowl of the sky, dotted with sparkling stars. Then look over the city spread out at your feet. Long lines of light mark its broad avenues. Crescents and rings of gas flames show its numerous circles, and constellations like those overhead tell the location of its squares and its parks.

Pennsylvania Avenue seems like the Milky Way as it cuts through the darkness. The red lights of the streetcars, herdic cabs, and private carriages make one think of the will-o'-the-wisps of the Dismal Swamp. In the distance shine the lights of Burlington Heights in Georgetown, and back of the Capitol one may catch a glimpse of those of Alexandria, across the Potomac in Virginia.

Sometimes I think that the Capitol is too fine a structure for the men who have the right to seats in its Chambers. The average Congressman thinks himself a great man, but he is only a public servant, after all. He is paid by the people to do the everyday work of their Government, which is already well organized. We have now all the laws we actually need. If it were not for the necessity of formally passing appropriations, our country might do better without Congress than it does with it.

CHAPTER III

Characters of Congress

I AM SITTING in the press gallery of the Senate. The Senators, in their various degrees of disorder, are carrying on their usual antics in the great pit, known as the Senate Chamber, just below me. I jot down, as I look on, such items of gossip as strike my fancy.

As I write, Coke, of Texas, has come to the chair of the President of the Senate, and his great bald dome shines directly beneath me as I lean over the gallery rail. I reach out my pen; the ink quivers on its point; a moment more and a black drop would spatter that rounded whiteness. But such a disaster would set the Senate in an uproar, so I draw back my pen over my paper.

Nearly one half of today's Senate is bald. The parchment pates of the great men shine up at the press gallery, and I see

19

enough bare skin on their crowns to cover half a dozen bass drums.

Senator Joe Brown, of Georgia, is bald from forehead to crown, and the top of his skull is as level as that of a Flathead Indian. Circling his bald dome, the long iron-gray hair falls straight, then wraps itself into a thin roll which caresses his collar and looks like the haircut of a schoolgirl from the country. The Senator shaves his upper lip and his chin, leaving his luxuriant beard fastened to his lower jaw, like that of a billy goat. This beard contains enough hair to stuff a small pillow, and when Mr. Brown grows excited his only sign of emotion appears in his continual clutching of it.

Jones, of Nevada, has ten thousand dollars for every hair on the crown of his head. He would give hundreds if he could thicken the fuzz at the top, but hair is one of those things not bought with money, and like Senator Brown, millionaire Jones also consoles himself with a long gray beard. Senator Hoar, of Massachusetts, has very fine hair, but the spot at his crown is as bare as a billiard ball, and it is as white as Boston beans are before baking.

Luke P. Poland is the only relic of the old statesman of the days of Clay, Calhoun, and Webster. He still clings to the swallowtail coat, with the bright gold buttons which were used by all of the fashionable men of that time. It is cleaner and prettier than the Prince Albert or the cutaway of the present. In fact the dress of men has been growing simpler and simpler during the past century. Washington, who died in 1799, had ruffles on his sleeves, and half of the men who signed the Declaration of Independence wore powdered wigs. Jefferson sported knee breeches, and Madison was proud of his originality in having worn an inauguration suit of clothes of American make.

Daniel Webster usually chose a suit of snuff brown, with a large soft necktie. Martin Van Buren was fastidious, appearing during the summer in the whitest of white linen. His suits

were cut in the very latest style and he wore high stock neckties, which almost engulfed his standing collar. Andrew Jackson also dressed well, though he did not make his clothes a
great matter. Henry Clay wore a swallowtail, and a standing
collar, extravagantly high, and James Buchanan was precise,
always appearing in full dress.

Today half of our public men go about in suits as business-
like as those of a bank cashier. William Walter Phelps, with
all his millions, wears clothes which cost about twenty-five
dollars a suit, and he likes a red necktie. Lyman, of Massachusetts, wears a green scarf; Orlando Potter's gray clothes would
not sell for five dollars to a second-hand-clothes man; and the
black ones of Colonel Woolford, of Kentucky, are shiny with
age.

Carlisle and Randall wear little inch-wide neckties, and both
are generally dressed in black. Both stoop a little and neither
is very careful as to his appearance. Judge Reagan, of Texas,
appears in a black diagonal Prince Albert coat and a turnover
collar, while Perry Belmont's small frame is clothed in
closely buttoned black broadcloth. And "Calamity" Weller's
clothes are as rough and crazy as his brain. His wild-eyed
face usually looks as though it needed a razor, and his hair
stands on end.

George Hearst, the millionaire Senator from California,
has been represented as an illiterate man, but Senator Frye tells
a story that illustrates both his education and his humor. He has
not played cards with the bluffers of California for nothing, and
like most of his brother Senators, he is by no means averse to
a bet. Not long ago he entered a restaurant in San Francisco and
on the blackboard at the back of the bar he saw the word *bird*
among the items of the day's bill of fare. Hearst called out to the
keeper of the restaurant, who was a noted California character,

"See here, Sam, that's a devil of a way to spell *bird!* Don't
you know any better than that? You ought to spell it *b-u-r-d*."

"I would have you understand, George Hearst," replied the restaurant keeper, "that I am just as good a speller as you. I'm willing to leave it to the best scholar in the room that you don't know any more than I do. I bet you a basket of champagne that you can't spell *bird* the right way."

"Done," said Hearst.

"All right," said the man, "and there is a piece of paper for you to put it down in black and white."

He handed over a sheet of brown paper and with a stubby pencil Hearst wrote out the letters *b-i-r-d.*

"But," said the restaurant keeper in dismay, "you spelled it with a *u* before."

The Senator threw himself back and looked at the restaurant man with twinkling eyes. "Now, Sam," said he, "did you really think that I was damn fool enough to spell *bird* with a *u* when there was any money in it?"

The worst speller in Congress is an Illinois gentleman. He is a prominent Democrat, and the chairman of one of the leading committees of this Congress. A few weeks ago, in speaking of West Point, he characterized it as entirely too classical, and asserted that there was not a young man in his district who could pass its entrance examinations.

Congressman Belford, of Colorado, is on the same committee and recently when a question was being argued between the two gentlemen, Belford said he did not propose to be dictated to by a man who spelled Rhode Island with a small *r* and without the *h*. Mr. Belford made the same remark on the floor of the House when he was engaged in another discussion with the above-mentioned Congressman.

It is high time that the public should know to what he refers. It is to the following note written by this illiterate Illinois Congressman. There is hardly a correctly spelled word in it, and even the proper name is misspelled. *Col.,* I suppose means *colleague.* I give it verbatim: "My col. is pared with Mr. Balco of rode iland. If he was hear, he would vote i." Schoolboys who are ambitious to become Congressmen need not despair because they do not spell well.

A most villainous picture is being published in some country papers, purporting to be a likeness of Senator Vance of North Carolina. It is a libel on one of the finest-looking men in public life today. Senator Vance is a tall, broad-shouldered, handsome man of fifty-four years. He has a large, pleasant, open face, bright fun-loving eyes, and luxuriant hair and mustaches of iron gray. He is a popular man among his fellow Senators, and he can tell more good stories than almost any of them.

North Carolina is full of the evidences of Vance's liking for a joke. One day when he was Governor of the state, it is said, he was riding on horseback along a highway some ten miles from the capital. A stranger overtook him, and the two travelers fell into conversation. The stranger, who had never seen Vance before, said he had gone to Raleigh especially to see the Governor but that when he had called at his house, the Governor was not at home.

"Did you see the Governor's wife?" said Vance.

"Yes," was the reply.

"And did you not kiss her?"

The man, very much astonished, replied, "No, but she was very pretty and I should have liked nothing better."

"Well, I've kissed her," continued Vance, "and I never meet her but that I do." And thereupon, after enjoying the man's bewilderment, he told him he was Mrs. Vance's husband, the Governor himself.

When Mr. Jones, of Texas, came to Washington he was about as raw a specimen as ever struck the town. He was the typical Westerner of the stage. He wore a woollen shirt and rawhide boots, and he showed not a sign of a collar or cuff. His red cotton handkerchief was often in evidence, as it still is today.

Congressman Jones lived in a second-class boardinghouse. Up several steep flights of steps, his little back room was meagerly furnished and it had no modern improvements. There was no gas and its only light, except candles, came from a jet in the entry, through a hole in the door. With such surroundings and his long silence at the first of the session, the impression obtained that Jones was a nonentity.

But one day an exciting political discussion arose in the House and to the surprise of everyone, Mr. Jones took the floor. He made a most eloquent speech, commanding the applause and attention of both Republicans and Democrats. It was full of good sense and possessed a certain quaint, old-fashioned humor that took the House by storm. Since that occasion, Mr. Jones has had a different status. His Washington experience has already improved him. He now dresses like a civilized citizen and has lost much of his Western roughness. It is not every man who is improved by his experience in Congress.

Who has not heard of "Pig-Iron" Kelley? He is sitting in his seat there in the center of the House. It is the best seat in the Chamber; at least Mr. Kelley thinks so, for he has chosen it of all the others. Mr. Kelley is the oldest member of the House, and as such he is the only one who has the right to a choice of seats. The other members obtain theirs by drawing lots.

Mr. Kelley is very tall and very lean, being the nearest approach to a skeleton in all the House. He has a red face, grisly hair and beard, and blue eyes surrounded by rose-red eyelids. His shoulders are stooping, and he bends over as he sits at his desk. Though sixty-nine years of age, he is still strong and active, and he is one of the most indefatigable workers at Washington.

The most noted thing about Mr. Kelley is his monomania on the subject of the tariff. He has studied tariff all his life. He comes here as representative of the tariff interests at Philadelphia, which he has represented for the last twenty years. His constituents have implicit faith in him, and he will continue to represent them to the day of his death, I suppose. If America should ever go for free trade, Mr. Kelley would die instanter. His soul is so wrapped up and saturated with "protection" that its withdrawal would cause an immediate collapse. Mr. Kelley thinks tariff, talks tariff, and writes tariff every hour of the day; a roommate of his tells me that he mumbles it over in his dreams during the night. When he goes into society he backs women into corners and asks them their opinion of the duty on steel rails. Such a case actually occurred here a few nights ago, and though the lady informed him she knew nothing about the subject, he persisted in giving her his views at length.

Mr. Kelley started out as a jeweler, working five years as an apprentice in a watch shop in Boston. He afterward studied and practiced law in Philadelphia, where he served for ten years as Judge of the Court of Common Pleas. He was elected first to the Thirty-seventh Congress, where he showed such strong tariff predilections that Philadelphia has kept him here ever since.

"Richelieu" Robinson, of Brooklyn, is also a hobby-rider of national note. His nickname, "The Twister of the Tail of the British Lion," has made his hobby-riding famous. Mr. Robinson is a striking character. Dressed in black, with a bronzed face and bushy iron-gray locks like those of the Negro statesman Fred Douglass, he sits hunched in his seat, watching the actions of the House with his keen eyes. The Congressman is a little deaf, but he can hear the words "England" or "Ireland," even when uttered in a whisper in the lobby, and such sounds call him at once to their place of utterance. He denounces England on every occasion in the House, for his whole soul is wrapped up in the cause of Ireland.

Ireland is Robinson's native country. He was born fifty-nine years ago in County Tyrone and was educated at Belfast. He left school to come to America, where he graduated at Yale. He served under Horace Greeley in the first days of the New York *Tribune,* and forty years ago he acted here as its Washington correspondent, signing his articles "Richelieu." He has since been continually connected with the chief newspapers of the United States, to which he is still a frequent contributor.

I watched Richelieu Robinson the other day during the reading of his buncombe ironical resolution proposing that the United States buy Ireland and annex it. His gray locks quivered with ecstasy, and his ironclad features lit up with smiles of satisfaction, as the clerk rolled his tongue around the denunciatory words regarding England's tyranny and Ireland's oppression. He rejoiced all the way from the beginning of the reading to the close, then left the chamber feeling he had done his duty for the day.

Down in Brooklyn, the Irish really think Richelieu is going to buy Ireland himself some day. They say they will keep him in Congress until he accomplishes its annexation, and they look on this resolution as one step in that direction.

What a homely old fellow is Senator William M. Evarts, our former Secretary of State. He is by all odds the ugliest man known to fame. Thin and bony, with slightly stooping shoulders, he has a face far worse than Frank Blair's, who was once given a knife because he was the ugliest man in the United States. If Blair were living now, he could rightly hand that knife over to Evarts.

Yet, Evarts' face, with its big rough nose, its sharply protruding chin and wrinkled cheeks, is full of character, and his keen eyes are extraordinarily bright. Though now sixty-five years of age, Mr. Evarts is strong and healthy; he could, I believe, run again the foot race he ran down Thirteenth Street in the days of President Hayes, and I am convinced he would win today.

There is no man in Washington who enjoys a good dinner more than Senator Evarts. He is one of the highest livers in the capital. Notwithstanding the fact that he is six feet tall and that he does not weigh 125 pounds, he can eat all around Piletus Sawyer, who weighs 300 and has a stomach so large you could roll Evarts up like a watch spring and coil him inside it with room to spare. Once when he was speaking at an assemblage in New York, a late comer asked the name of the man on the platform. "What," he exclaimed, "that lean little thing Evarts? Why, he looks as if he boarded!"

Major Willian McKinley takes a prominent place in the Forty-eighth Congress. He is one of the finest-looking men in the House, of medium height, very straight, and well proportioned. His complexion is dark, his face closely shaven. His head is not unlike that of Napoleon Bonaparte, with high, broad brow, short black hair, and a heavy jaw. Major McKinley, now thirty-nine years of age, was born in Ohio, enlisted in the Army as a private and came out a major. At the close of the War he practiced law in Canton, where he married the daughter of one of the richest men in the northern part of the state. He has now been six years in Congress, having been re-elected last fall. His Democratic opponent, Major Wallace, however, is now contesting the vote count, and it may be that McKinley will be deprived of his seat.

In addition to his salary, each member of Congress gets forty cents a mile for the distance he travels from his home town to the capital, which pay ranges all the way from $3.80 for those whose homes are in Maryland or Virginia, to $1600 for the Territorial Delegate from Arizona. When it is remembered that the latter sum is enough to pay a steamship passage around the world, it seems a good deal.

Our Congressmen are each paid salaries of $5000 a year. There are 325 of them, and about 25 of that number are worth their salaries. Most could not make more than half as much by the sale of their talents in any other capacity. If some of them were forced to live by the sweat of their brows, outside of politics, I imagine that many of them would go on a low diet, and not from choice either.

Look over the men of your acquaintance. How many of them earn $5000 a year? Pick out 325 men from any part of the Union

—men whose brain and muscle alone are worth $5000 a year on the market—and I will show you that they are of a far higher grade than those making up the body of Congress.

How did these men get here? In various ways. Some bought their seats, it is charged, and some hold them through their friendship with great corporations. Some got them by drinking in barrooms to cultivate the slum voters. Some hypocritically slid into them by praying in the churches at the same time. Others hold their places by the favor of certain district rings, and the mainspring which runs the successful machinery of still others is the sending out of seeds and government documents to their farming constituents.

A few members of Congress are really great men, but these I can count on my fingers. A few more are noble and upright, and now and then you will find one who casts his vote for his country's good, and not just because it will benefit himself. Most of the others swell about and pose as great men. I suppose they feel great, except at election time when they drink, truckle, and bootlick to maintain their greatness. Congressional greatness—faugh!

CHAPTER IV

A New President Is Made

THE PRESIDENTIAL SITUATION continues to be food for gossip and speculation. Opinions vary as widely now as they did three weeks ago. Garfield's Secretary of State, James G. Blaine, is conceded by all to be in the lead as the popular Republican candidate, but with this concession there is generally coupled doubt as to whether he could carry New York. The popularity of Senator George Edmunds, of Vermont, is growing in certain states, but the boom for General John A. Logan seems to have stranded for the time at least.

"Robert Lincoln's position at the present time reminds me," said a classically minded Congressman, "of an election which took place in Athens before the days of Christ. Each voter was to cast two ballots for ruler of the city, one as first and the other as second choice. Every man in the city voted for himself as first choice but everyone voted for one great Greek—Themistocles,

29

I think it was—for second choice. The result was that the second choice became the ruler. Lincoln, today, is second-best choice for all. He may even be first choice of the convention. His name itself means the battle half-won.

"He would make an excellent President," the gentleman went on. "I have been watching him ever since he came to Washington to take a place in the Cabinet, and I don't believe there is a man in the country who is growing so fast or has such a future. I hear nothing but good of him. He is much like his father in his actions and thought, though he does not look at all like him physically. He can, like Old Abe, tell a good story, and he likes to illustrate his points with anecdotes."

President Arthur evidently desires a renomination, though I have yet to meet a man to whom he has expressed such a wish. He has not said so to the members of his Cabinet, I know, but he would hardly choose them for confidants anyhow. They are too close to other men, and they have too many axes of their own to grind. Arthur has given us a good administration, but it has been negatively rather than positively good. He has done well, in other words, by not doing anything bad. This kind of goodness does not count for much in presidential campaigns, and it is felt here by many not connected with the Administration that his nomination would be unfortunate.

The Republican Convention is over and the ticket with Blaine and Logan at its head is in the field. It needs no words to tell what will be the nature of the campaign. The names of the men who represent it are enough to show that the Republicans, this year, mean business, and that they propose to fight the battle for all it is worth. The Republicans of the rank and file of the party from all the states were for Blaine. The politicians were for Arthur, and the conservatives for the dark-horse candidate.

The candidate for Vice-President, General John Logan, is a man in the prime of life, with straight hair and heavy mustache as black as a crow's wing. His face is almost the color of an Indian's; his black eyes shine out from under heavy brows. He holds a leading position in the Senate, where he sits on the front row.

Logan is a poor man. I do not think he has any resources beyond his salary. He lives at a boardinghouse while he is in Washington, and there he spends most of the time when he is not in the Senate. If the Republicans win the election, his wife, who has a reputation as an accomplished society woman, will be the central figure of the next administration.

James G. Blaine is one of the best hand-shakers in public life. He seizes your hand, gives it a hearty shake, and holds it firmly and rather confidentially while he is talking. During his stop at Bellaire, Ohio, the other day, he was shaking hands from the beginning to the end of his visit, and crowds gathered around the depot, anxious to give him a parting look or grasp of the hand before the train left. He was leaning out of the car window, shaking the hands of those on the platform outside, when, among others, a pretty Virginia girl came up. Blaine seized her hand with his hearty grip. Almost instinctively and at almost this same moment, an old friend of his engaged him in conversation. Blaine began to talk, still holding the girl's hand, not noticing, I suppose, that it was not the hand of the man to whom he was speaking.

After about a minute, the affair began to attract attention. The girl attempted to pull her hand away gently but Blaine, who was engaged in animated conversation, only tightened his grip and talked the faster. At this, the young girl's lover who, with red face, had been standing back in the crowd, came up and, twitching Blaine's sleeve, pointed out to him what he was doing. The genial presidential candidate let go the girl's hand at once with a word of apology, and the blushing maiden was led away into the amused crowd.

The Democratic party is in deep water since the declination of its once-defeated presidential candidate, Samuel J. Tilden. It is floundering around, turning its eyes upon the various candidates still left in the field. A majority of the men I have spoken with regard Governor Cleveland, of New York, as having the best chance. Senator Thomas F. Bayard is one of the cleanest candidates spoken of, but he is too clean and too cold to get the nomination. Living on the line between the North and the South, he was too lukewarm to be a Rebel and too timorous to be a Union man. He ended up by being the worst cross known in American politics, a Copperhead, or Northerner sympathetic to the South.

Coming home from the Chicago convention, I rode with one of Grover Cleveland's most intimate Albany friends, and had quite a chat with him in regard to the Democratic candidate for the presidency.

"Mr. Cleveland," he said, "is one of the hardest workers who has ever sat in the Governor's chair at Albany. He lives all alone in the big Executive Mansion, except for his housekeeper and his servants. He eats alone. He seldom entertains company. During his term, he has not invited any lady to preside over the hospitalities at the Governor's mansion. The receptions, which he gives occasionally, are all stag affairs, no ladies being invited or wanted.

"I do not think Grover Cleveland cares much for the society of women," he continued. "If he goes to the White House, I imagine he will be a very uninteresting social figure. He might have his sister, Rose Elizabeth, with him, but she is rather a sharp-tongued young lady with a predisposition to Woman's Rights. Also, I understand that she and Grover do not get along too well together."

I heard an unlikely story yesterday about one of the speakers at the Chicago convention just after Cleveland was nominated. The statesman was supporting Cleveland's nomination. He began with a flowery eulogy, speaking of him enthusiastically as a great and good man, and working up to a climax, when he expected to pronounce the candidate's name with a flourish. As he reached the final sentence, he could not remember the name of the nominee. In agony, he turned to a man on his right and said in a stage whisper, "What is the name of the candidate?"

"Cleveland," was the reply.

"I don't mean the place he comes from, I want his name," said the speaker. It was a full minute before he could get it into his head that the name of the Democratic candidate also was Cleveland.

Belva Lockwood, the first female candidate for the presidency, rides down street on a tricycle every morning on her way to her law office. She was the first lady tricyclist here, but there is a tricycle club now formed that boasts among its thirty-eight members nine ladies, some of whom are expert riders. Any admirers of the beautiful can see, as she goes whizzing by, that Belva has a well-turned ankle, and I could inform the Woman's Rights voters that their candidate wears red stockings.

Miss Lockwood is not a bad-looking woman. She has blue eyes, a fair face that still knows how to blush, and gray hair which she combs tightly back off her forehead in a style such as one sees in pictures of Queen Anne. Belva Lockwood is fifty years old, more or less, and though Susan B. Anthony considers her young and indiscreet, her eyeteeth are so well cut that she manages to make a living at the law. The cases she takes are chiefly those of breach of promise and divorce, although at times she has made arguments before committees of Congress.

Interviewed regarding the presidential situation, this Equal Rights party candidate declares her case is hopeful. She is evidently enjoying her notoriety, now and then making speeches, and bowing to the crowds which greet her ironically with cheers and waving hats.

Another day has passed and the election is still unsettled. Probably at no other place is the suspense so terrible as here at the nation's capital. In Washington the Republicans, from the first, have acted like sensible human beings, as the reports have come in from hour to hour, now in their favor, now against them. They have not howled themselves hoarse over success, nor wept themselves blind over apparent defeat.

The Democrats, on the other hand, have acted like a gang of Mississippi bulldozers or New York hoodlums. They have gathered from Alexandria and the nearby Virginia and Maryland towns, and from the first reports in Cleveland's favor, they have taken it for granted that he was elected. They have asserted loudly that they believe an attempt will be made to count him out, and have uttered threats against those who say he will never be inaugurated.

To hear them talk you would suppose that the Southern Democrats here represent the leading element in the party, and that they can bend the American people to their will. They are the same set of old Rebel brigadiers which agitated the country in 1860. Last night, when they were raging round the streets with torches and red flags, they serenaded several prominent Democrats and demanded speeches.

One of these was Senator Vance, an ex-Rebel general, and another was Dick Merrick, the lawyer for the Star Route trials, and a noted Copperhead.

"I give this warning to the Republican National Committee," Merrick shouted. "Terror will follow any such proceeding as the seating of Blaine. Cleveland has been elected President, and he is to be inaugurated, peaceably if possible, forcibly if must be. If this Government cannot preserve the rights of the people, it had better be torn to pieces."

The Negro element in Washington's population is vitally interested in the election. There are sixty thousand of them, and although some are well educated and possess property, a great many are ignorant and indigent. Those who have jobs in the government departments expect to be put out if Cleveland is declared elected. The most ignorant hardly know what to think or fear. They crowd about the bulletin boards night and day, and their spirits rise and fall with each rumor they hear.

Some even fear they will be dragged back into slavery, for the worst Democratic elements have cruelly tried to foment this impression. One Democrat in a restaurant on D Street offered a bet of a thousand dollars to seven hundred on Cleveland and yelled that he had already purchased ten Negroes on the strength of the reports so far received. Many a former slave has spent the past three nights on his knees.

The preparations for the inauguration of Grover Cleveland go bravely on. The outlook is that more than one hundred thousand strangers will be in the city. Where they are all to be accommodated is one of the vexing questions of the moment. Cots are being put up in the boardinghouses, and various residences in all parts of town will be thrown open to the crowd. At Buchanan's inauguration, thousands walked the streets all night after vain attempts to get lodging. It will be strange if the same does not happen again on the night of March 3, 1885.

The coming ceremony will be, if not the grandest, at least the most costly inauguration in our history. There will be no Democratic simplicity about it. The ball in the central court of the new Pension Building will be a gilt-edged affair, and preparations will be made to accommodate thirty thousand people. There will be twelve thousand tickets, each ticket, I suppose, admitting two ladies and one gentleman. One hundred ball officers will act as floor managers, and fifty mail carriers in uniforms will have charge of the cloakrooms. Bootblack stands and a shaving room will be provided off the ball corridors. And the new Pension Building, with its acres of dancing floor, its hundreds of columns, and its three wide promenades, will give an opportunity for splendor and variety of decorations never before seen in America.

The supper rooms will probably be situated just off the corridors, where food will be furnished by the notorious Ed Stokes, the man who shot Jim Fisk and who is now the proprietor of the Hoffman House in New York City.

The ballroom will be lighted by electricity and by gas. Fifteen hundred large flags will aid in its decoration, and the Botanical Gardens will furnish flowers and plants. In addition to these which will be free, there will be other decorations variously estimated as costing from five thousand to ten thousand dollars. The music is expected to cost about four thousand dollars, and the price of the supper would make a deep hole in Mr. Cleveland's salary if he had to pay the bill. The sixty thousand dollars the ball managers expect to receive from the tickets will almost all be consumed in the expense of the party.

The outside walls of the new Pension Building are already completed. They run up seventy-five feet, and with a single range of office rooms, form a rectangular square about the great central court where the ball is to be held. Canvas will be stretched over these walls, making a temporary roof for the whole ballroom. A waxed floor will take the place of what is now mud, piles of brick, little mountains of sand, and small lakes of steaming mortar.

The whole city of Washington will be extravagantly decorated. The electric display will be a new feature in inaugurations, and there will be also a great number of calcium lights burning at different points. It is intended to have ninety-two of these at a cost of fifteen hundred dollars, and it is said they will burn for five or six hours. They will shine all around the Capitol, along F Street between the Treasury and the inauguration ballroom, and down Pennsylvania Avenue—in short, in all parts of the city where crowds are likely to gather.

The fireworks display also will be fine. Japanese pieces, consisting of large bombshells thrown from mortars, will explode high in the air. Others will throw out colored illuminated lanterns, each two feet in diameter, while still others will produce sparkling chains and blue dew, thunderstorms and moon dragons in combat, clusters of colored grapes, white shooting stars and chrysanthemums, and huge weeping willows. There will be fiery animals from six to eight feet in height—fishes, birds, elephants, deer, and oxen—all shining against the dark sky.

The fourth of March is over. Grover Cleveland has been inaugurated. A hundred thousand strangers have come to Washington to see the show, and at least a million dollars have been left behind them.

The day broke, clear and sunny, with the thermometer high enough to remove overcoats and cloaks. Tonight the moon has contended with the fireworks in a grand display of brilliance. No President has ever had a finer day for his coming in than Cleveland has; no President has ever had so many onlookers and so cold a reception.

The crowd began to gather shortly before daybreak. There must have been more than one hundred thousand who were not favored with tickets to the galleries of the Senate, and who stood and gazed at the outer walls of the Capitol, trying to imagine what was going on inside. The Senate met at eleven o'clock, with a handsomely dressed company of ladies and gentlemen filling its galleries to see the Vice-President sworn into office.

When this ceremony was over, all adjourned to the acre of platform set up on the east front of the Capitol. The platform was built over the Capitol steps, rising about ten feet off the ground, and its front and its sides were completely hidden by drapings of American flags. Upon this the President took his oath of office and delivered his inaugural address.

From the Capitol plaza a sea of faces looked up at the great man. They peered down at him from the roof of the Capitol, and some even climbed into the lap of the massive naked statue of George Washington, whose marble finger, pointed up toward the sky, seems to be denouncing those who leave him with his uncovered breast exposed to the wintry blasts.

Farther back, looking down the three avenues which lead from the east into the Capitol plaza, were rivers of soldiers in dress uniforms, ready to take part in the inaugural procession. Their bayonets shimmered in the sunlight, and the hues of their uniforms filled the eye with three long streams of glitter and color.

When the new President came to the front of the platform with President Arthur beside him, a weak cheering went up from a few throats. The people in the space about twenty feet square just in front of him, took off their hats while the President spoke. The crowd that had been in the Senate Chamber was with Cleveland there on the platform, and the majority stood on their benches while he delivered his address.

As the President began to speak, the crowd on the plaza began to move, and short as the speech was, half of them had departed before he had finished. Some parts of his address—the platitudes —were applauded, and there were a half dozen cheers when he made his Civil Service Reform utterance.

The Democratic leaders did not seem particularly happy. Their every action today has shown that they feel they have a white elephant on their hands. They are apparently uncertain whether they can rule Grover Cleveland as they would like.

The most surprising thing about this inauguration is the scanty applause which attends Cleveland's presence and actions. The Democrats in the city today numbered scores of thousands, but hardly a corporal's guard applauded him. The cold response of the crowds on the streets has been noticed by everyone.

The Democrats have come here to look over the man they have elected, rather than to honor him. They are not yet proud of him, and they are afraid of how he may conduct himself, for the charge that they have elected a Republican is current among their leaders.

CHAPTER V

The Clevelands in the White House

WHAT A BIG MAN President Cleveland is! He must weigh nearly three hundred pounds, and a line drawn through the center of his stomach to the small of his back would measure at least two feet. He is under six feet tall, has a great width of shoulder, and his flesh, unlike that of most fat men, is solid, not flabby.

Soon after his election, so the story goes, the President made a trip south. A large crowd of country people had gathered at a railroad junction to see him, hoping perhaps to shake his hand.

One tall, lank old fellow stared long and hard at the great man. Then he pushed through the crowd and grabbed Cleveland's hand.

"Well, so you're the President," he said, looking him up and down.

"Yes, I'm the President, my friend." Mr. Cleveland could not help smiling.

"Well!" the old man exclaimed again. "I've voted for lots of Presidents in my time, but I ain't never seen one before." He paused, then he laughed and slapped his side.

"Well, you're a whopper!" he cried, to the delight of the President as well as the crowd.

President Cleveland dresses well. His usual suit is one of black broadcloth, with the coat double breasted and tightly buttoned about his body. He wears good boots that always shine brighter than those of his callers. His linen is white and he puts on a fresh turnover collar every day. His favorite necktie is black, modest in its tie. The President knots it himself, and he does not require the assistance of a valet in making his toilet. He trims his heavy brown mustache himself and shaves the rest of his face with his own hands every morning.

This man Cleveland is a hard worker. He rises at half past seven each morning. And here I would pause to say that George Washington used to get up at four; Jefferson jumped out from under the covers when the sun's rays first fell upon the clock in his bedchamber. John Quincy Adams had taken a walk and a swim in the Potomac before the time of day at which Cleveland is out of bed. And President Harrison used to go forth to do the White House marketing long before half past seven.

As soon as he is dressed, Mr. Cleveland reads the daily newspapers, and at eight he is ready for his breakfast. This is not a large meal, and the woman he brought from Albany with him knows exactly what he likes. She cooks for him oatmeal, beefsteak, eggs or a chop, with coffee to wash it down. After breakfast with no exercise, the President goes directly to his office, where he looks over his private letters and answers a certain number. He seldom uses a stenographer for any purpose.

Next the President takes up the business of the day. Perhaps he has an interview with a Cabinet officer or the Chief Justice, or some other prominent person, before the stream of ordinary callers begins. Eleven o'clock often finds a hundred office seekers waiting to see him. The President listens to their requests, but he gets through with each one in short order. Then at about one o'clock he is ready for his lunch.

President Cleveland goes through his midday snack at the same rate as a Wall Street broker; it rarely consumes more than fifteen minutes. He then goes back to his office and to work. He grinds along until three o'clock, at which hour, rain or shine, he goes out for a ride in the White House carriage. Colonel Lamont, his private secretary, generally rides with him.

The President is fast exploring the countryside in the vicinity of Washington. Now and then he drives out in the direction of Secretary Whitney's country home, which, I doubt not, in the future will form a rendezvous for the President and his Cabinet. It is several miles from Washington, out of sight of the newspapermen; thus it would make an excellent place to talk over matters of policy, and to reconcile the differences between Bourbonism and Mugwumpism.

After his ride President Cleveland has dinner. This is a plain meal, sometimes with wine and sometimes without, after which on many evenings he goes back to work. If you cross the White House lot long after midnight, you will often see a light burning in the President's study. Grover Cleveland is the only President in our history who seems to need no amusements whatever.

The President is a Presbyterian, and although he does not attend church very often, he recently declared he could recite the Shorter Catechism from beginning to end. When Cleveland came to the White House all Washington was agog to know whether he would attend church at all, and if so which one. Members of the fashionable New York Avenue Church, whose pastor had been a schoolmate of the President, confidently expected that he would come into its fold. For the first two Sundays of the new administration that church was crowded; then on the third Sunday it was announced that Miss Rose Elizabeth Cleveland, the President's sister, had gone to an unpretentious Presbyterian church in an unfashionable part of the city. A week later came the news that the President himself had attended services there, and that with this obscure congregation his worshiping was to be done in the future.

Nobody in Washington was more surprised at Cleveland's choice than Dr. Sunderland, the minister of the First Presbyterian Church on Four and a Half Street.

"All through the campaign," he said to me shortly after the President's choice was made known, "I denounced Mr. Cleveland as an irreligious man. I wrote against him and talked against him. And now this man, whom I said was not fit for the White House, heaps coals of fire on my head by coming through my church door.

"Of course I was surprised," the fiery old man went on, "for the President knew well what I had done. Everybody in Washington knows that I speak plain truths as I see them. Before the War, my church was always filled to the very doors. But when I began to preach against slavery and secession, my Southern parishioners left and have never returned. My congregation dwindled, but I never gave ground. Some have gone uptown to churches in more fashionable neighborhoods. Others have left town.

"I could not refuse to receive the President, even if I wanted to, any more than I could refuse any who might wish to sit under my pulpit. You know how it is in Washington. Now, the President's being here will attract crowds. No doubt my church will be filled once again, and my collection plates will run over."

The true answer to the enigma of Cleveland's choice is not his wish to win the good will of the minister who disapproved of him. The facts are that years ago in Batavia, New York, Dr. Sunderland was the pastor of the President's mother. Miss Cleveland remembered how highly her mother had thought of this earnest young minister. It was she who sent to the First Presbyterian Church for its diagram and selected the presidential pew.

Many thought that the Christian element of the United States received a slap in the face when Grover Cleveland was elected President. His past career, it was stated, would form a bad example for the youth of the land, and many thought his election materially injured the standards of American morals. His present actions are not likely to change the opinions of the churchgoers. This morning he returned to Washington from his vacation, having spent the whole of the Sabbath traveling.

When the President departed, he went on a Sunday, and his Cabinet followed his ungodly example in taking the Lord's day for gallivanting about the country. It seems to be the rule for this Administration to travel on Sunday. President Cleveland did not begin to attend church until he had been several weeks in office, and he has not put in appearance in his pew more than one-third of the time. Like Bob Ingersoll, the fact that he is the son of a preacher does not seem to have benefited him greatly.

It is easy for the ordinary man to see the President. He enters the front door of the White House without being questioned, crosses the big vestibule to the left, then turns right and goes on up a flight of winding stairs. At its head he finds Colonel Loefler, a little, wiry, gray-mustached man, with twinkling black eyes, who for the last twenty years has carried visitors' cards in to the President of the United States.

The cards he handles form a curious collection. Those I saw today, for example, were of all kinds. Some were neatly engraved on heavy cardboard, with beveled edges, while others were rudely printed in highly colored inks on tinted paper. One I noted had the words "Chairman of the Iowa Central Committee" below the name. Another was penned by a woman's delicate hand, and a third looked as though a schoolboy had written it.

The guards who admit visitors to the White House and who take in their cards have a great responsibility. They have to size up each visitor and decide whether or not he is a crank. You can have no idea how many cranks come to Washington, and how they invariably go to the White House at the first opportunity. Often as many as a dozen a week are turned away, but now and then one gets in. Harmless cranks, such as Dr. Mary Walker, clad in her trousers and high hat, are known and admitted. But the unknown one may be dangerous, and he must be disposed of by strategy or force, as necessity dictates.

During Mr. Arthur's administration a number of such visitors said they had come because they "were willing to marry the President." The Honorable Jere Black used to tell that, when he was Attorney General under Buchanan, he often received letters from women whom he did not know, who wanted him to undertake negotiations by which they could marry the bachelor who was then in the White House.

The President's sister, Miss Rose Elizabeth Cleveland, is now the First Lady of the land. She presides over the White House, bosses the servants, and occasionally holds an afternoon reception when the public is privileged to go and see her. At such times she stands in the beautiful blue parlor of the Executive Mansion, with a number of the most fashionable court ladies of Washington around her. The public visitors who come to see her are marched past in single file, with policemen and ushers alert to keep them from stealing the bric-a-brac of the White House. They shake her hand, glance into her eyes, then march out again. At state dinners, she sits in the great dining room like a queen, but she has to smile unconcernedly when a backwoods Congressman, dressed in his long frock coat, eats with his knife or drinks the thin lemon water out of the finger bowl.

Miss Cleveland ought to have the say as to whether wine is to be served at these state dinners. From her late temperance letters, I judge she would prohibit it, but Grover Cleveland has been a free liver and it is hardly possible that he would agree.

The President's sister is the baby of the Cleveland family. She looks to be between thirty-five and forty-five years of age. She is a woman of medium size, with square shoulders and a short neck. Her complexion is sallow, but her features are intellectual. From a high forehead, little brown curls cover her head with innumerable ringlets. Miss Cleveland dresses plainly and she wears few ornaments. She is at home in the White

House, and has created a favorable impression in Washington.

As all the world knows, Miss Cleveland has lectured in public. A friend of hers tells me that shortly before her brother was nominated for the presidency, she gave a prayer in public in which she asked the Lord to make the next mistress of the White House a temperance woman. Could she have meant herself?

The report is that President Cleveland is to marry Miss Van Vechten. There is no doubt that the young lady has been spending a great deal of time at the White House, and it would be strange indeed if the President had not paid her some attention.

The gossip about the President marrying springs up with every new girl to whom he pays a compliment. I doubt not that there are a score of Washington beauties who have set their caps for him. Matchmaking widows do their best ogling when they are in the President's company, and since he has been in the White House a full baker's dozen of ladies have been reported as sure to marry him.

Miss Folsom, of Buffalo, was here last winter with her mother, and was fawned upon by many as the White House lady in prospect. A few years ago, it is said, Mr. Cleveland paid his attentions to Mrs. Folsom, the widow of his dearest friend and law partner, the late Oscar Folsom. Gossips go on to state that Mrs. Folsom is, like the Vicar of Wakefield, a monogamist, with a decided prejudice against second marriages. Cleveland next turned his eyes from the mother to her charming young daughter. Miss Folsom is fair to look upon, and it may be that she will yet come to the White House as its mistress.

Old friends of Cleveland, however, take you aside and whisper emphatically that he will never marry. They tell you—and how true it is I do not know—that the only woman the President ever really loved has been in her grave for twenty-five years or more. He met her, they say, when he was a schoolteacher in a small town in New York, when the down had just begun to show upon his lip, and when she was sweet sixteen. They loved, but were too poor to marry. Cleveland went west to make his fortune, and while he was gone, his sweetheart fell ill and died.

The President's matrimonial affairs are the chief topic of this week's gossip over the tea tables of Washington. Half a dozen people claim to have seen letters from the Folsom family, into which the President is said to be about to marry. Miss Folsom is a beautiful young lady of twenty-two, who last year graduated from Wells College in Aurora, New York. Last October she and her mother made a short visit to the White House, and they are now traveling in Europe.

Veteran know-alls of the capital say the wedding is to take place this summer. They report that Miss Folsom is laying in a Paris trousseau of extravagant dimensions. Others hint that Cleveland is footing all the expenses of this European trip. One or two can even predict for you just how the wedding will be conducted. They declare it will be a quiet affair, something like that of John Tyler, who rushed off to New York one night and was married quietly in one of the churches there. Cleveland will perhaps go off one day on his vacation, and at our breakfast tables the next day we will read the announcement that the President has been married and that there were no invitations.

Well, the presidential wedding is over, and the gossips of the capital will have to find another subject for their whispering. The quiet ceremony in the Blue Room of the White House yesterday, which made girlish Frances Folsom the First Lady of this land, was witnessed by only a handful of guests, relatives, and members of the Cabinet. The curious crowds, keeping vigil on Pennsylvania Avenue and at the railroad station, were disappointed, for the publicity-hating bridegroom outwitted them by leading his lady secretly out the back door. Under cover of darkness he took her to the train that waited far out in the railway yards. A locomotive filled with indefatigable reporters followed the bridal train, but police guarded their privacy in their honeymoon cottage in the Maryland mountains.

Frances Folsom Cleveland has now become a bright star in the galaxy of White House First Ladies. She has the good nature and tact of Dolly Madison, the culture of Abigail Adams, the style and vivacity of Harriet Lane, and a beauty greater than that of any of the ladies of the White House still remembered by the old stagers of Washington. During her two years as First Lady, Mrs. Cleveland has taken a larger part in our social history than any New Yorker who has presided over the Executive Mansion.

Mrs. Cleveland is the youngest woman who has ever entered the White House as its mistress, and the figure 2 seems to be her lucky number. She was twenty-two years of age when she became Grover Cleveland's bride on June 2, nearly two years ago. She has had a wonderful success. Her social career has been as surprising as has been the political one of her husband.

Coming to the White House fresh from college, she ran the gantlet of the Washington society critics, but her natural tact and beauty made her at once the most popular woman in the country. Generals and Admirals who had made their bows before the court ladies of Europe went wild over her virtues. Statesmen, and statesmen's wives as well, carried her praises to the remotest parts of the United States. The interest of the American people has been shown in the sale of tens of thousands of photographs, and today you will find her picture in nearly every home.

The First Lady looks tired now, for the season has been a hard one. She has done much to save the President, standing by his side at four great receptions, and making thousands of people happy with her beautiful smile and cordial shake of the hand. She has instituted a popular innovation in her noon receptions, held on certain days of the week for the benefit of the multitude of strangers who wish to meet the President's wife.

The National Woman's Temperance Convention, which met at Washington the other day, adopted resolutions "protesting against the immoral exhibition of the faces and forms of noted women as trade-marks and advertisements." It also sent out an appeal earnestly requesting young women to "refrain from wearing the décolleté style of dress because it is immodest and fraught with dangerous and immoral influences." During the convention a telegram was sent to Mrs. Cleveland, and a copy of these two resolutions will no doubt be forwarded to the White House.

The action of the convention calls attention to an annoying persecution of Mrs. Cleveland by the patent-medicine men, pill-peddlers, soap-makers, and other unscrupulous advertisers who send out circulars apparently sanctioned by her. Many people outside of Washington actually suppose that Mrs. Cleveland has approved them, and she is powerless to convince them of the contrary. Copies of such advertisements are received daily at the White House, with indignant letters of protest. Preachers write about them, mothers object to them, and whole communities are excited over them.

A copy of one of the most atrocious of these circulars was handed me by Colonel Lamont, the President's secretary, this afternoon. It charges that Mrs. Cleveland's beauty is due to the constant eating of arsenic.

"This," said Lamont, "is false from beginning to end. It is only a sample of many outrageous statements. Such things are exceedingly distasteful to Mrs. Cleveland. It is unnecessary to say that she has nothing to do with advertisements of any kind. She feels the responsibilities of her position as the wife of the President, and she has a right to expect the courtesy which is due it."

The advertisement referred to covers a whole page in the periodical in which it is printed. It is headed in bold letters "THE PRESIDENT'S TRIP" and below is the line "Mrs. Cleveland's Remarkable and Beautiful Complexion, How Such Lovely Complexions Are Best Retained." It begins with paragraphs about the presidential journey and then come these words:

"Many have been the remarks during the trip about the complexion of the First Lady. In fact some of her close personal friends have even gone so far as to insinuate that some forces other than those supplied by Nature were brought into use by Mrs. Cleveland. But of course all this was only conjecture. The secret of her beautiful complexion has at last been given to the wife of a General, famous during the late War, while the Presidential party was in St. Louis. It is simply the use of arsenic, which can safely be taken and which can be procured from the New York doctor whose name is signed to this advertisement."

This paragraph, which pretends to be an extract from an obscure New York newspaper, is one of the most libelous lies ever published.

But what can Mrs. Cleveland do?

She cannot enter suit and put herself on the witness stand. She evidently feels that noticing such slander would be beneath her. She has no other course than to suffer this outrage in silence.

New Year's Day has come and gone and another winter season has begun. From now until Lent begins, Washington will be mad with merriment. The wining and dining, the calling and courting will go on from noon until midnight every day in the week. There are churches in Washington, but the beaux and belles do not always frequent them, and Sunday afternoon and evening are popular calling times here.

The New Year's receptions passed off as usual. The pretty girls looked their prettiest, and the dudes called upon them in their Prince Albert coats with flowers in their buttonholes. The swallowtail is not considered proper for New Year's calling, even the President receiving in a double-breasted frock coat with a rose on its lapel.

The White House reception was gorgeous, gay, and giddy. The Executive Mansion never looked cleaner or grander, and since it was open to any who might wish to come, the crowd has never before been bigger. The dear people came by the thousands. Of all classes, ages, and sizes, of all colors, sexes, and conditions, they formed long lines reaching from the White House door around the paved walk all the way to the War Department.

I saw the colored citizen, resplendent in his glory, bumping up against the department clerk with a baby in his arms. In front of these two stood the fair young girl who might have been an heiress, but who was in fact a milliner. The President's callers filled the White House portico and there was a look of New Year's gaiety on most of their faces. Many were strangers going to see their President for the first time. To these, I doubt not, the event was one of the greatest experiences of their lives.

In the tiled vestibule the Marine Band, clad in gorgeous costumes of red and silver, sat along the Tiffany mosaic wall which shuts off the corridor. Professor Sousa was at their head, beating time for the musicians as the visitors passed.

I have never seen the President looking better. His face is rosy and his eye is as clear as that of a boy of twenty. Mrs. Cleveland appeared in full dress. Her diamonds shone and her silks glistened as she rustled through the corridor on the President's arm. I noticed that the President grew tired now and then, but it was not so with her. She had a fresh smile for every newcomer, and I can assure you it is no easy matter to produce five thousand new smiles and no two alike. I watched her as she shook hands with General Sheridan, who bowed to her with the grace of a diplomat, his hand lingering in hers perhaps a second longer than was necessary. General Sheridan is fond of ladies' society, and he is one of the most popular officers in Washington.

The Army, the Navy, and the diplomats were out in all their gold braid. There were fully five hundred thousand dollars' worth of pearls at this reception, and the sparkling diamonds could have been measured by the quart. I note that dresses this year are better made and costlier than in past seasons, showing the wonderful prosperity of America, whose people are the best dressed in all the world.

Of course there were shabby visitors, too, at the White House reception. One curious figure was an old woman in a black veil, who moved along with an ear trumpet about a yard long. This horn, of shining white tin, gleamed against her black veil as she held one end in her ear and turned the other end up to the mouth of the person she was addressing.

What a change has come over the President since he was married! From being almost a recluse where the fair sex was concerned, he has become now almost gallant. In his first days in the White House, the stories of Cleveland's brusqueness were legion, but now tales are told of compliments and attentions to his feminine visitors, and the ladies speak almost as well of him as they do of his wife.

Mrs. Cleveland has accomplished much in little time. Her husband now dresses faultlessly under her watchful eye. He has become gentler and more polite and even seems to enjoy the pleasantries of social intercourse. Instead of appearing to be bored with his state dinners, he apparently finds them agreeable. At the last big evening reception, he did not look straight ahead and plunge unseeing through the crowd as before, but stopped now and again to say a gracious word to one or another of his guests.

CHAPTER VI

The President's House

GROVER CLEVELAND'S boyhood was spent in the economical quarters of a poor parson's cottage. His early manhood was passed at Buffalo where he lived part of the time in the jail as its keeper and part in bachelor quarters back of his office, taking his meals at a Buffalo hotel. Then he inhabited the big gubernatorial mansion at Albany. And now he resides at the White House in Washington. He has had many different homes, but it is a question whether his last is more enjoyable than those which preceded it.

The White House, with all its comforts, is by no means a desirable residence for a quiet man. Its occupant has little privacy, and such moments as he has are always spent with guards at his doors, amid an unceasing clamor from those who want admittance but must be refused.

The President's every action is watched. Crowds come to his

back doors and peep into his kitchens. They interview his servants. And the good public has the right at any time to walk through his great palace and make their remarks about his furniture and the way he keeps house. Fully half of his dwelling is given up to offices so that he has his work always with him.

Grover Cleveland has to entertain, and at his parties, which he pays for out of his own pocket, he has to invite people for whom he cares not a straw, people who will eat his terrapin and drink his champagne tonight, then go off and plot to break down his reputation tomorrow. The position of the President of the United States is not an enviable one. His head, as it lies on the soft pillows in the second story of that great white palace, must rest as uneasily as that of any monarch in Europe.

Let us take a walk through the President's house. A doorkeeper with a face like that of a statesman, and a form which would have made him a member of the giant guards, had he lived years ago in Prussia, opens the doors. They turn silently on their hinges of polished brass and we step in upon the tiled floor of the great vestibule. The back wall of this vestibule, which is a mosaic of beautiful stones and colored glass, reminds me of the jeweled mosaic walls of the Potsdam palace of Frederick the Great, which cost a fabulous sum and which was built to blind the eyes of the other monarchs of Europe to the actual slender state of his purse.

Many of the stones in the wall in the White House vestibule are set in the rough, in beautiful shapes, looking, so one visitor remarked, like all the broken wine bottles of the White House, cemented together in patterns. Tiffany constructed this mosaic wall, and our Government paid well for it.

At the left is the entrance to the hall leading to the East Room, which is probably the largest parlor in the United States. Eighty feet long and forty feet wide, it was originally intended for a banqueting hall, but now it is used solely for receptions. The walls are of embossed paper of white and gilt, and the ceiling, beautifully finished in oils, is three times as high as that of an ordinary house. From its richly decorated beams hang enormous chandeliers, each one of which is made up of six thousand pieces of Bohemian glass, and cost five thousand dollars. When the chandeliers are lighted, the eight massive mirrors, set into the walls of the vast room, reflect the brilliant lights, which bring out the richness of the old-gold satin furniture and the beauty of the soft mosslike carpet.

Between these mirrors are some fine oil paintings, set, like the mirrors, into the walls. Gilbert Stuart's Washington, life size, which cost two thousand dollars, is the picture Dolly Madison had cut from the frame and carried away with her when the British invaded the capital. A little farther along is a fine portrait of Martha Washington, which cost three thousand dollars.

The Green Room, which adjoins the East Room, and the Blue Room and the Red Room are furnished like parlors, in the colors indicated by their names. Full-length portraits of the Presidents, including Arthur, hang on the walls of the long promenade upon which these rooms open, and at its end is the spacious doorway into the conservatory, which is filled with the plants and flowers of the tropics amid coral rockery. Here palm trees, orchids and ferns, roses of a hundred different varieties, lemon and orange trees bloom away while the wintry winds blow outside and the temperature stands at zero. During receptions, the guests wander with oh's and ah's into this tropical paradise, meeting at intervals the guards who keep watchful eyes upon their fingers.

The State Dining Room opens from the conservatory. Here all the official dinners are given, and oceans of champagne, herds of fine beeves, thousands of turkeys, boatloads of terrapin, and Great Lakes of ice cream have been swallowed year after year for more than half a century. Jefferson was almost bankrupted by his White House entertaining, Jackson spent upon it more than his salary, and no President so far, with the exception perhaps of Andrew Johnson, has come out of the White House with more money than he had when he first entered its handsome front door.

President Arthur's dinners cost him a fortune. He usually served at least fourteen courses, at a cost of more than ten dollars a plate, and since there were always about forty guests, each dinner cost him up to five hundred dollars. Multiply this by nine, the customary number of state parties in a season, and you have the salary of a Congressman for almost an entire year.

Good food, you know, tastes better off delicate porcelain than heavy crockery, and good wine has more flavor if sipped from cut glass instead of a tin cup. The china which President Arthur used for his state dinners was the elaborate set of a thousand pieces, representing American fauna and flora, which Mrs. Hayes had made by Haviland in France and which cost the Government fifteen thousand dollars.

The White House is truly beautiful, but amid all its magnificence there are many bits of the commonplace, and in spots it is actually shabby. As we came up through the handsome porte-cochere, we looked over the iron railing and saw the President's servants ironing his nightshirts and other unmentionable garments in the laundry of the basement. At the entrance, we wiped our feet on a straw-colored cocoa door mat, and in one of the oval glass windows of the handsome walnut front doors we noted a square of common tin upon which, in black letters, is painted "Open 10 A.M. Closed 2 P.M."

Even in the fine mosaic vestibule, we found a mixture of the grand and the cheap. Two rough door mats lie upon the rich mosaic floor. The varnish is cracked upon the grained woodwork, and beside the door leading to the second story is a walnut umbrella stand that would be dear at five dollars. The hall and the stairs that brought us to the President's offices are covered with an old piece of Brussels carpet which was good once, but which has been patched, sewed, and resewed. It would not bring fifty cents at an auction. Against the wall in the upper hall stand a couple of three-dollar wicker chairs, and over the desk by the stairs hangs a calendar bearing the advertisement of a railroad.

As we wait in the office of the President's secretary, we see that the only chairs, besides his own, are two red-painted ones which look as though they were intended for a lawn or a front porch. The room is carpeted with yellow Brussels carpet, and a twelve-dollar walnut desk serves for Arthur, the colored messenger at the door. In one corner, a little four-gallon black water cooler stands upon a cheap oilcloth mat. Under its spigot sits a tin slop bucket to catch the drippings, and over the knob at the top is turned a jelly tumbler with thick, ragged rim which serves as a drinking glass. There are china spittoons, and the furniture is upholstered in red leather.

The President's private office is a large room, at one end of which he sits behind his flat mahogany desk. As we look about us, I cannot help thinking of the history that has been made here, for this is also the Cabinet Room. I think of the various Cabinet meetings from the days of John Adams to the present. Here, in this very room, Andrew Jackson fought the battles of Peggy Eaton; here Martin Van Buren hatched his fox-like schemes; here Daniel Webster laid down his policy as Secretary of State; here the bony Calhoun stormed and Henry Clay counseled with John Quincy Adams. Here Lincoln made the plans which put down the greatest rebellion in the history of the world. There is hardly a figure in United States history who has not spent some of the most important moments of his life in this room.

Here, now, every week the Cabinet sits in secret session. The library that adjoins the room is now cleared and locked whenever a meeting is held. When Daniel Webster was Secretary of State, it was noted that the Cabinet meetings were reported in full in certain newspapers. Various means were undertaken to try to discover where the leak was, but without result. Then one day Webster happened to go out into the library to find a book. The other members of the Cabinet talked on as usual, and Webster discovered he could hear distinctly each word they uttered. So the leakage was found, and the room was thereafter kept locked.

The President's stables are half a square below the Ordnance Building on Seventeenth Street, just south of the White House, hidden in the White House Park by a big clump of trees. They are not wonderful in either structure or contents, although the building is a new one-story-and-attic brick, tastefully built. It has two wings running at right angles with the main building, the space between them forming a court or stable yard.

In these two wings, the presidential carriages are kept. What a contrast they are to the equipages of the past Presidents! George Washington rode on official occasions in a gorgeous state coach drawn by six horses. In his tours about the country he used four horses, and when he drove to church a prancing pair drew his carriage. His coachmen were always resplendent in a livery of white with scarlet trimmings. Jefferson used to go rattling across the country behind a four-horse team. President Arthur never drove anything finer than a two-horse rig, and his livery was of a dull mouse color with silver buttons. The church he attended was within a stone's throw of the White House, but he generally rode even that distance.

Many a man in Ohio has vehicles just as fine as those of President Cleveland, which show no glint of gold or silver trimming. His horses are just good plain roadsters, worth perhaps several hundred dollars apiece. I counted six in the stalls when I looked into the front part of the stable. These stalls are clean and well kept, and there is a fancy iron latticework, painted red and brown, which separates them one from the other.

What does the White House cost to run? Most people believe that the $50,000 a year which the President gets as his salary is the sum total. This is a mistake. The estimate of the amount that Congress is to appropriate this year lies before me, open at the page relating to the President. I see that in addition to his salary of $50,000, $36,064 is asked for him to pay the salaries of his subordinates and clerks. His private secretary is paid $3,250, his assistant private secretary $2,250, his stenogra-

pher $1,800, five messengers each $1,200, a steward $1,800.
The doorkeepers each get $1,200; there are four other clerks at
good salaries, one telegraph operator, two ushers getting $1,200,
a watchman who gets $900, and a man to take care of the fires
who receives $864 a year.

In addition to this there is set down $8,000 for incidental ex-
penses, such as stationery, carpets, and the care of the presidential stables. And further on, under another head, there is a demand for nearly $40,000 more. Of this, $12,500 is for repairs
and refurnishing the White House; $2,500 is for fuel, $4,000
for the greenhouse, and $1,500 is for gas, matches, and other
household expenses. The White House, all told, costs the country considerably over $125,000 a year. But this is a mere baga-
telle in comparison with the cost of the residences of the other
governments of the world.

Saturday afternoon in the White House grounds during the
summer reminds one much of the gay scenes of a Sunday in
the public gardens of the greater capitals of Europe. The lawn is
then filled with a well-dressed crowd as cosmopolitan as you will
find anywhere, and the big Marine Band, one of the best in the
world, clad in flaming suits of red and gold, gives forth the
finest music. The concert is free and all classes of people
may be found in attendance. Among the crowd, you will find the
best-dressed and finest-looking Negroes in the world. You may
run against a Treasury clerk or a Cabinet officer, and you may
admire the toilette of the chief lady of a foreign legation or of
pretty little peachy Miss Smith, whose father is a messenger in
the Treasury Department. The flowers, the trees, and the long
stretch of beautiful scenery away across the river beyond the big
white Monument, make a combination of which any country may
be proud. George Washington builded well when he laid the
foundation of our national capital on the banks of the Potomac.

At the White House yesterday afternoon the roof of the main
portico was cleaned by throwing a stream of water upon it. The

result was a huge shower of spiders. Thousands of these creatures, of every species, had collected under the eaves and in the nooks and corners, so that the roof of the portico was actually discolored by them. The water, sent with the force of an engine, brought them to the stone floor below, and soon perhaps a million of them had covered it.

All kinds of spiders, big spiders and little spiders, black spiders and green spiders, brown spiders and yellow spiders, rolled and tumbled and swam around in the water which to them was a veritable flood of Noah. The spider most common is called here the "presidential spider." It has a round, plump body, a fuzzy pair of gray and yellow feelers, and six shiny legs. These spiders are as old as the White House, and their presence here dates back to that day where the memory of man fails to go.

As evening drew on, the spiders began to crawl back to their old homes and for a time the white pillars were so covered with them that they looked as though they were painted black.

Spiders are not the only invaders of the President's house. Mice and rats have long been a problem, and each year, at housecleaning time, special efforts are made to exterminate them. They disappear for a while, but before long they are back again in increased numbers.

This afternoon, I stood on the White House lawn and watched workmen raking dead leaves into piles and taking them to the great fountain, where the water has been turned off for the winter. They were shoveling the leaves into the basin to make a warm cover, so they said, for the masonry. Weighted down with evergreen trees, this blanket of leaves keeps the bricks and mortar snug and warm.

Other spectators, even more interested than I, were several mangy dogs, which could not be driven away. They are only waiting for the workmen to finish, to burrow in under this coverlid for the winter. There they will remain until spring, and even after spring comes and the water of the fountain makes their home uncomfortable, they will slink about the White House grounds. These dogs are wise in the way of the dog catchers. Although their number is somewhat less than when I was here last, I counted six today. The yellow dog that took part in Garfield's inauguration procession came from the White House fountains, and many a dog tramp of the Washington streets makes his way here when night falls.

CHAPTER VII

The Honorable, the Supreme Court

WASHINGTON is again going wild over a lord. In this year of 1883 it is Lord Coleridge, the Chief Justice of England. His lordship arrived last night and was met at the depot by a committee of the chief lawyers of the capital, who conducted him to Wormley's Hotel. Here the most noble gentleman had nine rooms reserved, of which to took possession by writing his name in a scrawling, nervous hand on the register. He signs himself "Coleridge, London, England," giving no other name nor title, as is the custom of English lords.

Attorney General Brewster was among the first callers. It was he who presented the Secretary of State when he came in a moment later, and the three went off to call on the President. At the White House they spent a pleasant half-hour, then went back to the hotel to dine. At night they had a reception at the

61

Secretary of State's residence, and all day today the lord has been feted and carried about Washington with a crowd in his rear, taking note of his actions. Perhaps the most interesting scene of all was at the Supreme Court, when he took a seat beside Chief Justice Waite for an hour, thus sitting upon the Supreme Bench of the United States.

Never before has a stranger sat upon our Supreme Bench, though our Justices have several times sat upon that of England. The scene was an impressive one. The courtroom was filled with sight-seers. Long before the Justices came in every available seat was taken, and many ladies were among the audience. Inside the bar sat the lawyers, among them famed Benjamin Brewster with his frilled cuffs, posing beside "Squire" Merrick, whose red face, surrounded by a great standing collar, made me think of John the Baptist's head on a charger. Old Judge Swain was also there, and in addition a score of young green limbs of the law, who looked importantly about, for all the world as though the audience had come there to see them. Even the elder lawyers put on a few airs as they took their privileged seats inside the red railing, and the solemn silent Negroes who attend the door walked around with more dignity and pomposity than usual.

At just twelve o'clock the crier arose. As the old-woman-like set of judges came in, in their flowing black robes, he shouted out: "Oyez, oyez, oyez; all ye who have business with the Honorable, the Supreme Court of the United States, are admonished to draw near and pay attention, for the Court is now sitting. God save the United States and this Honorable Court."

Eight of the judges were present, Justice Field's absence in New York providing a vacancy for the Lord Chief Justice of England. The visitor was easily recognized by the fact that he was the only judge present without a gown. His black broadcloth contrasted strangely with those who sat in shining black silk gowns on each side of him.

Think of the greatness of the occasion! There, side by side, sat the Supreme Justices of the two greatest nations in the world. Each seemed to me a worthy representative of the country to which he belongs. I have seen it stated that Coleridge does not look like an Englishman. This is a mistake. He is English to the backbone. He looks English, acts English, and is English. Chief Justice Waite is just as much an American as Coleridge is English. He looks like a hardy, practical, common-sense American; Coleridge, a scholarly, refined, aristocratic Englishman. The two men are diametrically opposite. They have not a feature in common. Coleridge is a pronounced blond; Waite, a decided brunet. Coleridge has a long, thin, intellectual face; Waite has a broad, practical one. Waite's hair is heavy and of a dark iron gray; Coleridge has only a fringe, which is of a fine silvery color. Waite's dark face is covered with a heavy beard; Coleridge has no beard at all and his rosy face has a high forehead untouched by a single hair. He is as bald as Scipio Africanus, and his crown shines like a baby's cheek.

Lord Coleridge is, I should judge, much older than Waite. I think he must be overtired with so much fêting, for he took a cat nap or two while he sat on the bench. Coleridge is a very tall man, and his shoulders are round and thin. Waite has broad shoulders and is of medium height, inclined to stoutness. These two greatest judges in the world are modeled on different plans, and Nature took no two pieces of clay from the same pile in their construction.

An amusing story has been told about Lord Coleridge's visit to Mount Vernon. It is said that on his remarking that it was a wonderful feat for George Washington to throw a silver dollar across the Potomac, Senator Evarts replied, "Yes, my lord, but you must remember that General Washington could make a dollar go farther than anyone else."

This is one version, but there is another which I do not believe. It states that Senator Evarts' reply was much more to the point, and that he said, "Yes, Lord Coleridge, I do not doubt that General Washington threw that dollar across the Potomac. He was a man of great physical strength. You will remember that he performed a much greater feat when he threw a British sovereign across the Atlantic in 1776."

The new official year always begins with the reassembling of the Supreme Court. More than once have I been present to witness the stately proceedings. The Supreme Court is the most dignified body of our Government. Its meetings are held in the old Senate Chamber, situated midway between the House and the Senate, just off the busy aisle that connects them. Its atmosphere of quiet dignity forms a strange contrast to the hurrying throng which is continually rushing past outside.

Stopping in this crowded hall, where a bearded Negro guard sits, you push slightly on the swinging door. Another well-dressed Negro inside pulls a cord and the door slowly opens without murmur or creak.

You are now in the Chamber of Justice, and what a wonderful chamber it is! It might be taken for the council hall of a king. Its fittings are red, so dark as to remind you of royal purple. The seats for visitors are covered with warm plush, and extend around the back of the half-moon-shaped room. The Court is seated on the rostrum in front, fenced in with purple, their chairs resting against Ionic columns of gray and black marble. The Chief Justice is in the center. His chair is under a purple canopy, and a mammoth American eagle of gold, holding the words "In God We Trust" in its beak, looks down upon him with fierce eyes.

The Justices, in their black gowns, have a wise judicial aspect. They are all fat and rosy, and they sit half lounging in their chairs as though they knew they had a soft job for the rest of their lives, and proposed to enjoy it. They get ten thousand dollars a year and hold their office until they die.

In front of the judges, in a space as large as a fair-sized ballroom, sit the lawyers. They are not a distinguished-looking set of men, and it seems as if Mr. Small-Brains might easily gain admittance to their circle.

Of all the people in Washington just now, the Negroes are the bluest. The better-educated among them understand well that the Supreme Court's Civil Rights decision of this year 1883, does not remand them to slavery, nor materially take away any liberties they now possess. But they are disappointed because this recent decision practically voids the Third Civil Rights Act of Congress, which was intended to guarantee for them the social rights they so much want.

Now, innkeepers, managers of public institutions, railroads, and other public carriers need no longer fear penalties for discriminating against the Negroes in the matter of accommodations. The basis for the Court's decision is, of course, the fact that these are not property "civil" rights, and thus that they do not belong in the domain of federal legislation but in that of the individual states.

How should the ignorant among the Negro population understand anything so far above their heads? It is not strange that they are frightened by the Supreme Court's decision. They are, indeed, badly frightened. They are convinced that a dire calamity has befallen them. By night they dream of the return of the whipping post and the branding iron. By day they are eager to be reassured and to have their questions answered.

Last night at Lincoln Hall, the largest auditorium in Washington, there was not even enough standing room for all the people assembled to hear this subject discussed. Several thousand, among them this correspondent, could not get into the hall. Bob Ingersoll was one of the speakers and Bob is as popular with the Negroes as he is with his fellow infidels.

Another popular speaker among the Negroes is the Honorable John M. Langston, ex-Minister to Hayti. A few nights ago he gave an address on "The Status of the Negro in the United States," before an audience of two thousand persons in the Congregational church. They were, with few exceptions, all

Negroes, and they were as well dressed and as well behaved as any white audience. Needless to say, there were few among them with a good word to say for the Supreme Court and its recent Civil Rights decision.

In Langston's opinion, this Republican Supreme Court has acted both unwisely and unfairly, and he hopes that the Republicans in Congress will remedy the evil result in the next session. He says he has no doubts about his people's ultimate success, and he urges his audience to protest every infringement of their rights in hotels, on railroads, and in the courts.

Among the curiosities that few people see in Washington is the time-worn record of admissions to the Supreme Court. At my request the Clerk brought it from the great vault in which it is locked up, and handed me the first volume, an ordinary-looking black book about a foot and a half long and some six inches wide. On its back, on a red label, are printed the words "Supreme Court of the United States."

The book's parchment corners are worn. Its paper leaves are of a poorer quality than that of the account books of a corner grocery. Originally white, they now have a rosy hue which come from the ancient pink blotters that lie between each two leaves. These blotters are now almost white, their color having been absorbed by the porous paper of the book's ninety-three-year-old pages.

This book contains the very first records of the Court. The earliest date is 1790, in which year not a single admission is recorded. At the beginning of our Government, the Supreme Court had almost no business. It was not then, as now, considered any great honor to practice before it.

The first entry recorded the names of John Caldwell and Benjamin R. Morgan on February 8, 1791, and the next that of John Harte Lowell on August 8, 1792. There were no more admissions until 1794 when W. C. Ullels was admitted. Then there was a gap until 1801, after which entries came in more frequently. The first two pages include all admissions up to 1816, on which date I see the name of Artemus Ward, spelled with an *i* and an *a,* Artimas.

In 1823 one Alfred Conklin was admitted, though I doubt much that he had as lucrative a law practice as the great Roscoe Conkling has today. Beside the date, 1822, I see the bold signature of Alexander Hamilton, showing that he, the most noted lawyer of his time, did not see fit to enter the Supreme Court Chamber to argue a case until he was sixty-five years of age. He had no business before the Court during the first thirty years of its existence, although most of that time he was practicing at the bar. On the thirty-fifth page, I see Allen G. Thurman's name, and I find that in these thirty-five pages all the admissions to the year 1840 are contained. Those who appeared during the next forty years fill several volumes.

In this first book the oath is written, not printed, at the top of each page. It is short and precise: "I do solemnly swear (or affirm as the case may be) that I will demean myself as an attorney and counselor of this court uprightly and according to law, and that I will support the Constitution of the United States."

Everything about the Supreme Court is old. The Clerk's room and the consultation room are furnished with old furniture. The glass doors of the bookcases are lined with green cloth after the custom in the days of the Revolution. A great round clock, like a Brobdingnagian watch, hangs on the wall. The legend is that Judge Story, becoming disgusted with the differences in the time displayed by the watches of his associate Justices, said, "I will fix a timepiece which all shall go by." And he ordered this gigantic clock in Boston. It was well made. It runs to this day as truly as it did when Aaron Burr, Daniel Webster, and Salmon P. Chase set their watches by it.

In the consultation room, where the Justices put on and take off their robes, there are a number of portraits of former members of the Court. There is John Jay, in his black gown with the broad red facings—the old gown which it has been declared never existed except in the mind of the painter. This claim has lately been proven a mistake. A few weeks ago there was shown to the present members of the Supreme Court that very gown, which is now in the possession of Mr. Jay, the great grandson of the Justice, who now resides here in Washington.

Here also are the portraits of Chief Justice Taney, who rendered the infamous Dred Scott decision, of Chief Justice Marshall, and several others. His portrait shows Marshall to have been every inch a judge, a dignified man of large size and classic features. While studying his portrait by Rembrandt Peale, I was reminded of a story of his latter days which I recently heard.

It seems that religious discussions flourished in 1830, as they do in these days of Bob Ingersoll and Henry Ward Beecher. One of the most popular subjects of argument in the hotels and the coffeehouses was whether there actually is a God and a hell. One night a party of young lawyers were sitting about the fireplace in a Virginia inn, when an old man arrived in a broken-down gig. He was plainly clad, his knee buckles were loose, and he looked like an honest old farmer who cared little for appearances.

The stranger took a seat near the fire and sat silently listening, with the meekness and modesty of a child, to the discussion of the young bloods. They seemed to be settling all the great questions pertaining to this world and the next. At last one of them turned to him, and, winking at his companions, said familiarly, "Well, old gentleman, what do you think? Is there a hell? And do you truly believe there is a God?"

The old man then opened his mouth for the first time. The abashed jokers who had thought to have sport with him were astounded at his eloquence and his unanswerable defense of the Christian religion. He took up each of their arguments and demolished it. He discussed Hume on miracles, and led them far, far beyond their depths. Not a word further did they say, but when the old man went off to bed, they inquired of the innkeeper who he could be. To their amazement they learned that he was the great John Marshall, Chief Justice of the United States Supreme Court.

CHAPTER VIII

The Foreign Legations

L ITTLE IS KNOWN in other parts of the country about the foreign legations at Washington. There are twenty-nine of them, and among the men who compose them are some noted diplomats. They are not those of world fame, perhaps, for the United States is considered a second-class mission, our rating providing only for Ministers Plenipotentiary and not for Ambassadors.

Diplomats do not consider Washington the most desirable post. Located so far from other great capitals, many foreigners prefer assignments in Europe. In Paris, London, Berlin, or Vienna the court society is gayer, and it is a short jump from one country to another. In Washington the entertainments are not so many nor so elaborate, and if one is not happy here, there is no easy way of getting out of this country for a vacation.

The oldest Minister in point of service, the dean of the diplomatic corps here, is the Minister from Portugal, Señor Nogueiras, who has the rank of a viscount in his own country. With him are his wife and his daughter, the latter a fine musician and one of the leaders of Washington society, who takes charge of the fashionable amateur operas given here each winter.

Minister Nogueiras receives a fair salary, as do most of these foreign diplomats in our capital. The other nations pay their representatives far better than we do. Sir Lionel Sackville-West, K.C.M.G., the Minister from Great Britain, has a salary of $30,000 a year, while our Minister to England gets only $17,500. England pays her Ambassador to France $50,000, to Germany $35,000, and to Russia $38,000. In Turkey where our Minister, Sam Cox, is now getting $7,500 a year, the British Minister receives $40,000 for doing the same work.

Foreign countries, in many cases, own houses at the great capitals of the world, which they furnish and give to their representatives rent free. Sir Lionel Sackville-West lives in a mansion on the corner of Connecticut Avenue and N Street that is owned by the British Government. It is elegantly furnished, and he has a large allowance for entertaining. Sir Lionel is one of the most popular of the foreign Ministers. He has long been in the diplomatic service, having risen from the ranks to his present position. He is a modest, retiring gentleman, but he entertains in splendid style.

The German Government also owns its own legation, an old-fashioned double brick dwelling of three stories on Fifteenth Street, not far from the White House. The Minister is Herr von Alvensleben, who was assigned to Würtemberg when Sargent was United States Minister to Germany.

During some difficult negotiations here, his predecessor, Herr von Eisendecker, offended Bismarck by foolishly giving in writing to our Secretary of State some instructions which he had received from the German Chancellor. Bismarck intended that they should have been delivered by word of mouth, in order, I suppose, that they could later be denied by the German Government if that should prove desirable. Black and white does not lie, however, and these written instructions caused trouble. The result was that Bismarck recalled Minister von Eisendecker, and appointed Herr von Alvensleben, taking him from Würtemberg, a third-class principality. No doubt this was in order to show Bismarck's contempt for the United States.

The Mexican Minister, Don Matias Romero, has attracted much attention of late as the friend of Ulysses S. Grant, loaning him a thousand dollars when Grant's own countrymen failed to come to his support. He is a polished gentleman, a fine diplomat, and useful to his country. He receives five thousand dollars a year and has his rent free. During the Civil War he was here as Minister, and Grant and he have been acquainted for a long time, having had joint railroad interests in Mexico.

Minister Romero's wife is a beautiful American lady, a member of one of the old families of Philadelphia. The Minister from Chile, Señor Don Joaquin Godoy, also has an American wife.

The South American nations are well represented in Washington, but the attitude of the European diplomats toward their colleagues from Latin America has always been slightly patronizing. There is an invisible line drawn within the diplomatic corps between the representatives of the effete monarchies and those of the young republics of the American continents. Washington is not the only capital where this dividing line is to be found; it exists in all diplomatic centers, but it has been particularly evident here where the Mexican Legation is the social center of the Latin American diplomats. They usually mingle with the Europeans only upon state occasions.

By far the most talked about among the diplomats in Washington just now are the Orientals. The dozen almond-eyed young men attached to the Chinese Legation are in great demand at dinners and receptions, and the parties at their own brown palace on Dupont Circle are popular.

For the sum of eleven thousand dollars a year, the Chinese Legation rents one of Washington's largest houses, which has been called "Stewart's Folly," but which is more generally known as "Stewart's Castle." With its green lawn and shrubbery the Stewart mansion occupies a triangular point of land between Connecticut and Massachusetts Avenues, and some of the finest vistas in the capital extend on all sides of it.

The great brick pile, which is faced with plaster and painted a warm brownstone color, was built by the silver king, Senator William M. Stewart of Nevada. This accounts for its third nickname, "The Honest Miner's Camp." The architecture, the decorations, and the furnishings are extravagant. Gables and deep bay windows ornament the wings, and a pointed circular turret crowns the central portion of the house, giving it the appearance of the Rhine castle upon which it was modeled.

When I attended my first reception at this legation, I walked under the wide porte-cochere, up a short flight of steps, and into the huge circular hallway. I found myself under the central tower, with its galleries from which the sleeping apartments open. With a throng of elegantly dressed guests and my silk-clad Oriental hosts, I passed through spacious parlors, the banquet hall, and the ballroom. The conglomeration of portraits by unknown Western artists, of gold and satin-covered French furniture, of Oriental wall hangings and soft divans made me feel like a character in the Arabian Nights or like Marco Polo at the court of Kublai Khan.

The retiring Chinese Minister, Chang Tsao Ju, has been well liked in Washington. His entertainments have been notable, with their strange Far Eastern delicacies and their fragrant tea, poured from quaint wicker-covered pots. Ju is a great lover of society. With his nephew, Mr. Chin, to serve as his interpreter, he has paid afternoon calls as assiduously as any society matron.

The Minister is over sixty, but strong, and healthy, and good for many another post. Few have seen his poor little nineteen-year-old wife, except as she peers wistfully from the window of her cloistered apartment. I am told that not even the legation attachés may call upon her, and that when she goes out to take the air, she scurries into her carriage through a covered passageway.

Minister Ju is a picturesque figure in his blue and black satin robes, his round bonnet, and long queue. It will take many days to pack his extensive wardrobe into his sandalwood trunks and boxes. The gossips say that his clothes alone are worth a hundred and fifty thousand dollars. How many different pairs of shoes he has cannot be estimated since they are always of the same type: black satin, shaped like a junk, with heavy, thick, white felt soles. Minister Ju will be missed, but it is said that his successor is wealthy, and no doubt the legation will continue to be a center of Washington society's attraction and interest.

The new Chinese Minister will arrive in Washington this week. A great fuss has been made about his unfortunate reception in California. He has himself, it seems, made a mountain out of a molehill, in considering his temporary detention at the port an insult. Collector Hogan has been damned from one end of the country to the other, but the truth seems to be that the Minister was as much at fault as he. Upon his arrival in San Francisco, the diplomat was asked for his passport, according to regulations. Due to an error in Washington, Hogan had received no announcement of the Minister's coming, so that his request for credentials was in accord with the law. The Chinese Government, of course, was well aware of this.

Hundreds of rich Chinese citizens come to San Francisco each year, attended by large suites of servants. Many put on quite as much style as Minister Woon, so that Collector Hogan's mistake was a natural one. Woon has about as much cause to complain about his San Francisco reception as he would if a bank which he might enter without introduction or identification, should refuse to cash his check for ten thousand dollars, even though he declared he was a Chinese millionaire.

The presentation of the new Chinese Minister to the President yesterday was a splendid occasion, or rather the Chinese visitors made a splendid spectacle. Their ceremonial dress consisted of flowing silk robes, adorned with gold and silver embroidery. Under their red skullcaps, each topped with its button of official aristocracy, their black queues shone like jet. Their credentials, which were rolled in outside wrappings of gorgeous colors, were carried with great dignity and reverence.

The punctuality demanded by Chinese etiquette, however, was not observed in the White House. It was nearly a quarter of an hour before the President appeared, and the other groups of curious sight-seers could be cleared out of the state parlors. But when the Minister had been presented, and the ceremony was over, he departed with a pleasant smile on his face, apparently not at all disturbed by his wait.

Even more ceremonious, I am told, was Minister Woon's reception by the staff of the legation. There the kowtow was observed, all the members of the legation prostrating themselves on the floor before this new representative of their Emperor, the Son of the Dragon.

Chen Yen Woon is about fifty years old, vigorous and active, with the shrewd look of a man who knows his business well. His announcement that there will be sweeping changes at the legation, and that his young men will no longer ape the ways of the West, recalls some of the scandals of past flirtations.

Not long ago, so people say, a certain Oriental Prince, nominally an attaché of the Chinese Legation, fell madly in love with an American debutante who lives not far from Dupont Circle. His valuable presents she received graciously, but his proposal of marriage she greeted with laughter. "How could you suppose," she said to her Celestial suitor, "that I would marry a man who wore a pigtail?"

Next morning there arrived at her door a carved sandalwood box in which was coiled the Prince's precious black queue. By this unprecedented act, he had renounced not only his rank but his country, and all for a girl who laughed at and scorned him. What happened? No one knows. Some say his body was seen hanging from a window in the legation. But the legation is Chinese territory, and the police had no right to make an investigation. Whatever took place, the poor Prince was not seen again in Washington.

At the Chinese Legation, the Secretary insisted there was no truth to the story. "Any one of our attachés could marry an American girl any time he chose," he declared. "We have trouble in keeping the Washington debutantes out. They come here in crowds just to see the attachés. No doubt they succeeded under the former regime, but Minister Woon will not permit it now. The story was probably started by some of the disappointed ones who have not been welcomed in the legation."

Washington ladies are delighted to learn that some of their number have been received by the wife of the new Chinese Minister. She greeted them in her boudoir on the second floor of Stewart's Castle, toddling toward them on her three-inch-long bound feet, and clad in handsome silken robes of pink, lavender, green, and blue. Tea and cakes were passed, but the conversation could not have been very sprightly since the Minister's wife does not speak English, and the only medium of communication with her is smiles and bows.

I am told that this little Chinese lady is curious about this strange foreign city, and that her husband is gratifying her wishes so far as he is able. Just now he is looking for a lion. His wife wants to see a real lion. The stuffed lions at the Smithsonian Institution have been suggested, but only a live lion that will roar and lash its tail will do for her.

The Korean Legation has been the sensation of the week in Washington, for this is the first time that country has sent a permanent delegation here. Coming direct from San Francisco, they have registered themselves as a legation, spelling their country's name with a *K* instead of a *C*. They burst upon the capital in gorgeous costumes whose splendor dims even that of the Chinese. Their yellow complexions, their many-colored silk robes, and their intelligent faces are the wonder of the natives. All Washington society wants to be introduced to Minister Pak Chung Yang and his suite. The American Secretary of the Legation, Dr. H. N. Allen, tells me that the mission will be lodged in a house near Scott Circle. As soon as the legation is furnished, the Korean wives will welcome calls from the ladies of Washington.

There are ten Koreans in the legation, and their rank can be told by distinctive details of their dress. The Minister is set apart by the gold button and little white feather on the side of his hat. His head is never seen uncovered except perhaps by his wife and his servants. He twists his long hair into a tight topknot, then covers it with wrappings of finely woven black silk. Upon this rests the tall black top hat, made of woven horsehair, which every Korean man wears, and a string of gold beads under his chin holds his hat in place.

Minister Yang's hat looks like one of Oliver Cromwell's time, though it is three times too small for his head. All the Korean hats seem too small, but that is the fashion in Korea, I suppose. The Korean man never cuts his hair. Until he is married it hangs in a braid down his back. Thereafter he coils it up on his head. From their headdresses I judge that all the members of the present legation staff are married men.

I wish I could describe the appearance of Minister Pak Chung Yang. As a rule the Koreans are not very tall, and he is a small man. His black, almond-shaped eyes are set under a broad forehead on either side of a straight, rather fat nose, and a sparse imperial beard adorns his chin. The Korean Minister dresses in silks. He first puts on breeches long enough to reach to his armpits, but these are so fastened at the waist that they hang loosely in folds. Then comes his jacket, and over this he wears a long flowing silk gown of a delicate hue. When I saw him last, his costume was violet, white, and green with a dash of crushed strawberry, with the gown neatly fastened with a bow at the front. He had Chinese shoes on his feet and his legs looked as though they were closely swaddled.

The Minister is now forty-seven years old. He is one of the very rich men of Korea, owning a number of palaces, and rice plantations that cover many square miles. He keeps several hundred servants. Like all these Koreans, he has but one wife, and he left her in his own country.

The ladies of the Korean Legation have at last made their debuts into Washington official society. They have succeeded in throwing off their homeland's restraints, which demand that they be kept in seclusion. Everyone in Washington has been curious to see them, and their appearance behind their lords and masters at recent receptions has caused a sensation. They are pretty and dainty in their curious costume, which consists of broad white breeches tied at the ankles like those of Zouaves. These breeches are cut like an old farmer's broadalls, save that the point of division begins at the knee. A short jacket of pale-colored silk tops these baggy white nether garments.

These Korean ladies do credit to the teachers who have been laboring with them over the intracacies of Western civilization. They have learned to speak English, and the other night at the reception at the legation they seemed entirely at ease.

The rumor that these legation ladies are concubines, and that the true wives were left in Korea, is false. It is true that, by old Korean custom, the real wife usually remains at home to look after the household, while the Number Two Wife, or concubine, goes with the husband as the companion of his travels. It is true, also, that the Minister's wife did not accompany him. But Dr. Allen informs me that the other legation ladies are the actual wives of the other officials, and that Washington hostesses may calm their doubts.

At the Japanese Legation, on N Street near Vermont Avenue, foreign customs and even foreign dress have long since been adopted. The Minister's wife dresses her hair and chooses her gowns after our fashions. Only the Chinese women bind their feet, and both the Koreans and the Japanese move easily and gracefully through Washington drawing rooms. Now that Japan and Korea have led the way, there is talk of the Chinese Government's permitting the wives of its representatives to follow their lords into official parlors. But the Chinese ladies still take their airings in closed carriages, and few people have yet seen them face to face.

It is curious that here in the capital of the United States there are many patches of land which do not belong to this nation, but to other nations, some of which are many thousand of miles away. All legation properties are considered foreign soil, and thus are removed from the laws of our land.

The United States may not condemn and repossess them, as is the case with other real estate here. No one may set foot upon them without permission of the legation officials, officers of the law not excepted. Not long ago when a policeman caught sight of a burglar entering the second-story window of one of the European legations, he himself broke the law when he rushed inside the house to apprehend him.

Then there is the matter of the personal immunity from arrest of all these foreign diplomats. Not long ago a certain Minister bought a thousand dollars' worth of fine clothes in New York, and ordered them sent to him c.o.d. by Adams Express Company. They were taken in at the legation, but pay was refused. Since there was no way to sue the Minister, Adams Express Company was just that much out of pocket.

Now and then the younger attachés make use of their immunity to run heavily into debt, some so heavily, indeed, that they become *persona non grata* and have to be sent home. The United States Government rarely interferes, however, in minor cases, on the ground that the tradesmen, knowing of this immunity, should look out for themselves.

A secretary of a certain Latin American country has been a flagrant offender against the laws of the District of Columbia. Night after night he paints the town red, visiting the variety theaters, becoming fighting drunk, and raising Hail Columbia. At first, when the police tried to arrest him, he pleaded immunity. Finally, however, they got the better of him. They now pretend they do not know who he is, and they lock him up for the night on the charge of disturbing the peace. Then they release him the next day with abject apologies.

Generally speaking, however, the foreign diplomats are well behaved. Such offenses are rare. The most evident breaches committed are, perhaps, in the matter of fast driving, the dashing young diplomats lashing their horses to a far greater speed than the law permits to other Washingtonians.

A young Russian may be seen almost any fine afternoon, driving a galloping stallion hitched to his droschky, and one of the second secretaries of the British Legation has a playful habit of riding his horse across the sidewalks to the very doors of the shops. In both cases the helpless policemen simply shrug their shoulders, knowing it would be useless to protest.

The chief restraining factor is that a young man who wants to make a career of diplomacy, does not wish to be declared *persona non grata,* nor to have a black mark placed on his record. Thus this question of diplomatic immunity is annoying rather than productive of serious damage.

CHAPTER IX

American Diplomats Abroad

LEVELAND has chosen the aristocrats of his party as his Cabinet officers, and the ordinary Democrats are left out in the cold. Thomas F. Bayard, his Secretary of State, who hates the Negro, never sits down to dinner in anything less formal than a swallowtail coat and a white necktie. His family has the bluest of blue blood in their veins, and I doubt not that the English *Book of Heraldry* has a place on their parlor table.

Lucius Q. C. Lamar, Cleveland's Secretary of the Interior, has also a distinguished ancestry, his fathers and forefathers having all been kid-gloved officeholders. Secretary of War William C. Endicott boasts that his pedigree goes back to the eminently respectable Governor of Colonial Massachusetts who burnt the witches. And even Postmaster William F. Vilas, from the wilds of Wisconsin, has a grandfather to whom he can point with pride.

80

In the President's selection of foreign ministers the same rule has been followed. Men have been chosen who have impressive genealogical trees, in most cases men whose ancestors have been important in our country's history. Edward J. Phelps of Vermont, who is named Minister to Great Britain, has one ancestor who was exiled from England for acting as the Clerk of the Court which sentenced Charles I to death. Phelps himself is known in Vermont as the aristocrat of his party in that state, which charge was used against him on the stump during his candidacy for governor some years ago.

Then there is George Pendleton, "Gentleman George," the aristocrat of aristocrats, the man whose body is nourished by terrapin and champagne, whose grandfather was Hamilton's second in his duel with Burr and an intimate friend of George Washington. George Pendleton's grandfather was a Federalist with the most patrician of tendencies, but he went back on his ancestral training in his youth and joined the Democratic party. The leopard, however, cannot easily change his spots, and Pendleton today, is so much a Republican in feeling and actions that his party in Ohio has practically repudiated him.

George H. Pendleton is now about sixty years old, and his health is perfect. One of the finest-looking men in the Senate, he stands as straight as a Lake Superior oak, his large head thrown back, his chest well to the front, and his paunch rising in a billowy swell under his closely buttoned coat. A line might be dropped down his back from the crown of his head and it would touch the heels of his brightly polished boots. He carries himself with great dignity, and his blue eyes smile in courtesy and his face shines with the oil of suavity when he meets a friend.

Senator Pendleton is wealthy. He has a house just off Scott Circle which is worth, I should say, more than fifty thousand dollars. His home in Cincinnati, with the large tract of land about it, could be sold for several hundred thousand dollars. Mrs. Pendleton is the accomplished daughter of Francis Scott Key, of Baltimore, the author of "The Star-Spangled Banner." With her the Senator has for years kept open house in one of the pleasantest homes in Washington. When "Gentleman George" goes to Germany as our Minister, it will not be his first trip abroad. At eighteen, in 1844, he sailed for Europe and made a two-year tour of the continent such as few Americans of that day had accomplished.

Sunset Cox leaves for Turkey today. The mail carriers of the city presented him with a magnificent gold-headed cane a short time ago. This cane is the most beautiful walking stick I have ever seen. Its staff is of ebony, its handle a crook representing an eagle's head and neck in carved gold. Two rubies form the eyes and the eagle's bill is hooked.

The initials of Minister Cox are S. S. but they do not stand for Sunset. His name is Samuel Sullivan Cox, and his nickname is the result of his facile pen. Years ago, shortly after he became editor of the *Ohio Statesman*, in Columbus, Sam Cox wrote an elaborate, sophomoric description of a very fine sunset. He waxed eloquent and effusive in lauding the beauties of the evening sky, so much so that the other editors commented upon the article with ridicule. They referred to him often thereafter as "Sunset" Cox, and the name stuck. Sam Cox can take a joke, however, and he likes the sobriquet.

The Secretary of State is absolutely right in asking that the dignity of our most important diplomatic representatives abroad should be raised to the status of an ambassador. This proposal will probably bring forth once again the cheap hue and cry about the "simple dignity of American citizenship," about the "foolish pomp of the effete monarchies," and so on *ad nauseum*. But the United States owes it to its citizens that their representatives at foreign capitals should have a rank equal, at least, to that of the diplomats of lesser powers. It would be less humiliating for us to give up this diplomatic business entirely than to continue to conduct it so that we appear to be a third-rate power in the Congress of the Nations.

Congressman Richelieu Robinson, the tail-twister of the British lion, is bound to keep himself before the public. His last move as to regulating the dress which United States Ministers shall wear in the courts of Europe, is a great stroke, and will satisfy his Irish constituents that he is doing his duty. It is a small business, and Congress may have sense enough to let it die without action.

The general idea of the diplomatic service is that it is a soft berth for wealthy young men who enjoy court society. Congress seems to have little idea of the real duties and obligations of a minister to a foreign country. They do not reflect that, in many cases, treaties are made over a tea table as well as in a council chamber. The minister who represents his country well should be not only a statesman, but a person of social culture and education such as gives him equality with any courtier in the world.

Robinson wants our ministers to wear "the simple dress of an American citizen." What is the simple dress of the American citizen? Is it a Prince Albert coat and breeches cut high at the instep? Is it a colored shirt with breeches held up with a belt strap? Is it a short cutaway, or a half roundabout? Or is it a steel-pen swallowtail, which makes the wearer look like a Shanghai rooster?

Richelieu Robinson wears a swallowtail when he goes to parties here, but in Congress he puts on a Prince Albert. I think he wants our ministers to wear a swallowtail, the same dress worn by court servants all over Europe. An American minister so clad might easily be asked to perform some menial office by those who have not been introduced to him, and who perhaps have not realized that the American citizen is equal to any king.

Mr. Richelieu Robinson's resolution has not even the virtue of being original. This dress-for-a-minister question has been raised many times and small men have made capital of it as

Richelieu does now. Marcy, who was Secretary of State in 1853, at the time Buchanan was Minister to Great Britain, sent a circular to all our legations, directing them to appear at Court in the "simple dress of an American citizen." The announcement fell like a bomb into the United States offices abroad, and a large amount of correspondence ensued.

The Minister at Paris wrote that he thought it would not seriously impair the relations between the two countries; the Berlin Minister obeyed the order; Buchanan reported trouble with British protocol; and August Belmont, who was then at The Hague, wrote enthusiastically that he had even danced with the Queen in this "simple dress of an American citizen."

The dress question hung fire in London for five months. There were no Court levees until Parliament met, and Buchanan absented himself from its opening. In the London papers it was reported that the matter of dress was the reason for the American Minister's absence. At the Queen's Assembly this month, Buchanan appeared in a swallowtail coat, with the addition of a small dress sword. He created a sensation, but was well received. He describes the reception in a private letter to his niece, Harriet Lane, dated February 24, 1854:

"The dress question, after much difficulty, has been finally and satisfactorily settled. I appeared at the Levee on Wednesday last in just such a dress as I have worn at the President's one hundred times. A black coat, white waistcoat and cravat, and black pantaloons and dress boots, with the addition of a very plain black-hilted dress sword. This last is to gratify those who have yielded so much and to distinguish me from the upper servants. . . . I knew I should be received in any dress I might wear, but could not have anticipated that I should be received in so kind and distinguished a manner. As I approached the Queen, an arch but benevolent smile lit up her countenance, as much as to say "You are the first man who ever appeared before me at Court in such a dress. . . ."

So ended the trouble in England.

The American Embassy in France also reported trouble.

Henry S. Sandford, of Connecticut, was Secretary of Legation, but he was for a time also acting as chargé d'affaires. Sandford was a stickler for American dress, and he resigned when Minister Mason, newly arrived, went to Court in a coat embroidered in gilt, with a sword at his side and a cocked hat under his arm. This invention of a Dutch tailor in Paris was borrowed chiefly from the livery of one of the attachés from a minor Continental court.

Six years later, after Mason had left, Sandford still had this matter of clothes on his mind. From Connecticut he wrote to Cass, then Secretary of State, that the new Minister to France, Faulkner, should have his dress dictated for him before he departed.

"Some of our Ministers abroad," Sandford wrote, "conform to the instructions of June, 1853, some consult their own individual notions as to the dress that is most becoming. One, to my certain knowledge, has the constellation of our Confederacy embroidered in emblematic stars on the collar of his coat. Another adopted the uniform of the United States Army, still another that of the municipal Controller of Paris—a black velvet suit with rich embroidery. One Minister has all his buttons fashioned after the National Shield, with spread-eagle attachments, and I hear of still another proposing to have a gorgeous suit manufactured out of the Star-Spangled Banner."

The idea of clothes making the minister dates back to Ben Franklin, who appeared in citizen's dress at the courts of Europe about the time of the formation of our Government. Later ministers did not follow his example, and in 1817 American diplomats wore "a blue coat lined with white silk; straight-standing cape embroidered with gold; single-breasted coat with straight or round buttonholes, slightly embroidered; buttons plain or, if they can be had, with the artillerist's eagle stamped on them, i.e., an eagle flying with a wreath in its beak; cuffs embroidered in the manner of the cape; white cassimere breeches, gold knee buckles; and a three-cornered chapeau."

Picture, if you can, how our ministers then looked! I cannot! But this habit was continued, I think, until the days of Andrew Jackson who prescribed the following change in the interest of economy:

"American Ministers at foreign courts shall wear a black coat with a gold star in each side of the collar near its termination, the under clothes to be black or white at the option of the wearer; a three-cornered chapeau de bras, with a black cockade and gold eagle; and a steel, ornamented sword with a white scabbard."

CHAPTER X

Washington High Life

THE EXTRAVAGANCES of the past social season would make Andrew Jackson turn over in his grave, and the economical soul of John Adams quiver with indignation at the wicked waste in the circles of Washington's high life. President Adams could not have swallowed his oatcake and lemonade if he had read about a luncheon like that given by Mrs. Senator Stanford, at which Pacific Coast ladies ate from china plates that cost a hundred dollars apiece and drank tea from a pot of solid gold.

The dinners of Washington could not be more expensive if their pepper and salt were grains of gold dust. They make one think of the Roman epicure, Apicius, with his banquets of nightingales' tongues. Just to glance at their bills of fare is to make your mouth water.

Mrs. Stanford's luncheon took two and a half hours to serve. Its twelve courses consisted of raw oysters, consommé in cups, baked bass and potatoes, macaroni, roast beef and tomatoes, Roman punch, brown squab, salad, olives and cheese, fresh strawberries and cream, charlottes, ices, coffee and sweets! Still, it was only a luncheon. The dainty eaters put it all away quite easily, in spite of their hearty breakfasts and the fact that their dinner is their main meal.

At the dinner that Secretary of the Navy Whitney gave for the Honorable Joseph Chamberlain and Sir Charles Tupper recently, many courses of English, as well as American, dishes were featured. There were English hares, dressed with truffles and mushrooms, and American wild turkey, stuffed with roast chestnuts. The terrapin was served in small silver saucepans, with long handles and removable silver lids, engraved with a W. Then came cheese soufflé, canvasback duck, ice cream, café mousse, and coffee.

It is not in their food alone, however, that these Washington dinners are remarkable. The serving and preparation of the table are quite as important. At state dinners at the White House the table is a veritable bouquet, both cook and gardener proving themselves to be artists. The cook sculptures his figures in sugary confections; the gardener creates monumental floral decorations. Corsage bouquets are always found at the plates of the ladies, and not long ago these were all orchids, which are by no means a poor man's flower.

Take the decorations at Mrs. Leland Stanford's dinner for Mrs. Grant! The center of the table was covered with an old-gold satin scarf, bordered with blue plush, and embroidered with patterns of begonia leaves. Along the table were silver vases filled with Jacqueminot roses, and tall silver candelabra, for each of which a silver brick was consumed in the making. The names of the guests were on cards upon which were painted the flowers of California.

At a recent reception at Mrs. Senator Hearst's, the walls and mirrors were draped with rose-colored silk, and the mantels were decorated with poinsettia blossoms and Annunciation lilies. In a doorway between the parlor and the ballroom there was an umbrella covered with California moss, sprayed over with carnations, with a pendant fringe of gilded cypress cones. In the back parlor, the mantels were draped with Nile green silk, held up with bunches of silver and gold pine cones, with pampas grass suspended in the center.

The hall and the library were filled with palms and calla lilies, and the tower room off the main parlor was fragrant with roses on tables and stands. And yet the man who owns this house began life in poverty. I doubt not the day has been when he thought the prettiest flowers in the world were the potato blossoms on his father's farm in Missouri.

A curious feature of the wining and dining of Washington is the craze for giving entertainments of special colors. It is not necessary that these hues should match the dress or the hair of the hostess. A Senator's redheaded daughter might, of course, have a white tea in honor of the horse which is supposed always to accompany her. But seriously, these colored dinners, luncheons, and teas are worthy of comment. I was invited to a pink tea last week, to an orange reception the week before, and I have even attended blue and purple affairs.

Not long ago Miss Bacon, the daughter of Representative Bacon of New York, gave a red luncheon at which the shades of the candles and glass globes were red, the bread and baked potatoes were tied with red ribbon, and a cushion of red tulips formed the centerpiece. The souvenirs were Japanese bonbons with dwarf red roses springing from their tops. Even the ice cream was red, in the form of strawberries in little red candy hampers.

The most elaborate of all was the violet dinner which Mr. and Mrs. Roswell P. Flower gave last night. There were violets everywhere, and violet color predominated in the decorations. Bowls of the fragrant purple flowers were set on the mantels, and even the fireplaces were filled with masses of stevia and violets. On the center of the damask tablecloth, on a strip of old Duchess lace, stood a filigree silver basket overflowing with purple blossoms. A broad violet satin ribbon ran in a zigzag pattern up and down the long table, while great heaps of violets at each end proved to be made up of corsage bouquets, one for each lady, with her name painted in gold on the long violet ribbons which tied it. The cheese straws and cakes were tied with violet ribbons, and the entire dinner service was of violet and gold. The only variation was in the men's boutonnieres, which were lilies of the valley and Jacqueminot rosebuds.

An innovation at the recent luncheon of a Western representative's wife has caused much comment. The hostess placed before each guest a little cup filled with red, white, and black beans, announcing that the one who guessed nearest the correct number would receive a prize. Mrs. Stanford, who guessed two hundred, won.

The cost of entertaining is constantly on the increase here in Washington, and the days when a Congressman could entertain like a prince on his five thousand a year have long since gone by. Today you cannot get any kind of a housemaid for less than three or four dollars a week, and the good women cooks command twenty dollars a month. French chefs are paid from a hundred a month up, and it is a poor coachman who does not receive his dollar a day with board.

It is well known that Washington hostesses hire the china for their large balls and receptions. Almost every china store in this town has stocks of plain white dishes which go out and come back many times during the social season. I asked one of these merchants why the dishes used for this purpose were so plain.

"It is not because people like them," he explained, "but because their guests cannot so easily tell that this is the same china they ate from the day before at another house. Suppose you were to notice some brightly ornamented Japanese plates at Mrs. Senator B's tea. Then the next afternoon you were served cakes upon exactly the same kind of plates at Mrs. Representative C's. You might remark to a friend that Japanese dishes were all the rage here in Washington, but she would shake her head and whisper into your ear the one damning word 'hired.' "

The President gave his second White House evening reception of the year just this week, and a thousand bare backs and bare necks gleamed under the gaslight of the East Room's magnificent chandeliers. A thousand men were in danger of colds in their claw-hammer coats, and the archdemon Pneumonia had plenty of chance to pick out his victims.

Washington, more and more, apes the courts of Europe, and a fair share of the sixty billion dollars which the *World Almanac* says the United States is now worth, is put into the dress of its people. We are lavishing fortunes on clothes. There is enough silk worn here every winter to carpet a whole state; there are pearls by the bushel, and diamonds by the peck.

At the White House the other night there were at least five hundred women wearing diamonds of various sizes. I counted fifty pairs of solitaire earrings whose stones were as big as the end of my thumb, and thirty diamond stars and pendants any one of which would buy a large farm. One brunette beauty, dressed in a flowing red gown, had by actual count eighty-five diamonds on her person. Some of these, set in bracelets and rings, were not unusually large, but the solitaires in her ears were as big as hazelnuts. She shook at least five thousand dollars this way and that every time she moved her head.

Jewels are worn here not only by the young and beautiful but by the middle-aged and the wrinkled. The day of the old-fashioned grandmother has passed, and you will not see one old lady in a lace cap. The older the woman, the more giddy she seems to be. She cuts her dresses an inch lower at the bust for every extra ten years, and I blush for the fair sex when I look at the décolleté corsages and fat bare backs of the powdered old dames.

I do not believe the charge that some of these fine ladies of Washington hire their jewelry, just as they hire the china for their entertainments. Of course much that is worn now is shoddy and cheap, and half the brilliants you see at the White

House receptions are surely rhinestones. The gems worn by Senators' wives and other millionaires' daughters are supposed to be pure. But who can tell? The fact that such highly placed females wear them would, if they were paste, make them pass for real.

By all odds the finest collection of real diamonds is that of Mrs. Leland Stanford, who wears a dozen different sets every season. She has some amazing stones, as big as pigeons' eggs, which once belonged to Queen Isabella of Spain. Another set of clear yellow diamonds glow like golden fire under the gas flames of the East Room, and she owns still a third, made up of purest blue-white stones, which shine even brighter. The gossips say Mrs. Stanford keeps her sixty different diamond rings on a string of common black tape.

Mrs. Senator Jones of Nevada owns some of the most elegant pearls seen in Washington. One of her choicest possessions is a necklace of large, perfect pearls with a splendid diamond pendant made to represent an oyster shell. A single exceptionally fine pearl is affixed to this glittering shell on the spot where a pearl in an oyster is usually found.

The Washington nabobs are a strange conglomeration. Some have the bluest of blue blood in their veins, education acquired in the best of schools, and manners polished by long sojourns in Europe. Such persons have, as a rule, many friends among the great public figures of the day, and have little trouble about getting into the swim.

There is, however, another class who have nothing but their money to recommend them. Their vulgar ostentation marks them as *nouveau riche,* and when you meet them at large receptions you have no difficulty in recognizing them. Many use bad grammar; the men cannot avoid mentioning their wealth; and the women, whether their figures make it advisable or not, dress in the most extravagant extremes of fashion. Stories of the crudities of such people are legion.

There is one lady whom I shall call Madame Newrich, whose husband has made a fortune in trade, and who has installed his family in a splendid mansion here in Washington. Not long ago Madame Newrich sat at a formal dinner party beside one of the most noted generals of the late war. The General, himself none too careful of his table manners, used the point of his knife to convey a bit of food from his plate to his mouth. His dinner companion gave him a nudge in the ribs.

"I beg your pardon, General," she said in a loud whisper, "but when my husband makes a social blunder, he is glad to have me correct him. I know your wife, at least, will thank me when I tell you not to eat with your knife. People in Washington are queer. They eat only with their forks and their spoons."

The General looked at the busybody with astonishment. He said not a word, but turned away to talk with his neighbor on the other side.

The great charm of society in Washington is that it is not entirely founded on wealth. Its principal interest comes from the fact that the most important and successful men in all branches of activity come here. Instead of there being one lion to roar at a party, there may be ten or twenty or thirty. So many men and women of brains and brilliance give Washington gatherings a sparkle that is found nowhere else, except perhaps in the capitals of Europe. There is a frankness and simplicity and a lack of snobbishness as regards wealth and fashion. While there are extravagant displays in the homes of the rich, these are no more frequented by people of real importance than are the more modest establishments of the officials of moderate means.

Washington hostesses, in the main, depend upon their own gifts for entertaining. There are no one or two great caterers such as hold sway in New York. Nor are there any social dictators who decide who shall be and who shall not be invited to parties. It would be hard to imagine any of the important families here turning over their invitation lists to some social agent to blue-pencil. Washington has been called provincial, and in many ways it is, but it has today the only real cosmopolitan society in the United States.

The officers of the retired Army and Navy forces are always in great demand. One of the old stand-bys is General Van Vliet. You will find him at every reception, at nearly every big dinner. You may have heard the story of how General Sherman, who is nearly as constant a dinner-goer as General Van Vliet, one night forgot at which house he was scheduled to dine. Seeing Van Vliet walk past his door in full dress, Sherman decided to follow him, being sure that the General would lead him to the right party. He was not disappointed.

Like many another member of Washington society, General Van Vliet is able to change his politics at will. During Arthur's administration he was such a strong Republican that now it is surprising to find him thick as thieves with the Democrats. Everybody likes Van Vliet, and the excuse is made for him that no Army man should hold any political views. The day after Cleveland was inaugurated, the General called at the White House to tell Colonel Lamont how he and the President should conduct the Administration's social program. After he had finished speaking, one of the other visitors spoke up.

"And pray how long have you been a Democrat, General?" he asked, smiling.

"Since yesterday noon," was the old gentleman's unruffled reply.

During nearly every administration since the beginning of our Government, Washington has been agitated by questions of protocol. They began when the capital was still located in Philadelphia and New York. They existed during the stormy days of John Quincy Adams and Andrew Jackson. James Buchanan had social troubles added to his presidential problems, and only last year there was a fight between Mrs. Carlisle, the Speaker's wife, and the ladies of the Cabinet. As usual their difference of opinion was as to who ranked whom. This question of who should pay the first calls, the ladies of the Senate or the ladies of the Cabinet, has long been a burning question.

The "court" at Washington has different rules from those of the drawing-room circles of other cities of the United States and its customs also differ from those of the court circles of Europe. It has, in short, an etiquette of its own, and now for the first time the unwritten laws of its usage have been put into a book. Mr. D. B. Randolph Keim, a Washington correspondent and litterateur, has published a little volume containing a full exposition of the subject with its thousand and one petty rules and distinctions.

Mr. Keim's little brown *Handbook of Official and Social Etiquette and Public Ceremonials at Washington* lies before me as I write. It is a neat pocket volume of 230 pages, well printed and gilt-edged. It divides the social world of Washington into three classes: first the official class, including the President and all his important employees, the officers of the Army and Navy, Senators and Congressmen; second the quasi-official class, or the foreigners who represent other countries in our capital; and third the nonofficial class, including residents of Washington, strangers, and visitors.

Of the official class, of course, the President comes first in rank, the Vice President next, then the Supreme Court, the Senators, the Cabinet, after which are the foreign ministers and Congressmen. Other officials, such as Army officers, Navy officers, and heads of departments are scattered along down the list until twenty-five degrees from the President we find the order of chiefs of departmental bureaus. Think of it! Twenty-five grades in the official circles of this Republic! This is almost worthy of being a part of Sunset Cox's book *Why We Laugh.*

Once every season, there is a reception at the White House for the Senators and Representatives in the Congress. Usually, handsome cards of invitation are sent out for such an occasion, and only once has a different procedure been attempted. In place of such cards an announcement was printed in the newspapers of Washington, extending the President's invitation to the members of Congress. The witty wife of an Eastern Congressman said, when she was presented to the President that evening, "Well, Mr. President, you advertised for me, and here I am."

Will Cabinet calling last? I suppose so, for Mrs. Secretary Blaine is, so far as I know, the only Cabinet wife who ever seriously objected to this custom of opening her door to the wives of Tom, Dick, and Harry every Wednesday during the season. On most Cabinet days, Mrs. Blaine will receive none but her own friends, other callers being told that the wife of the Secretary of State is not at home.

After all, isn't Mrs. Blaine justified? Why should our Cabinet wives have to dress up one day every week and put themselves on parade to be looked over by people about whom they don't care a penny? Mrs. Fairchild, the wife of the Secretary of the Treasury, received eight hundred calls in one afternoon, and even tried to return them. But luckily for her, many of the cards bore no address, nor could the names be found in the City Directory.

The expense of such receptions is often three times or four times the salary of a Cabinet official. Many of their wives would drop the custom at once if they could, but there are others who insist that they enjoy it.

The chitchat at Washington social gatherings is often vapid. The charming ladies rush from one acquaintance to the next, hardly realizing to whom they are speaking. A funny story about a noted Admiral and a society matron is now going the rounds. The lady prides herself on her charm and her manners. She exerts herself mightily to make everyone she meets, even strangers, feel that they can be at home with her.

As she sat down beside this Admiral last year at a big dinner, she gushed, "Why, my dear Admiral, how nice it is to see you. And how is your wife?"

"My wife is dead, madam," was the famous sea-dog's reply. The good lady apologized, as well she might for the fact was well known that the Admiral was a widower.

Again, just last week, the two found themselves partners at dinner. "Why, my dear Admiral, how nice it is to see you," the lady repeated her patter. "Do tell me, how is your dear wife?" She was thrown into confusion by the Admiral's dry reply, "Madam, she is still dead."

CHAPTER XI

Fashions and Fads

MISS BAYARD'S DEATH is another offering on the funeral pyre of Washington society. There is no doubt but that Kate Bayard was killed by too many parties, and the terrible strain of her social duties. Mrs. Endicott also has not been well, and a number of the young ladies of the higher circles here have suffered greatly from their nightly wining and dining, their dancing, and their reception giving and going.

The décolleté dress has grown lower and lower. Dresses were low enough in President Arthur's time to sprout the seeds of consumption in many a fair woman's chest, but it is even worse this year. In many cases there is nothing but a strap over the shoulder to hold up the low-cut corsage. Society people here remember how Miss Kitty Beach, whom it was said young Alan Arthur was to marry, nearly caught her death at the White House one night. Clad in a very low-necked dress she went with young Arthur into one of the colder halls or onto the porches, I forget which. The wind blew upon her and she was ill for weeks.

It is no wonder that these Washington belles should be injured by their mode of dressing. During the day they wear the heaviest of cloth dresses and flannel underwear. When they go on the streets they cover themselves with sealskins, and if they do not wear such cloaks, they have their shoulders and chests covered with heavy wraps or furs. Warmed even to perspiration by such dressing, in the cold evening air they throw off their heavy clothes, and so far as warmth is concerned, they might as well be attired in the summer costume of an Indian squaw.

Annie Jenness Miller, the authority on dress reform, says she gets letters about the décolleté dress question from nearly every state and territory, and from England, Sweden, Norway, France, and Germany. They invariably ask "Do you approve of the décolleté dress?"

Those whose morality is offended by the so-called indecent exposures in the nation's ballrooms are disappointed with her replies. For Mrs. Miller is not so shocked at the sight of a semi-nude society woman as are the dear souls from the small towns where all necks and bosoms are covered.

"It is not so much a question of morals as of custom," says Mrs. Miller. "Where such fashion is the custom, there can be nothing wrong about it. It is only when the wearer blushes at exposing her neck and breast that there can be criticism. The fashion will undoubtedly continue, for every lady knows that her silks and laces are more becoming by the exposure of a beautiful throat and neck. I answer all my enquirers by saying that there is a great difference between the women who wear such dress as a matter of course, just as they wear fine jewels and costly raiment because they are born to it, and those who would have to put aside their own convictions and prejudices to wear it with a sense of shame."

In connection with the anti-décolleté dress resolution passed at the recent convention of the National Woman's Temperance Union at Nashville, a report is being circulated that Mrs. Cleveland intends to establish the fashion of high-necked dresses in Washington this winter. There is no truth in this report. Mrs. Cleveland, while she will use her own judgment as to her own dressing, has no thought of dictating the dress of others. She usually wears her dresses just a trifle open at the neck. She has a beautiful neck and arms, but she has not, so far as I can learn, ever expressed any decided opinion upon the low-necked dress question. Along with Mrs. Whitney, the wife of the Secretary of the Navy, she evidently thinks this matter should be left to the individual taste of each person.

A story having to do with low corsages is being told by the wife of a Justice of the Supreme Court. It seems that the Korean Minister last night attended the reception at the home of Mr. Fairchild, our former Minister to Spain. Minister Pak was seen talking with his host, who at one point became convulsed with laughter at some remark of his Oriental guest. Being pressed to share the joke with others, Mr. Fairchild explained, "The Minister was commenting upon the décolleté dress of the ladies, and said, 'Doesn't it seem to you, Mr. Fairchild, that these ladies are very much above their clothes?'

The use of enamel as a cosmetic is growing more and more common in Washington society. It used to be that only the oldest and homeliest put enamel on their faces, and in such cases it rarely extended below the neck. Now many young girls enamel, and with low-cut dresses they must, to carry out the illusion, enamel arms and bust as well as face and neck. A sort of enamel powder is now used, I am told, which is rubbed into the flesh until it shines like polished wax.

This is well enough when the maiden has the form of a Mary Anderson, or the neck and bust of a Venus de Milo. But when she is of the rangy build, all angles and no curves, the effect is horrid. There are nine thin girls to one plump one in Washington society, and for them, I think, most men would vote for no enamel, no low-necked dresses, and for sleeves buttoned tight at the wrist. Fortunes are spent here in paint and powder every season, and had I the income from the rouge alone, I would not have to work to support myself.

A few years ago the short-hair craze struck Washington. Pennsylvania Avenue of a bright afternoon was filled with the daughters of noted men, who walked along the sidewalks dressed in sealskin coats, fine dresses, and nobby hats, under which their hair, cut like a boy's, showed forth. A few looked better for the new style; others were made uglier than they already were. A pretty girl is well enough with short hair, for her plump rosy cheeks, her soft, round white neck, and jauntily poised head are emphasized by the rakish cut. But with short hair the thin, scrawny, scraggy-necked girl looks thinner, scrawnier, and scraggier than ever. The ugly sisters appear to better advantage with the new style of coiffure which is being worn by Mrs. Cleveland.

Her fashion of wearing her hair in a low knot on the nape of the neck, now called à la Cleveland, was adopted by Frances Folsom more from necessity than from preference. One of her schoolgirl fads was to have her hair cut very short and her neck shaved. This low knot was chosen to hide the untidy short hairs when she let it grow again. Seven out of every ten women in Washington have copied her and the style has been adopted throughout the country.

A small fortune is spent in hairdressing here every season. The bills for this item of the toilet run from thirty to ninety dollars a month, according to the number of times the hair is dressed every day. There is a peculiar touch of the professional hairdresser which is unmistakable, and woe be to the society beauty whose fair acquaintances lift their eyebrows as they look at her hair and whisper, "Her maid undoubtedly does it." Most ladies of fashion have their hair dressed by an artist for every evening reception, and some call for his services twice in one day.

Washington is a photographers' paradise. Glass cases containing their wares are found on every block of Pennsylvania Avenue, and their pictures of public men are sold in the Capitol itself.

Statesmen are like college boys in that they enjoy exchanging photographs, and while Congress is sitting the photograph galleries are crowded. A prominent person can have his picture taken for nothing, for it is understood that the photographer can sell copies to the general public. The photographer will send a cab for a Senator or Representative, and expect to make his profit by selling his pictures to the great man's admirers.

The society belles say they dread the camera, but as soon as the rosebuds have made their debuts, they rush off to have their pictures taken. They want themselves reproduced in all varieties of costume, and the latest fad is the placing of a white fan at the back of the head.

Women are the same the world over. It is not hard to convince the homeliest maiden that she is strikingly like the most famous beauty. Tell a Senator's plain daughter that she looks like Mary Anderson, the beautiful actress, and she will twist her form like that of an India rubber man in the circus, trying to assume Miss Anderson's graceful pose. She will gather her thin hair into a wispy Grecian knot, and she will grin like a cat chewing wax, as she tries to imitate the smile of Mrs. Grover Cleveland.

Attorney General Garland's action in not attending the state dinners at the White House is construed on different grounds by the different groups in Washington society. Mr. Garland's friends say he excludes himself from social Washington on account of bereavements in his family. Another explanation, however, is that Garland has made a holy vow that he will never wear a full dress coat, that such a thing has never been known in his family, and that he does not propose to be the first to introduce it.

The matter of the swallowtail has been a troublesome question to many a public man before Garland. Senator Joe Brown worried his soul about it for months before he gave in. Then he compromised by having a swallowtail made out of chinchilla beaver cloth, and wearing a red flannel chest-protector under his shirt bosom. It is said Brown was influenced as much by his fear of taking his death of cold as by his fear of the displeasure of his constituents. Ex-Secretary Kirkwood would not wear a dress suit even at the White House. He often appeared at the formal evening receptions there in coat and pantaloons of black broadcloth, shining with age, and with a black string necktie, frayed at the edges.

Senator George, of Mississippi, is another man who affects that phase of snobbishness which causes a man to dress less well than he might. George promised the folks back home that he would neither wear a dress coat in Washington nor ride in a carriage. He has kept his promise religiously, going about on all occasions dressed in business clothes, and always using the streetcars.

In speaking of this matter of dress a prominent Senator said to me just the other day, "Public opinion has changed. Today people want their representatives dressed like gentlemen. To underdress is a greater weakness than to overdress, and it will hurt the man who affects it in greater degree. The day of 'Blue Jeans' Williams has gone. The standard of intelligence of the American people is now too high for dirt and rags to represent greatness. In twenty years you will hear no more of the buncombe statesman whose chief capital is a dirty shirt, a slouch hat, and a shake of the hand. The day of respectability has dawned, for people have seen that rough clothes do not make the good democrat, any more than the rich attire of the dude makes a gentleman."

The fad for autographs prevails in the capital. Each day you may see the page boys in Congress running from Representative to Representative and from Senator to Senator with long morocco-covered books in their hands, asking for autographs. Most of the great give a scratch of the pen willingly; some even write pieces of poetry, or "yours truly" in addition to their names.

These albums do not belong to the pages. The boys are paid by strangers and others five dollars apiece for carrying them around. Or the books may belong to the members of Congress themselves. New members do not always understand this, and Congressman Moore, of Tennessee, thought for a long time that the autographs were sought by the pages for themselves. He wrote some good advice in each book, and in one he set down these words: "Be a good boy and you will become a great man." He signed his name with a flourish, and was pleased with himself until he found out that that particular autograph book was the property of the distinguished Senator Edmunds, of Vermont. Edmunds told the story of Moore's advice to him, all around the Capitol with great enjoyment.

I am now looking at such a book which has been left in the Press Gallery for the signatures of the correspondents. It belongs to McCarty of the *Baltimore Sun,* and is to go to a lady in California. He tells me that he has been two years already in gathering its signatures. The book began with President Arthur and his cabinet. Arthur wrote with big up-and-down scrawls that jump from one word to another without his pen leaving the paper. He was evidently glad when the end of his name was reached for he closed it with a flourish, and the final "r" takes a shoot right through the "Arthur" and crosses the "t".

No one would imagine Secretary Frelinghuysen's autograph was written by a man, for it is more like the signature of a palsied old woman. Robert T. Lincoln's name has an "R" bigger than the rest of all its letters, and the middle initial "T" is monogrammed with the "L." Brewster, the Attorney General of Arthur's Cabinet, writes with the same boldness as that of his dress. The ink flows in rivers, and every curve says: "This is the great Brewster, with his coat of arms, his frilled shirt, his white plug hat, and his aristocratic head."

John A. Logan's signature takes up half a page. It looks like the hieroglyphics on the subterranean tomb of Ti in Egypt. It is as cold and aggressive as Logan's own character, and he closes it with the dashing curve like that of the sword which he carried during the war. Senator Edmunds has also an illegible signature, but it looks more like the sign on a Chinese tea box than the Egyptian scrawl of Logan.

But, taking the Senators all together, they are as good a set of penmen as you will find in any similar body. As a rule they write more plainly than the members of the House, some of whom can hardly read their own writing.

Ben Perley Poore, who has been in Washington for the past fifty years as a newspaper correspondent, has perhaps the most valuable collection of autographs in the United States. It contains the handwriting of sixteen thousand prominent men. It represents all parts of the world and dates back several generations. Poore has them all classified and subclassified. One volume is devoted to the Army, one to the Navy, one to authors, one to editors, one to clergymen, and one to the ladies.

In the volume of the European autographs you will find the most famous names of France, England, and Germany. And in the volumes labeled "United States" you will see the handwriting of the great men of several presidential administrations. I asked Ben Perley Poore when he first began to collect autographs.

"It was in 1836," he replied, "when I was visiting Andrew Jackson in company with my father. We were present together one morning at the opening of 'Old Hickory's' mail. As he read a letter he turned to us and said, 'Here's a curious thing. This woman wants my autograph, and she's not the first to ask for it. I don't see why men want other men's handwriting. I have been afraid to send my signature out for fear that some one might write something above it and cause me trouble. But I have solved the matter by this card.'

"Jackson then showed us some cards which he had covered entirely in writing his signature, and he handed one for me to keep. That was my first autograph and I have been collecting them ever since."

Just here I would say that I do not believe in this fad of autograph collecting as it is now practiced. Signatures should not be collected any more than should one collect the teeth of famous men, or the parings of their fingernails. The mere writing of the name means nothing unless some message accompanies it.

CHAPTER XII

Somewhat Scandalous

WASHINGTON SOCIETY is trembling over the possible scandals that may be lurking under the thin veil of the upper crust. A month ago one of our dudes who parted his hair in the middle and who called himself B. Shephard White was the petted of Senators' daughters and the boon companion of Generals' sons. A few days later he was revealed to be a cheap defaulter and was captured in Kentucky in the very presence of two of our most brilliant society leaders.

We had imagined that he was an aristocrat and the son of an aristocrat. We were sure that his blood had the tinge of the sky, and now we are horrified to find it charged that his father was a Boston dishwasher, and that some of his most distinguished ancestors ate their meat on the banks of the Congo.

This young man was a seven-hundred-dollar-a-year clerk,

and he cut a wide swath here on thefts amounting to less than a thousand dollars. He now rests in the Washington jail, and the fair ones who have corresponded with him are lying awake at night wondering whether their love letters have been destroyed or whether they will be brought forward in evidence. An effort will undoubtedly be made to prevent his case coming to trial, but such hopes are vain, and he will probably wear a louder suit than he has yet had in his wardrobe. In other words, he will wear the black and white stripes of the penitentiary.

On the heels of this scandal comes the marriage of Admiral Porter's grandniece to one of the waiters of a Washington hotel. The story of how the young couple met at the seashore, and how the knight of the dinner table, by tidbits of soft-shelled crabs and delicious morsels of tenderloin, wooed and won the fair hotel guest, is being rolled about on the tongues of statesmen and their wives. They discuss it, however, with fearful hearts, and ask themselves as they look at their own daughters, "Who next?"

This runaway match of Admiral Porter's grandniece is to a certain extent history repeating itself. The Porters have always been bold in their love-making, and Commodore David Porter, the father of the Admiral, bulldozed his sweetheart's family into allowing him to marry her. Porter was a Commander at the time, and Miss Evelina Anderson, the daughter of William Anderson, a rich member of Congress from Pennsylvania, was visiting the Navy Yard. The two fell in love, but her family did not approve. Miss Anderson's brother, a brave young man, was deputed to receive Commander Porter when he called to ask permission to marry his beloved.

"You come on a fool's errand," young Anderson told him. "My father sends you word that he will not receive you into our family."

Commander Porter jumped from his chair. His eyes flashed fire as he said, "Sir, you are meddling in a matter that does not concern you. I came here to marry your sister, and damn you, if you don't call your father, I'll throw you out of the window."

The frightened brother rushed to summon his father, telling him Porter would surely cut all their throats if he could not have Evelina. The result was that Father Anderson came into the parlor, talked with Porter, and liked him at once. A week later he gave his consent to the marriage. His wedding present to the young couple was a handsome house on the banks of the Delaware, which is, I think, still in the family. Admiral Porter himself is my authority for the above story.

Washington is a curious medley. Consider the shocking affair at Stewart's Castle last week. It was the big ball of the season, and the guests were all invited ones. Among them was young H——, the son of the chronic objector in Congress, who became disgracefully drunk. Staggering into the ballroom, he rudely seized the bare arm of one of the young ladies. He blew his brandied breath into the face of the pure young girl and tried to force her to dance with him.

A member of one of the South American legations who tried to protect the frightened belle, got a blow in the face from H——'s fist for his pains. Policemen had to be called to drag the drunken young fellow out of the house, and his hat and his overcoat were thrown after him. The next day the foreigner sent a challenge to the offender who, sobered up, replied with an abject apology.

Then there is young M——, who was refused a drink at his hotel because it was evident that he had already had too much liquor. He tore up the hotel register, and made rags of the parlor curtains. At the close of his spree, he tried to shoot one of the Negro servants and sent a bullet through the arm of a second. It is said that this young beau-about-town has been so drunk for the past three months that the servant whom he shot has been putting him to bed almost every night.

Within the past few years punch has become so popular in Washington that you will now find a big punch bowl at almost every fashionable gathering. It is quite an art to make a good Washington punch, and it takes very little of it to cause the knees to quiver and the head to swim. One recipe gives the ingredients as whisky, rum, claret, champagne, sugar, and lemon juice. Add just a little water to this and you have a drink that will put an old toper under the table with half his usual allowance. Still, this strong stuff is offered to young men and maidens at Washington parties. Is it any wonder that some of them take too much and that we have such scenes as the disgraceful one at Stewart's Castle?

This scandal at the fine mansion on Dupont Circle has called the attention of the capital to the vices which stalk with brazen faces through every part of it. There is a great deal of drunkenness in Washington, and society winks at it in a friendlier manner than it did a few years ago. More and more woman appear in public in décolleté dresses cut shamelessly low, without the illusion of lace and flowers to hide the swelling bust. At an evening reception not long since a lady appeared with a low-cut pink dress so made that the shoulders were perfectly bare. She looked like a life-size living marble statuette bust, set in a bouquet of pink flowers.

When such a state of affairs prevails in the fashionable Northwest, what can you expect on the other side of the Avenue? There are more of the demimonde in Washington now than ever before. No law is put into force to stop them. They parade Pennsylvania Avenue in scores every bright afternoon, dressed in their sealskins and silks, either walking or driving in some of the best-looking turnouts in the city. They even enter the galleries of Congress. I have spotted them in the private galleries reserved for the members' families, where a member of Congress must have furnished the ticket for their admission.

Washington society is so constituted that it is impossible to guard it with anything like the restrictions of McAllister's

Four Hundred of New York, or those of the bon ton society of any other American town. Here every season the people change. Every Congress a new batch of maidens and a new set of hangers-on appear on the capital stage. Every four years a new administration turns the social world topsy-turvy, and the old order gives place to the new. Under such conditions anyone can make his way into society.

The introduction of a Senator or a Representative or a politician is the opening wedge, and this, in these democratic days, is free to all. A number of well-placed ladies in Washington society, with more blue blood than money, have for a consideration taken up other ladies whose venous fluid is less aristocratically colored, and have pushed them into society.

I know many people who rank here far higher than they could in their own state. I could point out some who are even ostracized in their home towns, but who, in Washington, move about on the topmost layer of the upper crust. The skeletons in Washington closets are legion, and the paint and powder that adorn many a beautiful face cannot cover up the story which lies underneath. But Washington seldom bothers itself about the skeletons in its inhabitants' closets. Lucifer himself will be welcomed if he will dress well, keep his hoofs hidden in patent leathers, and his tail out of sight.

Conservative mammas are inclined to look with alarm upon the attentions of the young men of the foreign legations to their innocent daughters. It is not that the foreigners are given to drink, they say. On the contrary in their use of liquor, they set a good example for the sons of American families. But they have the reputation of being decidedly wicked in other, perhaps even more harmful ways. In justice it must, however, be said that they usually practice their vices in secret.

It is seldom that such a scandal comes to light as that told of two attachés of a certain embassy, now recalled to their own country. Between them they plotted to drug the wine of a well-known and lovely young girl, so that they might carry her off from an evening party. Fortunately they were as imprudent as they were wild, and they discussed their plan in the ballroom. Confident that none of the other guests near them could understand their language, they outlined aloud all the details of their nefarious scheme. It happened that their surmise was wrong, and that a guest who spoke their language overheard. With the help of the host their wickedness was exposed. The two young attachés had all but achieved their purpose when they were caught in the act and unmasked in disgrace.

In spite of their polished manners, many foreigners do not regard our girls with the respect shown by their American beaux. There is frequent criticism of their free and easy ways, and of the risqué conversation in which they indulge. The young diplomats excuse their objectionable remarks by pleas of not knowing English perfectly. Under cover of this subterfuge they can try out their fair companions. If offense is taken at some suggestive expression, they can plead ignorance; if no objection is made, they can go a step farther.

In defense of the foreigners, it should be said that there seem to be young ladies in Washington society who themselves often go too near the line in their conversation. Have you heard this story from a Massachusetts Avenue drawing room? A young diplomat was chatting with a debutante who asked him whether he had gone to church the day before.

"No," he said, smiling, "I stayed at home and broke the Ten Commandments."

"Oh! Oh!" The forward girl looked archly into his eyes. "Did you break every one of them?"

Or have you heard of the disgraceful behavior of the giddy daughter of a Congressman some years ago who entertained seven men in her parlor one evening with a wholesale flirtation? In turn she allowed each one to sit upon the sofa with her and put his arm round her waist. At the end of five minutes she would say, "Now, Mr. Jones, your time is up. It is Mr. Smith's next." She excused herself by saying that down South at home she was accustomed to permit this to her one lover.

Here in the capital, where she had so many, it seemed only fair to divide her favors up evenly.

The elopement yesterday of E. Berry Wall, "King of the New York Dudes," and Miss Salome Melbourne of this city, is the day's gossip. Everyone knows about E. Berry Wall. His hundred suits of clothes have filled columns in the newspapers. His taste in dress has been the envy of the high-collared Anglomaniacs of New York club life, and his wardrobe, from the top of his exquisite derby to the toes of his round-toed, well-varnished shoes, has been to the fashionable young bloods of today what that of Beau Brummel was to the English nobility of nearly one hundred years ago.

Both Beau and Berry lavished fortunes on clothes. Both moved in the highest circles, and either would have been horrified to have made a mistake in their dress. All men, however, change when they are in love, and Berry's infatuation brought about the awful necessity of his having to be married in a traveling suit.

The story is really too utterly awful, don't you know, and it reads like a romance. The heroine is a beautiful girl, just nineteen, tall, slender, and well-formed, with pretty eyes of dark blue and a profusion of dark auburn hair. She is a bright conversationalist, dresses elegantly, sings charmingly, her musical education having been acquired in Germany, London, and Paris.

Miss Melbourne made her debut in Washington society last season. She is not a professional singer and has not appeared on the stage. But she has sung here and in London at private musicales, and her performances at parties given by Mrs. Vilas, Mrs. Nordhoff, and at the Chinese Legation attracted attention. She is modest, and sensible enough, perhaps, to work a radical reform in her club-loving husband.

There is no doubt but that E. Berry Wall is much in love, for he has already turned over a new leaf. Colonel Henry Watterson of the *Courier-Journal* invited him to have a drink with him last night when the two met at Chamberlain's Clubhouse where Berry is stopping with his bride. "I can't do it, Colonel, I've quit," Berry replied. "I'm a married man now and I expect to give up club life." "And this," said the friend who told me the story, "is a good deal for Berry to do, for he belongs to sixteen clubs in New York, and his clubs have been his home."

Berry Wall laid his plans to outwit the objecting mother of Salome with great care. Mrs. Melbourne was sending her daughter off to Europe, and he persuaded his aunt to give a party for her before she sailed. During the reception he intended to slip away with Salome and be married, and she then would have remained in New York. Mrs. Melbourne, however, stuck so closely to her daughter's side that the couple had no chance to escape.

It was in Baltimore that they finally succeeded. Mrs. Melbourne had certain customs formalities to arrange there, and Berry came to the train to see them off in a cutaway coat and a low stiff hat. He decided to accompany them from New York to Baltimore and he started off on his journey without even one Saratoga trunk.

On the train he laid his hat down too near a steam pipe, and it was drawn out of shape. When the party had arrived at the hotel, with a wink at his future bride, he excused himself to go out and buy a new hat. Miss Salome was quick to understand. She said she was tired and that she would lie down. So Mrs. Melbourne thought it was safe for her to go to the customs office. She had no sooner left the hotel than Berry Wall returned and took Salome off ostensibly for a walk in the park. Thus it happened that the dude and the debutante were married without ceremony or wedding costumes.

Washington has as many and as attractive saloons as any city of its size in the world. Those of the better class are elegantly furnished. Mirrors of heavy plate glass reflect decanters and goblets of Bohemian manufacture. Sparkling champagne bubbles up through long-necked glasses, old bourbon shines out seductively with an amber glow, and the red wines of France burn side by side with the crystal gins of Holland and the white wines of the Rhine and the Moselle. The floors of the saloons are of marble, and their polished wood and gilded trimmings gleam under brilliant lights, inviting the weary statesman, the disappointed lobbyist, or the unsuccessful claims agents to come in and drown their sorrows.

The Washington bartender is a nobbily dressed, lively, wide-awake man, full of spirit, often understanding several languages, and as entertaining as a barber in his conversational powers. He knows human nature, and he can generally tell a dead beat at a glance.

While waiting for a Congressman in one of these gilded palaces of sin the other night, I fell into conversation with one of the older bartenders of Washington. He was a man who had mixed drinks for Presidents and had carried Senators to their rooms in the days when a statesman was considered queer if he did not drink too much once in a while. I asked him about the prevalence of drinking in the Washington of today.

"Most of the Congressmen and Senators drink," he replied, "although there are many more total abstainers than there used to be. The Southern and Western members drink most, and they always want whisky. Now your Northern and Eastern men indulge more in wines and beer, and the foreign ministers, though they drink wine, seldom come to a bar.

"We have some curious drinkers among the present members of the House," the bartender continued. "There is one from South Carolina who takes on the average about forty drinks every day. He fills his glass to the brim and tells me his sight is bad and he doesn't know how much there is in the glass until it runs over. He always drinks whisky and he takes it straight.

"A House member from Kentucky wants three lumps of sugar, a tablespoon of water, and a pint of whisky for his usual dram. Dust a little nutmeg over this, he says, and it makes a drink for the gods. This man can drink this several times in one day and can repeat it during the evening.

"Then there is a Texas Congressman whom the boys call 'the brewery.' I don't know how much he drinks during the day nor what he drinks elsewhere, but here he always orders beer and he takes it before breakfast. Every morning, as soon as he gets out of bed, he comes here and drinks four 'stove-pipes' or schooners of beer, gulping them down one after the other.

"I suppose Washington has more dead beats than any other city," the drink-mixer declared. "Some dress as well and are as clean and portly as a Senator. Why, only the other day an ex-judge and an ex-territorial governor tried to beat me out of two drinks. They came in at six-thirty in the morning, looking rather seedy. While I was mixing their drinks, the judge wrote their names on a card and handed it to me saying they would pay when they came back at ten o'clock. The dodge was too old. I set their drinks back behind the bar, and replied that I would keep them for them until they came back.

"There are a half dozen dead beats who come here regularly, and we have nicknames for them. 'Colonel Lunch' buys five cents' worth of beer and eats forty cents' worth of free lunch at this bar every day. So it costs him only ten cents a day for his food. Five cents worth of beer pays for his breakfast, and a glass of Milwaukee lager at some other free lunch counter pays for his dinner.

"'General Hot Scotch' is a lawyer by profession and a drinker by practice. His favorite drink is hot Scotch whisky, and he always finds someone to give it to him. He is a small, clean, eighty-two-pound man, with a tall hat, a nobby cane, and shabby genteel clothes. He comes in with a smile and says, 'I want a drink! I need a drink! And I'm going to have a drink!' If he hasn't the money and I refuse to trust him, he appeals to the other drinkers at the bar. He does it so charmingly that someone always pays, and he does get his drink."

Washington has been agitated by temperance feelings of late, and the liquor lobbyists are fighting the proposed increase in the cost of a saloon license. The license is now a hundred dollars, but it is planned to increase this to two hundred. The saloon owners are up in arms, but the probability is that they will have to pay it.

The better saloons here make large profits. They can easily afford the increase. Those of a lower class are dives and doggeries, and the sooner they are done away with the better. Drinking in the capital may not be so bad as it was in the early days, but it is still bad enough. There are saloons in every block, and all over the city. It is a strange quarter in which you have to take ten steps to get a drink.

The Senate adopted a rule yesterday that no intoxicating liquor shall hereafter be sold on the Senate side of the Capitol and a lively discussion was held. In Pecksniffian speeches several of the tipplers in the august body declared their abhorrence of liquor. One or two avowed themselves teetotalers, and one who is known to keep always a supply of bourbon in his committee room, proclaimed himself a supporter of the new rule.

The discussion, however, announces to the public how disgraceful has become the use of whisky and wines in the halls of Congress. For the next month or two, I suppose, our statesmen will be careful to do their drinking at home; after that the rule will be relaxed and the old habits resumed.

CHAPTER XIII

The Burning Question
of Civil Service

THE WASHINGTON HOTELS are crowded, and office seekers are as thick as shells on the beach. They make a motley crowd, and long hair, red noses, and shiny clothes are seen in all public places. At Willard's Hotel the gang appears especially seedy and desperate; and among them guarded denunciations of Cleveland's civil service ideas are not infrequent. The city will be overrun with these office seekers until Cleveland has firmly established that Civil Service Reform is to prevail, not only in spirit but also in fact.

The Republicans much doubt that the President will be able to enforce the Civil Service Law by his present plan to leave the matter entirely in the hands of his Cabinet. Two former secretaries have told me that if the heads of the various departments are inclined to follow the spoils system, they can make the changes and Cleveland will be almost powerless to prevent it.

It may even be done without his knowledge. If complaints are filed, the secretary can assert that the changes were all made for cause, the dismissed officeholder will be told so, and that will end the matter. The clerks in the various departments are not feeling secure. They do not sleep well of nights, and they fear to go to their offices in the morning lest they find the sentence of official decapitation upon their desks.

If Senator Pendleton should be defeated in the coming election, it will be more on account of his Civil Service Reform Bill than of anything else. The whole organization of his Democratic party is antagonistic to the idea of civil service.

Have you ever looked into the records of the early Presidents on this question? In every case the Democratic party has supported the idea that "to the victor belong the spoils." Look at the record! Washington was a civil service man, and he made only eight dismissals during his term of eight years. John Adams was the first President to appoint a relative to office, but he also was imbued with civil service ideas, and his dismissals were only ten. Then comes Jefferson, whom the Democrats claim as the grandfather of their party. Jackson, I suppose, they would call its father.

How many removals did Jefferson make? The record puts it at forty-two. But even Jefferson acknowledged the propriety of civil service, and he had a civil service examination of sorts. Next comes Madison, less of a Democrat and more of a reformer. In eight years he dismissed only five persons. Monroe made nine removals in eight years, and John Quincy Adams, the last of the patriots, made only two during his entire term.

Democrat Andrew Jackson, who succeeded Adams, held his forces together and gained his election by promising to make a clean sweep of the government offices. When he was elected, many of the office seekers who swarmed about the

White House, were accommodated. Some seven hundred removals were made.

There was no pretense then of seeking a cause for dismissal. It was cause enough that the incumbent had not voted for Jackson. During his entire term of eight years, the spoils rule was openly followed, and his successor Van Buren riveted it upon the country.

Since the days of Jackson, the spoils system has been the controlling idea of the Democratic party, so that it is not strange that they should be disgusted with Senator Pendleton who has struck a death blow to it. Pendleton is in fact too much of a statesman for his party. In every reform for the past years he has been in the front rank; no more high-minded, honest Democrat has ever sat in the United States Senate.

A prominent Democratic Congressman talked freely to me last night and defended the spoils system at length. He denounced Cleveland's policy of not replacing Republicans in office with Democrats as detrimental to the country and ruinous to the Democratic party.

"The fate of the party and the Administration lies in the crossroads post offices," he said. "It makes little difference to the country at large what they do with the jobs here in Washington, or those of our diplomats serving abroad. But if the postmasters are not changed, it is as though there were no change in administration.

"When you think of the close relationships in a small town you can see how such a principle acts. Take, for instance, the town of Pinhook in my district. It has about three hundred people, a couple of stores, a blacksmith shop, and a post office. Its population is about equally divided between Democrats and Republicans, and it is always a question which way it will go in an election.

"Smith, the present postmaster, is the leader of the Republicans, and he works well for the party. He has his little row of post-office boxes at one end of his store counter. Everyone comes in to get his mail, and they buy from him rather than from the other store, which is run by Democrat Jones. When Smith puts up a pound of sugar, the paper he uses is a tract on the tariff. If he sells a cake of soap, tales of Republican greatness are printed on the paper in which he wraps that purchase. He sees that the Republican county newspaper gets all the new subscribers, and when subscriptions to the Democratic organ run out, he does not hurry to notify the editor. Oh, he is useful to the party, all right.

"Across the road in the other small grocery and general store is Jones, as ardent a Democrat as Smith is a Republican. He has worked for the party through every campaign since 1860. At every election he has sent me, as head of the Central Committee, twenty-five dollars for campaign expenses, has kept me posted on how the sentiment of the town is shaping up, and what we can do to be sure it votes Democratic. For years, however, the Republicans have won, and Smith, who is not a bad friend of his, has crowed over his success.

"Now at last the Democrats are in, so Jones decides to go to Washington and see about getting the postmastership as his just due.

" 'Is there anything the matter with Postmaster Smith?' the Postmaster General asks. He has in mind the orders from the President that the fact that a man is a Republican is not enough cause for his removal.

" 'Why,' Jones replies, 'Smith's a Republican. He's the rankest, radicalest Republican in Wayback County, and he's been working against our party for years. I'm the Democrat. Of course there's nothing wrong with Smith; he's good and honest. But the people of Pinhook think he's been in office long enough. They want a Democrat.'

" 'Well, now, if Smith had stolen a mule, or if he didn't do his job of sorting the mail properly, then I could help you. But just that he is a Republican doesn't count now.'

"So Jones goes home in disgust, and every time he gets his mail in Smith's store, he curses the Administration under his breath. The Democratic voters of Pinhook do not know what to make of it. The Administration has not changed for them, and when the next campaign comes around they have no leader, and no contribution comes to headquarters from the disgruntled Jones."

My friend the Congressman grew more and more vehement.

"The civil service idea is the most ridiculous thing ever attempted in the domain of politics," he fumed. "If it governs the choice of the country postmasters, it should be equally good for higher offices. Take George Pendleton, the advocate—some say the engineer—of this damnable civil service plan! He spent three months in Washington after the election, and the result is that he turned a good man out of his job as Minister to Germany and got himself appointed there.

"Or even take the President. On this theory, Cleveland should have said to Arthur on March 4th, 'Mr. Arthur, it's true the people have chosen me to fill your place. But I believe that when a man is in office and is doing well, he should not be disturbed. Everyone says you are a good President, so I'll just go back to my law practice in Buffalo and leave you in the White House.'"

Well, now that the Civil Service Commission is at work, an end will probably be put to a certain class of advertisements which have been common in the Washington papers. If one should judge the past system merely by these advertisements, there would be little doubt but that a systematic brokerage of government positions existed. The constant recurrence of such advertisements leads to the presumption that they are answered, and I have heard of cases where assistance so gained has been attended with success. The success, however, was due not to the influence of the assistant, but to the fact that he understood how to use the applicant's recommendations to the best advantage. In these, as in other cases, the assistant was a dead beat who bled the applicant as long as possible.

The advertisements make interesting reading. The following were clipped from the pages of the two most respectable Washington papers:

WANTED—A RELIABLE GENTLEMAN will furnish the best political papers and will pay $150 to any one who will help him secure a position of any kind in Washington. Address, in confidence, Capt. A. Y. R. Devere, Philadelphia, Pa.

WANTED—A GOVERNMENT CLERKSHIP at a salary of not less than $1,000 per annum. Will give $100 to any one securing me such a position. Address, Box 68, Star Office.

WANTED—A POSITION IN GOVERNMENT bindery by a lady. Will give half first month's pay and $50 after in monthly payments. Address Mrs. A. B. M., Republican Office.

$100—WILL GIVE $100 FOR A PLACE as clerk or messenger in any of the departments; first-class references. Address, CONFIDENCE, Republican Office.

WANTED—BY TWO YOUNG LADIES situations in Government office; will give first month's pay and $10 monthly as long as retained. Address A. B. & L. X. Georgetown Post Office.

WANTED—A young lady will give $150 to $200 to anyone securing her a position in any of the departments, paying from $60 to $65 per month. Capable in every respect. Address, Discretion, Star Office.

I might multiply these advertisements ad libitum by a reference to the newspaper files, but an idea of the practice can be gotten from the above.

It will not be long now before every government clerk will have to know how to use the typewriter, and no doubt there will be a special civil service examination to prove his skill. For the typewriter is rapidly coming into use. In nearly every department you will hear it clicking as you pass along the aisles. In the Department of Justice alone there are twenty machines; I suppose, all told there are as many as a thousand in use in the city, and the agents of both the Remington machine and the Caligraph tell me their sales are increasing daily. Already typewriting is becoming a business and there are a number of offices here devoted solely to it. These are, in many cases, operated by ladies who will copy a speech, take down a letter from your dictation, or prepare copies of documents at a fixed price. The rate now prevailing is six cents per hundred words, and some operators make as high as ten dollars a day. The average is, however, two to three dollars a day.

The typewriter is now found in almost every lawyer's office, and in many of the large business establishments. A number of newspaper men here use them in preference to the pen; and these words are being written on a Caligraph. I expect to see the day and that not very far distant, when the great part of business correspondence of all kinds will be done upon typewriters. The world is too fast for the pen, and life is too short for a writer to waste valuable time in manual labor.

I have received several letters asking for information on Pitman art of phonetic writing, which is also called "shorthand." I find on investigation that shorthand writing is fast becoming another of the leading professions of Washington. In the days of Andrew Jackson, hardly a public man possessed the luxury of a private secretary, to say nothing of a shorthand amanuensis. Now there is scarcely a man in public life of any prominence who has not a phonographic secretary accompanying him on all occasions.

Senators Seward and Sumner were among the first to bring shorthand to aid in their work. This was early in the fifties. Now all the leading lawyers and businessmen, together with nearly every head of a department or bureau, dictates his letters, speeches, and arguments.

Amanuenses and private secretaries of prominent men, lawyers, etc., paid by the year, make all the way from five hundred to two thousand dollars annually. Many of these amanuenses in Washington are ladies, some making very pretty salaries. Miss Sprague, the sister of the authoress of *The Ear-*

nest Trifler, who was once a shorthand writer here, is now, I am told, making five thousand dollars a year by practicing her trade in New York. Mrs. Palmer, of Utica, makes eight thousand a year, and Miss Jennie Balestine, of Rochester, makes five thousand.

Two hundred hands are now busy working on the immense new granite building devoted to the State, War, and Navy Departments. The hammer of the mason and the whistle of the steam engine can be plainly heard in the Cabinet Room of the White House across the street. This mammoth building at Pennsylvania Avenue and Seventeenth Street is at last approaching completion. It has already cost about nine million dollars, and its aggregate will foot up to at least ten million and a quarter. This is the greatest building in Washington. It is said to be the largest granite structure in the world, and it covers about four acres and a half, or an acre more than the Capitol. It is so built that it will almost outlast the ages. Its composition is of immense blocks of gray granite, weighing all the way from a quarter of a ton to twenty tons each.

The building is perfectly fireproof. It is made entirely of iron and stone, with the exception of a skin of boards laid over the stone floors of the offices for comfort, and of the doors themselves, which are of polished mahogany. The door casings, however, are of iron, and there are five hundred and forty-five tons of iron in the window frames and door frames of the east wing alone.

This great structure lies to the west of the White House, facing the Potomac and looking down upon the moss-covered farmhouse of Davy Burns, who used to own much of the land upon which Washington is built. The architecture of the building is of the Roman Doric order, married, I should say, to the French Mansard. Stop for a while and study the structure in its immensity, and again in detail, and you may begin to form a new application of Ruskin's expression "poems in stones."

Enter one of the offices of that part of the new State, War,

and Navy Department building that is now finished and occupied. You will see pale-faced clerks, bending over desks writing and figuring their lives away, in order to obtain that
which sustains their lives. A clerk seldom gets more than this,
and under the Civil Service Reform scheme, the government
clerk is becoming more and more of a machine, and less and
less an active, thinking, growing man.

As I stand here on this marble pavement and think of the
lives that will be eaten up in this building, and of the enterprise
shriveled into inertia, it makes me shudder. Young men will enter it full of hope and courage, full of brains and energy. When
they begin, their thousand or more dollars a year will seem good
pay to them, and they will work with a will, hoping to rise
through the various branches until their earnings will equal
those of a Cabinet minister. It will not be long, however, before
they will find that they are fighting the windmills, and are lost
in the old grind of copying other men's writings, or posting dead
books, where they have not the opportunity for the exercise
of an original thought. Their brains will waste away from
lack of use. The lazy hours of from nine o'clock till four will
eat up their energy until some day in the future, they will
wake up to the fact that they have been swallowed by that great
monster cannibal called the Government, which not only eats
up men's bodies but their souls as well.

At this time some of them may attempt to cut themselves
loose, but their efforts will be as futile as those of the Laocoön.
The roots of habit and inertia have wound themselves about
their frames. They will mark time until at last death will come
to take away what it thinks to be of so little value as to be
hardly worth the taking.

This will be the case if the Civil Service Reform prevails.
If it fails, the government clerk's position will be none the better. He is bound to be dependent upon his superiors at best, and
the lack of civil service rule makes him all the more of a syco-
phant and a toady. There is no worse employer than the Government, and I would rather work for a Scrooge than for
Uncle Sam.

———————————————— ⊰◉⊱ ————————————————

CHAPTER XIV

Among the Literati

———————————————— ⊰◉⊱ ————————————————

WHAT A GREAT AMOUNT of literary work is being done by our public men, and what a valuable amount of material is being laid up for the American historian of the future! Senator Blaine's book promises to be as full of historical meat as Thurlow Weed's memoirs or George Ticknor Curtis' life of Buchanan, while "Sunset" Cox is about to write a book containing the true inwardness of Democratic workings since 1856. But Cox and Blaine are only two of a host who are now engaged in literary work in Washington. Proctor Knott and Ainsworth L. Spofford, the Librarian of Congress, are getting along slowly with their history of American humor, Mr. Knott's duties as Governor of Kentucky taking up most of his time.

Congressman Kasson, formerly Minister to Austria, and the finest scholar in Congress, is writing a diplomatic history of the Civil War, but it is impossible to find out anything as to the nature of the work. George Bancroft is just completing his last edition, and his final one, of his great history. Charles Murray, Washington correspondent of the *Philadelphia Times*, has about completed a new novel which Carleton and Company are to publish. It is not at all like *Sub Rosa*, his tale of Washington life, which has gone through a half dozen editions and still sells. Henry Adams, the offspring of a line of Presidents, and the son of Charles Francis Adams, who with his wife wrote *Democracy*, is engaged upon a new satirical monologue about Washington life.

Joaquin Miller, the poet of the Sierras, has built a log cabin here and will make this the center of his literary work hereafter. Horatio King still keeps up his writing of historical articles for various magazines. So literature is fast becoming a feature of Washington life. There are as many literary societies and socials as fashionable gatherings. Mrs. Ransom of Cleveland gives receptions every Friday which are attended by many literati, and Horatio King's Saturday night literary treats are one of the institutions of the capital. Besides these there are the Classical Society, which embraces such men as George Bancroft and Judge Shellabarger, the Travel Club, which John A. Logan often attends, the Literary Society, the Unity Club, and a half dozen others.

George Bancroft was working among his roses when I called upon him the other day. The rose is the historian's favorite flower, and he has the finest rose garden on the North American continent, situated back of his house on H Street, and embracing a greenhouse as well as outdoor beds. Mr. Bancroft came into the house as I entered. He was clad in black broadcloth, and his iron gray hair was covered with a slouch hat, which he removed as I followed him into his library.

A fine specimen of the best intellectual workers is the Honorable George Bancroft. Over eighty years of age, he has a frame of iron and a brain as bright as that of a youth. He is of middle height, lean and wiry. His thin, thoughtful face is lengthened by his long, silky beard of silver white, and his thin gray hair is combed back from a broad, high forehead. He has light blue eyes, and a complexion which has been darkened by the winds during his daily horseback rides.

On horseback, the old historian wears a short black velvet coat, above which his long white beard falls like silk lace. A soft felt hat shades his eyes, and his legs are encased in a pair of well-fitted pantaloons. His groom is dressed in as fancy a livery as the servants of any of the rich in Washington. As straight as a bean pole, this man looks very fine in his tall black silk hat, his pleated waistcoat, chamois knee breeches, and high-top boots. Both of the riding horses had their tails cropped short, and they were cantering up Fourteenth Street as I watched them the other day. Mr. Bancroft attributes his long life and good health to his daily horseback rides.

Mrs. Bancroft, who is of nearly the same age as her husband, I understand, has a great talent for needlework and embroidery. I saw specimens of her handiwork in every room, upon a set of chairs cushioned entirely with her embroidery, upon a beautiful piano cover, and on table covers, screens, and tidies which add beauty to rooms already artistically furnished. One particular feature about this house of Bancroft's is its comfortable homelike look. It seems as though it was made to be lived in and enjoyed. The pictures on the walls, the plate glass mirrors here and there, do not give it the cold and stately look you get during a visit to the house of many a newly made millionaire. Here, everything seems meant for use, and the little home touches give it a welcoming warmth.

Bancroft's *History of the United States* has been the work of a lifetime. He told me today he was well satisfied with the last edition, just published. "I want my history to be correct in every statement and in every particular," he said to me. He has been working a long time to that end, longer indeed than the average man's life. It is that part of Mr. Bancroft's life work which will live longest after him, forming a more impressive monument than could all the granite in New England.

This aged historian is one of the most courted men in Washington. It is more of an honor to have his company at dinner than that of the President. He is the only private citizen who has ever been given the freedom of both Houses during sessions of Congress. His country has honored him often, and he was Secretary of the Navy under Polk, and afterward Minister to the Court of St. James.

Mark Twain and George W. Cable have been reciting extracts from their works to large audiences here this week. I dropped in Monday night to hear them, and spent the pleasantest evening I almost ever had at such an entertainment.

The two men are as different as the poles, and both are surprises. George W. Cable is under medium height, very straight, very slender, and as sallow as many of the Creoles whom he portrays in his novels. His face is effeminate rather than manly, and his beard of silky black and his long drooping mustache, whose ends hang down below his chin, carry out this illusion. His nose is straight and small, his eyes bright, black, and piercing, and his forehead medium high. His hair is the color of jet, and as glossy as oiled ebony.

Ten years ago, the world knew nothing of George W. Cable; now he stands in the front rank of the American literati. At one time he was a merchant, then tried newspaper writing on the *New Orleans Picayune*, and while doing so began to study the early history of New Orleans. He wrote several sketches about the Creoles there for the *Century Magazine*. These attracted attention and he found this field well worth developing. He has shown himself to be an accomplished novelist, and his reputation will last.

Mark Twain is just as big and awkward as Cable is small and graceful. His huge head is joined by a long neck to a pair of round shoulders. He came onto the stage as though he were half asleep, and he looked to me as though Nature, in putting him together, had somehow gotten the joints mixed. He has a big face, a nose prominent enough to represent any kind of genius, and eyes large, black, and sleepy. His thick mane of hair is now iron gray, and his bushy mustache overhangs his whimsical mouth. As he stood on the stage he reminded me of a mammoth interrogation point, and as he drawled out his words, with scarcely a gesture, his voice made me think of a little buzz-saw. He did not laugh while he uttered his funniest jokes, and when the audience roared, he merely stroked his chin or pulled his mustache.

The humorist could not help being satisfied by his reception. He must have been struck by its contrast with his first struggles in Washington. When he came here years ago, he had hard work to make money enough to pay his board bills. Mark Twain used to drink a good deal in those days, and was hardly considered a reputable character. It was shortly before this that he had taken the trip from which he produced *Innocents Abroad*. This book he wrote in Washington from the notes he made during the tour.

Innocents Abroad made Mark Twain both famous and wealthy. His manuscript was rejected by several prominent publishers, and he was about giving up in despair when a Hartford company took hold of it. The result was that they made seventy-five thousand dollars off the book, selling more than two hundred thousand copies. It was after this that Mark Twain tried editing the *Buffalo Express*. A man who worked on the paper at the same time told me today that this venture of his was not a success. He loafed around the office, guying the office boys, and telling jokes and stories instead of writing.

The only fruit of Mark Twain's Buffalo experience was his marriage which, like *Innocents Abroad*, turned out well. His wife brought a pot of gold into the family, and when he got to Elmira, he found that his father-in-law had made him a present of a brownstone front, and had thrown in a coachman with a bug on his hat. Mark Twain did not remain in Elmira, however, but went to Hartford, where he wrote *Roughing It*, which also was successful and which established his fame. He is a hard worker. While at Hartford, he writes in his billiard room in the attic, and like Trollope, he believes that there is nothing like a piece of sticky shoemaker's wax on the seat of his chair to help an author to turn out good literary work.

William Dean Howells, the greatest of American novelists, is spending a month or two in Washington. When I called upon him yesterday, I found him different in appearance from the impression conveyed by his pictures. He is short and stout, and his every feature is that of a college-bred businessman, rather than that of the unconventional author. He is free from egotism and he looks on his profession much as a merchant does on his store.

The great writer dresses in business clothes. This morning he had on a pair of light pantaloons and a dark cutaway coat with vest to match. His white collar was a turnover and his necktie a scarf which entirely filled the front opening of his vest. As he chatted, he gestured now and then with his hands which, I noticed, were remarkably small, and free from the ink stains of the ordinary literary man.

Mr. Howells was modest in speaking of his work. He told me he does not believe in the word "genius." He thinks he has a natural bent toward literature, but that his success is due to hard work. He works right along the year round, and prefers to take his rest day by day rather than in a lump. In response to questions as to his average day's work, Mr. Howells said:

"I produce about a page of *Harper's Monthly* or an editorial column of a newspaper. I do not like to write fast, and I write, rewrite, and change both words and matter over and over again. I don't think anything pays a writer so well as going over his own work. Some of my novels I have entirely rewritten, such as, for instance, *The Foregone Conclusion*. I consider that one of the best pieces of work I have ever done, and its revision improved it greatly.

"I have never written a book simply for the purpose of producing something for people to read," Mr. Howells continued. "I have always tried also to give them something to think about which might better themselves or the world. I do not believe in the theory of art apart from morals. This couplet of an Italian poet, which keeps running through my mind, expresses my idea in this regard:

> "Our work of making books is all in vain
> If books in turn do nothing to make men."

Joaquin Miller, the long-haired poet of the Sierras, has just moved into his log cabin. I called on him there this morning and found him a tall, well-made man of forty-five, with blue eyes and curly brown hair flowing out from under his slouch hat. His pantaloons were tucked into a fine pair of boots, and he had a good-natured air of the Western wilderness which fitted his picturesque surroundings.

The Miller cabin is on the highland at the head of Sixteenth Street, the great avenue of the Washington of the future. "The President's house is at one end of Sixteenth Street," says "Waukeen," "and mine is at the other, but while I own a cabin, the President has only his cabin-et."

Sixteenth Street is a broad street paved with asphalt, and lined with fifty-thousand-dollar mansions and fifty-dollar Negro huts. The White House, almost bathed by the Potomac and faced by Lafayette Park, is its starting point. Halfway up toward Joaquin Miller's cabin is a green plot in which a bronze equestrian statue of General Scott looks at the Executive Mansion. The street rises steadily from old St. John's Episcopal Church, past George Pendleton's mansion, Negro laborers' shanties, Senator Cameron's great palace, and a like mixture of houses, until it reaches the Boundary of this town. There the land jumps to form a fifty-foot hill, or plateau, running back into the country. On this wooded plateau, Joaquin Miller has bought land and put up his log cabin.

It is built on the wild Western plan, without a nail in it. The oak logs are hewn on the inside, but left rough on the outside. They are notched and joined, one on the other, until they have risen a story and a half. A ridge roof covers them, and from the two windows in front there is a beautiful view of the whole city. Bright red and white curtains hang at these windows, and a latchstring hangs from a hole in the only door which is made of plain pine.

This latchstring was left out for me, and I stepped into the interior of a typical frontier home. It was a large room, sixteen feet wide and some twenty-two feet long. A blazing fire of hickory logs burned upon the open hearth. Three split-bottomed rocking chairs were drawn close, and a plain poplar writing table, littered with writing materials and two bunches of cigars, was nearby. Two smaller tables made of pine boards, with legs set crisscross, stood at either end of the room, covered with bright squares of red felt.

On pegs driven into the log walls of the cabin I saw hanging rifles, a Mexican saddle, and the white goatskin pants in which "Waukeen" rides on his Western mustang. Through the African cloths that form the curtains between the two rooms, I spied the poet's bed, covered with a fur robe. Here the poet sleeps and dreams, and I am sure he sleeps well, for I am told that its springs are of the most modern, comfortable type. Miller likes good living, and in this rough cabin he wears a fancy dressing gown and embroidered slippers. On his hand I saw a solitaire diamond of purest water, bigger than any owned by the belles of Washington.

"I need to be alone to do good work," Joaquin Miller said to me. "In the solitude of this cabin I can accomplish far more than if I were down in the city. Even here I am troubled by visitors, and on Sunday I have to lock my front gate. I no longer permit telegraph boys to come here. A curious thing happened the other day because of this. Some friends of mine, passing through the city, telegraphed me an invitation to dine with them. A few days later I received a letter from them enclosing the wire, on the back of which was written 'Miller refuses to receive telegrams. Threatens to shoot boys. Signed, Western Union.' "

Literary women abound in Washington. Their name is legion, and they provide some of the brightest lights of the society of the capital.

Frances Hodgson Burnett is still a young woman, full of life, and a vivacious and interesting talker. Of medium height, she has dark auburn hair, a broad forehead, and pleasant blue eyes. I had a delightful chat with her this afternoon about her literary work.

"I was fifteen years old when I published my first story," she told me. "It was titled 'Miss Carruther's Engagement.' I sent it off to *Ballou's Magazine* under a pseudonym, and asked them to address their answer to me under cover of a friend. My brothers teased me a great deal about my writing, so if I failed I did not want them to know. In a short time I received an answer. The magazine would publish it, but they could not afford to pay me for it. Of course I wrote them to return my manuscript. Young as I was, I knew that if the story was good enough to publish, it was worth paying for. I next submitted my story to *Godey's Lady's Book*. Its editors doubted the originality of my tale, so to convince them, I sat down and wrote another story. For the two I received thirty-five dollars, and my vocation in life was fixed. I have been writing from that day to this."

Mrs. Burnett is not working so hard now as before her recent illness. The only writing she is doing is on a child's continued story for the *St. Nicholas* magazine. Its title is *Little Lord Fauntleroy*, and its scenes are located in both this country and England. This author lives quietly here in Washington. Her husband is a doctor, and their home is a plain three-story brick on I Street. Her workshop is in the attic, a large room hung with paintings. A tiger skin lies in the middle of the floor, and warm red curtains tone down the glaring light of the Washington sun. A desk, half a dozen easy chairs, and a sofa make up its furnishings. Amid these surroundings Mrs. Burnett has written most of her recent works.

Mrs. E. D. E. N. Southworth's writings have not improved with her advancing years. She writes the same wishy-washy sentimental tales now as those she indited with fear and trembling for the first of her sixty-five books. At that time, some thirty-five years ago, she was a schoolteacher. Now she has made herself independent by her own pen, and she still finds a ready market for her wares. Mrs. Southworth lives in quiet comfort on the Georgetown heights. She is not, like some writers, subject to fits of genius. She can write at any time, and she turns out books as others manufacture machinery.

Mrs. Southworth says it costs her little effort to write a book. When she has outlined her plot, she just lets her pen flow on and on, page after page, until she has enough manuscript for her purpose. Then she bundles it up, with scarcely an erasure, and sends it off to her publisher.

Rose Elizabeth Cleveland's book, *George Eliot's Poetry and Other Studies*, is meeting with considerable criticism. Had it been launched while she was a private citizen, or if she had published it anonymously, it would undoubtedly have gone begging for a publisher. It is a smart money-making stroke to put it out just now. She will probably make enough out of its sales to give her pin money for years to come. I confess I am one of those who do not like to see her fame in being the sister of the President of the United States being exploited by peddling her book on the news counters.

In many a Washington family today, the binding makes the book. Young girls may safely bring home the most sensational cheap novel, provided it is hidden under a National Library cover. In its paper-backed book-counter form, it would quickly be thrown out of the window.

A young lover of such cheap romances said to me recently,

"My mother doesn't think a book can be bad when it is bound in the neat marble paper and red leather cover of the Library of Congress. Last week I bought a paper-backed book called *Her Honor Saved*. But just because it had a yellow paper cover, my mother took it from me before I had finished the second chapter. I got the very same book in the National Library in proper binding, and she not only made no objection but read it herself."

And it is true that the trashiest romance, sent to the Library of Congress for copyright, looks quite as respectable, in its uniform binding, as do its neighbors—*Pilgrim's Progress,* and the other religious books on the Library shelves.

There is a great deal of talk just now about the dangers of the immoral French novel and of this paper-backed literature of which the modern girl is so fond. I asked a number of our well-read Washington women what they thought of the present craze and what effect it may have on our daughters.

The question seemed to have considerable interest for Mrs. General Sheridan, who devotes much time to the education of her three girls.

"My own daughters," she said, "are too young to be allowed to read novels, so the question has not yet been forced upon me. But I do not approve of indiscriminate indulgence in modern novel reading for anyone. It drains and enervates the mind, making it unfit for more solid food. In my opinion no young girl should be permitted to read such light literature until she has attained the age of eighteen.

"In my youth the unformed mind was not allowed the wide license in reading which now is granted to girls in their teens. George Eliot and Ouida fascinate them by the beauty of their style, veiling evil with a mantle of choice language, and so deceiving the unsuspecting young reader until she cannot tell the good from the bad. The literary merit of George Eliot tempts many to place her works on a footing with the best authors, but her moral influence is corrupting, or at least confusing.

"The writings of Tolstoy, of course, should not be allowed

in any decent home." Mrs. Sheridan spoke with strong feeling. "His *Kreutzer Sonata* was written with no higher aim than to depict vice in alluring colors."

Mrs. General Miles agrees with Mrs. Sheridan on this point.

"I think two of the worst novels I ever read were *Anna Karenina*, by Tolstoy, and *The Quick and the Dead* by Amelie Rives," she said to me. "*Anna Karenina* is without doubt the most pernicious book on the market. It should never be placed in the hands of any young man or any young woman.

"Among modern writers," Mrs. Miles continued, "I enjoy Bret Harte, whose stories deal with life on the free Western frontier with which I am so familiar. Then what could be finer than Frances Hodgson Burnett's *That Lass o' Lowries*? I find Mary Cecil Hay's novels elevating, and so also are some of the works of 'The Duchess,' although her books are light and frivolous."

CHAPTER XV

The High Cost of Washington's
Works of Art

ANYONE who has visited our capital knows that many of the paintings and statues which adorn its public parks and buildings have been chosen more because of the efforts of lobbyists than because of the approval of competent art critics. Buying the naked Washington in front of the Capitol, at a cost of $42,170, was worse than throwing money away.

For the past forty years and more, people have laughed at the chilly air and naked form of George Washington as, in marble, he sits opposite the east front of the Capitol. He has been the butt of the jokes of Senators, Representatives, strangers, and guides for the past four decades. Still this statue has a longer history than any other at the Capitol. Ordered by Congress at the end of Andrew Jackson's first term, it took eight years for Horatio Greenough to make it. He did the work in Florence, Italy, where he chiseled out the Father of our Country in a sitting posture instead of standing, as the Act of Congress demanded.

When the statue was completed, in 1840, the next question was how to get it from Italy to America. Congress haggled over the matter for weeks, finally sending a man-of-war to bring the statue across the Atlantic Ocean. But the marble George weighed twelve tons, and it took twenty-two yoke of oxen to haul him over the Italian roads. It is said that the peasants thought this statue the image of some saint; that here and there they knelt and crossed themselves as it went by. When the statue reached Genoa, it was found to be too large to be put into the hatch of the man-of-war which was to carry it to Washington; so a merchant vessel had to be chartered. When it arrived at the Washington Navy Yard, Congressmen were horrified to see that our great hero had been carved, sitting in a chair, nude to the waist. The Virginia statesman General Henry A. Wise remarked at the time, "The man does not live, and never did live, who saw Washington without his shirt." And the country applauded the sentiment.

Now the Navy Yard is not the Capitol, and it cost $5,000 more to bring the statue from there to the Rotunda, for which it had been designated. At the Capitol doors, it was found that the statue was too large again. The masonry had to be cut away and the door enlarged. When it was finally installed, the Rotunda floor began to sink, so a pedestal was built under it to support it. It was soon decided that the Rotunda was not a suitable place for the statue, and at last, after a number of removals, it was taken to where it now stands, in the bitter cold, bleak air of the Capitol plateau where the winds howl out Washington's agony at the fiasco.*

Originally this statue was to have cost $5,000. It has already cost $42,000, which sum is considerably increased by

* Today, Greenough's Washington is in the Smithsonian Institution.

every removal. One jokester, commenting on the outstretched sword in the figure's hand, says he is sure Washington is crying, "Take my sword if you will, but bring me some clothes!"

A great deal of the money which Washington has invested in its outdoor art may be looked upon as a mighty poor investment. The statue of Freedom on the Capitol Dome cost $23,000. Clark Mills received $20,000 for casting it and Crawford, its designer, was paid $3,000. The lady is nearly twenty feet tall, three times the height of the tallest man, and she weighs fifteen thousand pounds. When Crawford designed her, he intended to put a liberty cap on her head, instead of the bunch of feathers which she now wears. But Jeff Davis, who was then Secretary of War, objected on the ground that this cap had been worn by the freed slaves of old Greece. He suggested the idea of feathers, saying, "We could split the American eagle open and fit it on the head of Miss Freedom as an appropriate cap." And Jeff Davis was so important in those days that his counsel prevailed.

Lately, electric lights have been fastened upon the top of the Capitol dome, and a great wreath of fire hangs about the statue's feet. It may have been that these electric wires carried the lightning which, a day or two ago, struck Miss Freedom, running up her bronze skirts and tearing a hole a foot square in her thigh. As yet, nothing has been done to repair the damage, and the gaping hole still looks out over the city.

Clark Mills received other great sums from the Government, though he died comparatively poor. Fifty thousand dollars was the price paid him for Andrew Jackson, who sits upon a rearing horse opposite the White House. It is said to be the first equestrian monument Mills had ever attempted to model. When he was making the statue his friends said it would never stand upon its heels, as he planned; but by making the front part of the horse hollow and its hind legs and tail solid, he has secured perfect balance. The strongest wind blows against it in vain.

Mills received another $50,000 for his equestrian statue of General Washington in Washington Circle. A third $50,000 statue is that of General Thomas, in Thomas Circle. It must make the taxpayer happy as he looks at this last statue to know that Congress paid $25,000 just for the pedestal and that the four bronze lamp posts around the base cost $4,000 apiece.

The historical paintings in the Rotunda of the Capitol, by Trumbull, cost the Government $32,000. They are not interesting as works of art, but they are valuable in that they are actual portraits of many of the men they show. Today these portraits look fresh and new. A Washington artist has just retouched them, and has repaired those which were cracking with age. Some have been actually transferred to new canvases.

Each of these Rotunda pictures has a history. The faces of the women in the older ones were taken from sittings of famous society belles who reigned in the days when they were painted. Many a noted woman, and others not so noted, has thus had herself preserved at the expense of the Government and the generosity of the artist. It is like the original head of Liberty on the silver coins made at the Mint, which was taken from the head of a Philadelphia maiden. Or like the homely girl on the banknote. It is said that a designer for the Bureau of Engraving and Printing used his own daughter's face on one of our greenbacks. Had his daughter been pretty, it might have escaped notice, but, alas, she was not, and her full sensual lips ill became the character she portrayed. A great deal of fun was made of it until the head was finally changed.

There are many inconsistencies in the Rotunda pictures. Miles Standish, in the "Landing of the Pilgrims," has a foot which belongs to a man at least eight feet tall, and Standish, of course, was of middle height. The picture which represents the "Signing of the Declaration of Independence" was dubbed by John Randolph of Roanoke the "Shin Picture," because in the row of statesmen in knee breeches, sitting in front of the speaker, each had one leg thrown over the other knee. This comment attracted so much amused attention that the artist was directed to change it, which he did by painting tables in front of some of the statesmen to conceal their legs.

Above in the dome is Brumidi's famous fresco, with Washington on the right and Victory on the left, and with thirteen female figures representing the thirteen original states. Brumidi was paid for this $50,000, and he put in his own work at $39,000. The artists is said to have been a free liver, and the story is told that the thirteen fair faces which look down into the Rotunda include those of certain ladies of questionable reputation with whom he was acquainted.

Chief Justice Marshall's bronze statue, which was dedicated Saturday and which cost $40,000, is a valuable addition to the art works of the capital. The audience that celebrated the dedication of the Marshall statue was made up of the most noted men that one could find, gathered together. The Cabinet, the Supreme Court, the Senate, and the House were present, together with the leading literary and social lights of the capital.

A trio of famous old men sat together on the front row: George Bancroft, W. W. Corcoran, and Robert C. Winthrop, of Massachusetts. Bancroft, as old as the century, with his long white patriarchal beard, his thin face, and slender frame, sat erect during the exercises, and at their close stepped around, lively as a cricket, shaking hands with everyone.

W. W. Corcoran, who sat beside him, is not nearly so healthy, though he is much fatter. Mr. Corcoran is now nearly eighty-six years old. He was a cobbler's son in Georgetown before the capital was laid out, and he has lived to see Washington City grow into the social, political, and intellectual capital of the nation. He commenced life as a merchant, failed in that, then turned to banking. During the war with Mexico he became the banker for the Government, and thus it was that he laid the foundation for his fortune. An old Washingtonian once told me that Mr. Corcoran is proud of being a self-made man and that, far from trying to conceal the fact that his father was a shoemaker, he boasts of it and treasures his father's old cobbler's sign as one of his choicest possessions.

W. W. Corcoran has always been liberal in his benefactions. He has, it is estimated, given away not less than four million dollars. One day when I was having an interview with this great philanthropist, I asked him whether he felt that the immense sums he had given, had repaid him in satisfaction.

"Indeed, yes," he replied. "The pleasure I have had from doing good with my money is far greater than that which would have resulted from the retention of any sum, however large. My feeling about giving reminds me of the epitaph on the tomb of Edward Courteney, Earl of Devonshire:

> "What we gave, we have,
> What we spent, we had,
> What we left, we lost."

It was Mr. Corcoran, you remember, who gave Georgetown the valuable tract of land on the banks of Rock Creek for Oak Hill Cemetery. The only part he retained was "his last home," as he has labeled the photograph he showed me of the handsome Greek mausoleum whose marble dome bears in chiseled letters his name, "Corcoran."

A curious incident took place before my eyes the other day in the Corcoran Gallery of Art. I was standing beside the well-known statue by Vela which is called "The Last Days of Napoleon." The dying Emperor is represented at St. Helena, seated on a marble chair, with a map of the world on his lap. His stony but expressive eyes gaze off into space. His emaciated form symbolizes his tragedy. The great feeling of sadness and frustration expressed in this statue is commented upon by all who see it.

As I stood there, two country citizens walked to my side. They still had the red mud of Virginia on their shoes, and they seemed somewhat bewildered by their surroundings. They gazed at the statue for several minutes in silence. Then one said to the other "That's Napoleon Boneparty. He looks bad, don't he! Ain't it a pity he couldn't have been took when he was well?"

A similar happening occurred while I was noting the handsome face of the young Caesar which stands at the entrance to the bronze room. The bust is a fine one, representing one of the very handsomest of men. The face is truly beautiful, and the lips are especially large and well-chiseled. An old woman, accompanied by a red-cheeked girl, stopped in passing and took a long look. Then she said in a loud voice, "Mary Jane, look here. Here's a fine-looking feller. He's got a good mouth fer kissin', now, ain't he?" A cracked laugh came out of her wrinkled mouth, and the girl's cheeks grew even redder.

Mothers hurry their young daughters past the exquisite nude statue of "The Greek Slave," the work of the famous sculptor Hiram Powers, and one of the greatest treasures of the Gallery. About fifty years ago, Powers began his career here in Washington. At first he modeled chiefly the busts of the great men of the day, including President Jackson. Then, in 1837, he removed to Italy and set up his permanent studio in Florence. The classic sculptors of ancient times inspired his late works, of which "The Greek Slave" is undoubtedly the most admired.

The statues in the Corcoran Gallery are more daring even than the paintings of nude women. Again and again, prudes have raised anguished voices against them, declaring that they are "traps for the young." Their objections, fortunately, have not prevailed and works of such beauty as Powers' "Greek Slave" are still there to be enjoyed.

CHAPTER XVI

Houses with Histories

FOR AN HOUR or two this morning I visited the oldest house in Washington, and nearby I walked through the ruins of what was the finest mansion in the United States thirty years ago. David Burns's* ancient farmhouse still looks toward Arlington from its site on the banks of the Potomac below the White House, and his daughter's square palace still stands there beside it. Both are now like whited sepulchers; the life has gone out of them. Their furniture has been removed. Dust, desolation, broken plaster, and tarnished brass have taken the place of the splendor, the glamour and glitter which were theirs during the days of the Presidents from James Monroe to Martin Van Buren.

The story of these two old houses is the great romance of Washington. The farm cottage, whose two smokeless chimneys

* Carp's spelling; the name was really Burnes.

146

stand sentinel over the hollow shell between them, was here more than one hundred years ago. It was then owned by David Burns, a crusty, obstinate old Scotchman, whose family for three generations had held the land surrounding it. Originally they owned but six hundred acres along the Potomac. Their little plantation, which was scorned by the Carrolls, the Lees, and the Custises, at first went by the humble title of "The Widow's Mite." But the Burns family were Scotch, and they thriftily added to their farm until the estate comprised all the land between Georgetown and the Capitol.

Nearly every foot of this land is now covered with valuable buildings. It includes the best part of the city of Washington. The White House, the Treasury, the Post Office, the State Department, in fact all the important public buildings except the Capitol are located on Davy Burns's land. Business Washington has risen on a portion which must have been too swampy to farm. Its outskirts, bordered with the great houses of ex-Senators Blaine and Stewart, now constitute the most fashionable quarter of Washington. A sheet of greenbacks large enough to cover it would hardly equal its value; the extra hundred million in the Treasury would not more than pay for it.

David Burns was not anxious to have the Federal City located on his farm. He had little faith in George Washington and did not hesitate to tell him that he "would have amounted to nothing if he had not married the rich Widow Custis." General Washington, however, persuaded Burns to sell part of his land, and to accept a price of about sixty-six dollars an acre. So the capital was built here on the Potomac River and this old Scotch farmer became one of the wealthiest men in the country.

The old Burns farmhouse was probably a fair country home in 1779. In it pretty Marcia Burns grew up to young womanhood. Her father gave her a good education, and she was just nineteen when John Adams and his court moved into the unfinished White House. This was seven years after the location of the Federal City was fixed, and David Burns and his wealth were known throughout the land. His daughter Marcia, his only heir, was looked upon as the great catch of the country.

Marcia was pretty, too. As fair as a lily, they say, with roses in her cheeks and a pleasant fire in her eyes. Washington still talks of her witty conversations, and her elegant manners. In those early days, the bachelors of the first Congresses gladly visited this farmhouse. Washington and Adams accepted invitations to dine at its table, Tom Moore, the poet, slept under its roof, and pretty Marcia, with her beauty, her wit, and her wealth, had no lack of suitors.

Among her admirers was a Congressman, General John P. Van Ness, who came from one of the old Dutch families of New York. Jack Van Ness was at this time a bachelor of thirty. He had had a classical education, and had studied law, but had given up his practice for politics. He was a handsome young man, a good talker, and his money flowed like water. While he pressed his suit, his sweetheart's father died, and she was left alone in this old farmhouse by the river. This brought matters to an issue, and on the ninth of May, 1802, when the birds were mating in the great trees around the old farmhouse, Marcia Burns married Jack Van Ness, thus putting into his hands half of the city of Washington.

General Van Ness appreciated his good fortune, and right royally did he enjoy it. Deciding to build the finest house in the United States, he employed Mr. Latrobe of Baltimore, the man who had designed the White House, to help him. Latrobe, given carte blanche, made plans on the most extravagant scale. The costs were so great that even the General grew alarmed. Latrobe replied to his remonstrations by saying "I have nothing to do with the cost of your house. It is your business to furnish the money; I have only to draw up the plans and to build it."

The result was that the Van Ness Mansion, when completed, was the finest private residence in the New World. It was the first to have hot and cold water in all the bedchambers, and its fame was so great that it was almost as much of a curiosity as the White House itself. Its cost, in those days of Madison and Monroe, when a silver dollar seemed as big as a cartwheel, was from fifty to sixty thousand dollars, and it was furnished in a manner to correspond with the elegance of its construction.

I walked through it today. It is an immense square house of two stories, with brick walls two feet thick, covered with stucco. In front, facing the White House, and in the rear, looking to the Potomac, are portes-cocheres with Ionic columns. Two porter's lodges stand at the entrance to the spacious grounds, and a high brick wall surrounds its gardens.

Finished in 1820, when Monroe was still President, the Van Ness Mansion was for thirty years the seat of continuous hospitality. The General and his beautiful wife entertained like royalty and fashionable Washington delighted to do them honor. Clay, Webster, Madison, and Monroe had been the guests of Marcia Burns in her farm cottage home, so they doubtless visited her also in her new mansion. Until 1832, when she died, she was a social leader in Washington; after she was gone, her husband kept up his interest in society, giving a dinner each year to all the members of Congress.

After the death of General Van Ness, in the days of President Polk, the mansion was bought by a wealthy Virginian, one Tom Green who loved wine better than money. For years he lived in it, drinking the old wines which were stored in its great cellar. After the Civil War, the estate came into the hands of ex-Governor Swan of Maryland, who still owns it. It now comprises the six acres of land about the house, and its owner is holding it to be worth a hundred thousand dollars.

Since the days of Mr. Green, ruin has been rapid. Time is eating into the mansion as fast as its devouring teeth, aided by disuse, dust, and destruction, can demolish it. The house is now used as a low kind of beer garden, if not indeed something worse. A Negro family has it in charge, and what used to be Tom Green's office is the barroom of a doggery.

The grounds and the house, too, are often rented to picnic parties, and the parlors where Andrew Jackson, John Quincy Adams, and Dolly Madison danced the minuet with Marcia and her General, are now used for Negro frolics. Today, while I noted the faded splendor, a laughing colored girl was being swung by her sporty lover high into the air under the trees that hang over the cottage of David Burns. These grand old trees were casting their shade over two long picnic tables spread with food, watched by twenty pairs of sloe-black eyes, while brown faces grinned, showing white teeth in anticipation of the meal to come. Near them, beside a winding avenue of old boxwood, a cheap band was playing.*

One by one, the old historic mansions of Washington are passing away. Today I read an advertisement for the sale of Kalorama, once the residence of Colonel Washington, but better known as the home of Joel Barlow, the father of American poetry. The estate is on a hill not far from the western end of the P Street Bridge over Rock Creek, where Joel Barlow watched his friend Robert Fulton demonstrate his unbelievable models of boats to be run by steam.

Kalorama was a handsome residence in the days of Joel Barlow. A large porter's lodge, now overgrown with green vines, stands at its entrance, from which a long winding avenue of noble trees leads up to the mansion. As I walked up the driveway, I saw a score of cows grazing in a nearby field; beyond them chickens were cackling. The grass, poorly kept, was covered with the falling leaves of autumn, but the old house itself, with its thick brick walls, looked as well as in the days when Joel Barlow first moved into it.

During the War, when Kalorama was used as a hospital, a fire burned out its interior. But the walls were not damaged, and they stand today as solidly as some of the ruins of old Rome. The house has long since been rebuilt, and with its semi-

---

* The Pan American Union now occupies the site of the Burns farmhouse and the Van Ness Mansion.

French roof, it has a modern look. Inside, beyond the eight iron pillars of its porte-cochere, one finds some twenty-five rooms; and from its windows there is a view over the whole city. A grove of fine oaks fills a ravine in front, and all about the house are forest trees of various kinds.*

The Octagon House, in which President Madison signed the Treaty of Ghent, lies within a stone's throw of the White House and just a few blocks above the old Van Ness Mansion. It, too, faces the Potomac, with a beautiful view across the flats to the river and the Virginia hills.

An immense eight-sided structure of brick, the front of the Octagon House is an oval which rises from the ground to the roof. This is like a two-story bay window or a gigantic round tower cut in half, fastened to the face of the house. Into its walls at the second story are set narrow old balconies with iron railings A high brick fence surrounds the back yard where a huge mahogany tree rises to throw its branches over the roof. The front door opens from a wooden portico whose marble steps are battered and broken. Its doors, curved to correspond with the shape of the front, are adorned with huge brass door knobs, tarnished with age, and their keyholes are nearly two inches long.

Enter the front door and you will find yourself in a circular room, in the small alcoves of which are the queerest old stoves imaginable, and the floor of which is laid with large squares of marble. All four doors of this room are curved, and one has a high window above it, like that in an old country church. The room in which Madison slept was just above, also of round shape. He came to the Octagon House after the White House was burned by the British in 1814, and with his wife, Dolly, he made it ring with his festive dinners and receptions.

The Octagon House is known to some as the Tayloe Man-

* Long since vanished, Kalorama stood on the height not far from the French Embassy of today. On the grounds of the estate streets were laid out and today's fine houses built.

sion, for it was built by Colonel Tayloe, one of George Washington's friends, sometime between 1790 and 1800. This Colonel Tayloe was at that time one of the few millionaires in America. It is said he had an income of seventy-five thousand dollars a year and that he spent a third of it on his race horses. He owned five hundred slaves who farmed his lands in Virginia, worked in his iron mines, built ships, and made iron plows. While he lived in this interesting eight-sided house, Colonel Tayloe also entertained like a prince.

Now and then I hear tales of the ancient ghosts in the Octagon House. Ringing bells was the way they used to haunt the old mansion, and every night at exactly the same hour their din would be heard. Various methods were tried to discourage these unhappy spirits, even to having a priest come to exorcise them. But the family got rid of them only when they took down their bells and hung them in other locations.

The Octagon House is now occupied by an art school. Its front bears the extravagant sign "National Academy of Fine Art." The walls inside are hung with pictures, some of which are of more than ordinary merit, and the mistress of the house, Mrs. Morill, gives weekly receptions to such lovers of art as may wish to come. She has the idea that the United States should buy the Octagon House and establish it as a National Academy. It is priced at thirty-five thousand dollars, but its thick walls will probably crumble before Congress will pass an appropriation to buy it.*

In the Decatur Mansion, on Lafayette Square, John R. McLean, the editor of the *Cincinnati Enquirer*, was married this week to Miss Emily Beale, the daughter of General Beale, and a granddaughter of old Commodore Decatur. The marriage forges another link in the chain of friendship between the McLeans and the Grants, for Generals Beale and Grant were a second Damon and Pythias, and the Beale Mansion

* Expertly restored, the Octagon House is today the home of the American Institute of Architects.

was General Grant's headquarters in this city. During President Grant's last term there was no family closer to the administration than the Beales, and Miss Emily Beale, now young Mrs. McLean, was a central figure at all the White House dinners and receptions. The Beale family is one of the oldest in the country. Miss Beale's great-grandfather was Commodore Thomas Truxton, one of the first six naval captains appointed by General Washington to guard the commerce of the United States.

Among Commodore Truxton's subordinate officers was a midshipman named Decatur whom he loved dearly and who married his daughter. This young man became Commodore in later years, and it was he who built the house in which his granddaughter was married this week. Decatur was living here when his duel with Commodore Barron took place, and the wedding march now ringing in those old halls wipes out the impressions left by the funeral dirge which on a cold March morning sixty-odd years ago marked Commodore Decatur's death.

The old Decatur Mansion is full of interest. Latrobe was the designer of this three-story mansion on the corner of Lafayette Square and H Street. A wide hall runs through the center of the spacious structure, and its parlor is one of the largest in Washington.*

Commodore Decatur furnished his home with his naval trophies and curios he collected in foreign lands. At the time of his death he held a high position in American life. He was finely educated, a man of great culture and wealth. The night before his duel with the man he had helped to court-martial, he gave a grand party in this old house. The guests had not long been gone before he slipped away from his wife's side. After breakfasting in a little hotel near the Capitol, he betook himself to the Bladensburg dueling ground to meet Commodore Barron. Decatur barely lived to be carried back to his

* In 1956, by bequest of Mrs. Truxton Beale, the Decatur House became the property of the National Trust for Historic Preservation.

mansion on Lafayette Square. He died that same night and the President and the other great man of that day followed him to Kalorama, where he was consigned to the old Barlow vault.

Across Lafayette Park, on the opposite corner from the Decatur Mansion, is the house where Dolly Madison held court after her husband died. The big brick mansion, with its bay window at the back, was built by Richard Cutts, her brother-in-law, even before the Corcoran House was erected. It is said that Cutts had to borrow money from Madison to pay for building his house, and that he was never able to remove the debt. It was thus that the house came into the hands of the President's wife.

Dolly Madison, the queen of Washington entertainers, never forgot a name or a face. Stories are still told here of her remarkable memory and of her kindness. A story now current is about a green youth who was standing alone at one of her receptions at the White House. Dolly Madison, seeing that he was greatly embarrassed, decided to try to make him feel more at home. When he saw Mrs. Madison approaching, the boy had in his hand a half-drunk cup of tea. He tried to gulp down the rest, and he was so frightened at the thought of having to shake hands with the President's wife that he put the cup and saucer into his pocket. Dolly Madison engaged him in conversation as if nothing strange had occurred. She asked about his family so kindly that the youth forgot his embarrassment. He even managed to bring his cup and saucer safely out of his pocket and drink a second cup of tea.

The lot on which the Madison Mansion stands once belonged to Henry Clay. It is said that he sold it to Commodore Rogers for a jackass, and the story goes like this. The Commodore had brought with him from the Mediterranean a shipload of finely bred Andalusian jackasses. There was one of these which Henry Clay coveted for his farm at Ashland, Kentucky, and he tried his best to buy it from the Commodore. At first Rogers refused to part with the animal, but he became tired of Clay's importunities, and one day he said in fun, "Well, Mr. Clay, there is just one thing you own which will purchase my jackass, and that's your lot on Lafayette Square near the White House."

"It's a trade," Clay replied. So Rogers got the lot and Clay got his jackass. The land is now worth a whole army of jackasses, and the mansion upon it would, I venture, sell for more than the estates of all Clay's descendants.

Mrs. Madison, it is said, spent a great deal on dress, her turbans alone costing a thousand dollars a year. In her later years, through the excesses of her son, Payne Todd, however, she lost her fortune and was at times dependent upon one of her old Negro servants for the very necessities of life. Her poverty forced her to move from her house on Lafayette Square so that it might be rented. When she died it was bought by Admiral Wilkes, and the last important milestone in its history is its recent purchase by the Cosmos Club.*

It is now several years since newspaper editor Frank P. Blair died, but his magnificent mansion, which has for years been one of the social centers of the capital, is still in the hands of his descendants. The old Blair Mansion is an immense white brick with a flat face of dirty white sandstone, looking across Pennsylvania Avenue to the War Department. Its windows are large, wide, and old-fashioned. Its door in the center is reached by a flight of steps of heavy stone, and there is a big yard at the back entered by a servants' door at the side.

The house was built in 1820 by a Dr. Lovell, the Surgeon General of the Army, a native of Boston, and for years one of the leading citizens of Washington. Frank P. Blair, who had come from Kentucky and was making a fortune editing An-

* Occupied by the Cosmos Club until 1952, the Dolly Madison House is now owned by the United States Government.

drew Jackson's newspaper organ, the *Globe*, bought the house from him. Blair lived in it for years, occasionally renting it during an administration to some Cabinet officer, until 1853, when his son, Montgomery Blair, took possession. Since that time it has been in the hands of this branch of the Blair family.

The Blair Mansion has had many distinguished tenants.* George Bancroft occupied it when he was Secretary of the Navy. Then came the elder Tom Ewing, Secretary of the Interior under President Taylor. While he was there, a noted wedding took place, that of General Willian T. Sherman and the Secretary's daughter, Ellen Boyle Ewing. President Taylor and his entire Cabinet were present, and among the guests were Henry Clay and Daniel Webster, to name just two of the host of famous men.

Three months after the wedding, Zach Taylor died, and Tom Ewing gave up the house to one of the members of Fillmore's Cabinet. This was Tom Corwin, then fifty-six years old. Corwin was a Kentuckian who earlier in his career had gone to Ohio, where he was elected to the legislature. Ten years later he came to Washington as a member of Congress, and he served until 1840 when he became a candidate for Governor of Ohio in his celebrated "log cabin" campaign.

Throughout his campaign, Corwin spoke from the step of a log cabin mounted on wheels. It was carted over the state from one town to another, and old stagers declare his speeches were the most eloquent in our political history.

If spirits there be, and if these return to earth, I doubt not that the jolly ghost of Corwin sometimes revisits the old Blair Mansion where he lived at the height of his fame. It may be he is there now, hobnobbing with Frank P. Blair and old Tom Ewing, and that the trio are retailing their reminiscences to each other. As Longfellow writes in his poem "Haunted Houses"—

* Now the United States Government's guest house, it is often used to house dignitaries from abroad.

All houses wherein men have lived and died
Are haunted houses. Through the open doors
The harmless phantoms on their errands glide
With feet that make no sound upon the floors.

There are more guests at table than the hosts
Invited ; the illuminated hall
Is thronged with quiet inoffensive ghosts,
As silent as the pictures on the walls.

CHAPTER XVII

Curiosities and Cranks

WASHINGTON is a paradise for curious characters. My latest discovery is a man who lives in a tree. He is an eighteen-hundred-dollar a year clerk in the Pension Office, one A. B. Hayward. Mr. Hayward is a black-whiskered gentleman, a pleasant one-armed bachelor of about forty years of age. His aerial habitation is situated just outside the boundary limits of the city, between Fourteenth and Sixteenth Streets, and within a quarter mile of the cabin of Joaquin Miller.

This tent-like house stands on a pine platform between two oak trees. The platform is perhaps twenty-five feet square, and as high above the ground as the first story of a business building. Upon this rise walls of pine boards about eight feet high, and over the hollow square which they form is stretched a ridge roof of two thicknesses of the strongest weatherproof
158

canvas. Before the door, which opens to the west, is a porch where the owner can sit on warm summer evenings, and on which I today saw his rocking chair and a water bucket.

Mr. Hayward's platform is reached by a ladder twenty feet long, but very light. When he goes to work at the Pension Office he carries it with him to the nearby farmhouse, where he gets his meals. The house in the trees is comfortable, heated with a small oil stove, with carpet upon the floor, a bed, a bookshelf, and a writing table. The weather here has not been cold enough to prevent Mr. Hayward from sleeping in his tent-home all winter. In summer, with the cool green leaves of the spreading oaks to give shade, it must make a more pleasant home than the average room of a city hotel or boarding-house.

Even more curious is the filthy hole of the Washington hermit that was sold this week for ten thousand dollars. For forty years, in the heart of the capital, in the shadow of the Patent Office, midway between the White House and the Capitol, this man has been living his hermit's life. A veritable savage in the kernel of civilization!

When Washington was a village, John Birch bought his little lot, twenty feet wide and sixty feet deep, in the poor quarter of the new town. Here, with his sister Sarah, he lived in a little one-story shanty. Stately brick buildings rose all about them in time, but they kept out of sight of their neighbors. By the time the massive Post Office structure was built, the wooden shanty collapsed, no doubt in shame.

Birch propped up the crumbling walls with old lumber. He had long since hidden his hut behind a high board wall, and he used this and old bricks to enclose one musty room about nine feet square. In this cell he has lived until today.

Curious indeed is this home of the Washington hermit. Two beds, two rickety chairs, a rusty stove, and a wood table are crowded into it. Few people ever caught sight of its owner. Fewer, having seen him, wished a second sight. Birch looks like a savage. Of medium height, his dirty shirt is open at the neck, and his hairy chest shows out beneath his pale face, animated by his wild, fierce black eyes. He cannot read nor write, nor does he know his age.

John Birch is, however, a genius in a musical way. For years he has made his living by repairing musical instruments. At a hole in the wall of his home, his sister Sarah has talked with those who wanted work done, but none of Birch's customers has ever set foot inside. This musical genius, it is said, has invented an instrument with a deep bass tone, deeper far than that of a bass viol. Its principle is that of a low whistle. Some Washington musicians think it would be interesting, both for use in a band or a large orchestra.

The Washington hermit's fondness for liquor is the cause of the sale of his property. He had for years refused to give up his shanty home and move elsewhere. But recently when he was happily inebriated, certain persons persuaded him to transfer it to them for the sum of five hundred dollars. This transfer would not hold in court, of course, but it enabled the property to be put up at auction, which was done today.

Birch's lot is on Tenth Street just beside Ford's old theater, where Lincoln was assassinated. That night, so Birch says, he saw several men sneak up the alley back of his lot, leading a horse that was saddled and bridled. One of these men was undoubtedly John Wilkes Booth. Birch saw the people later run out of the theater but he did not know of the shooting until the assassin had galloped away, well out of reach.

Old booksellers, since the time of Samuel Johnson, have been noted for their acquaintance with the great men of the day, and their memories of those of the past are interesting. Such a man is Joe Shillington, who for the past forty years has kept a bookstore on the corner of Fifth Street and Pennsylvania Avenue.

Ten years ago, when this location was the heart of the fashionable quarter of the capital, Mr. Shillington's store was the rendezvous of the statesmen and literati of Washington. Since then the city has moved toward the Northwest. Now, though his trade is probably larger because of the immense business establishments around him, times have changed, and his honors are divided with Brentano, Free, and other booksellers farther up town.

Mr. Shillington himself is a character such as Dickens would have delighted to describe. Of medium height, with a large rosy face, kind blue eyes, and the funniest little curl of red hair covering his baldness, he can tell stories by the hour about the days and men of the past. He describes them so vividly that they move before you, and you feel they actually exist.

It was just a few doors from Shillington's bookstore, for instance, that P. T. Barnum exhibited his notorious woolly horse here many years ago. When I referred to how Congressman Benton unmasked the fraud, the old bookseller laughed heartily.

"I remember it as though it were yesterday," he said. "Barnum was here in my shop some time before the event. With a friend he was watching an old horse trotting along on the avenue. 'I'll bet you five hundred dollars I can take that horse and make a pile of money out of him,' he said. The friend laughed and replied 'Well, I'll take that bet. The money is mine already.'

"Soon thereafter there began to appear in the newspapers glowing accounts of a wonderful horse captured by General John C. Frémont during his Western expedition. The articles described the horse as being covered with long woolly hair, and declared that its like was not known either by men or in books. Then it was announced that P. T. Barnum, the great showman, had bought this unnatural wonder, and that he would exhibit it all over the country.

"Washington was flooded with handbills exalting the 'Woolly Horse,' which was soon to come to town. Barnum rented an empty store just down the street from here. He posted a big sign outside stating that his woolly horse had been captured by Frémont, and day after day crowds paid well to look at it. There was a long line at the door one morning when Tom Benton passed by on his way to the Capitol. When the showbill caught his eye, he turned to a fellow-Congressman with whom he was walking and cried out:

" 'I'm going to put an end to this infernal swindle.' (Benton was, of course, General Frémont's father-in-law.) The ticket taker barred the way to the two Congressman, but Benton pushed him aside.

" 'I've had enough of this foolishness!' he cried angrily. And striding past him, he jumped over the rope that separated the woolly horse from its pop-eyed audience. With a slash of his pocketknife, he skinned half of the woolly cover off the animal. There it stood, once again just a bony old bay steed whose hide was just like that of all the horses in the world. The affair was the talk of Washington for the next nine days. No, I don't know whether Barnum collected his five-hundred-dollar bet or not."

Auctions are among the curiosities of the capital. Combining, as they do, the sales of furniture of Senators, Generals, and ministers of foreign countries, they attract all classes of bidders, from the very rich to the very poor. Fine furniture always sells for as much as its real value, and if it happens to have belonged to a prominent American family, it often brings more.

The rage for antique furniture continues, the auction prices mounting each year. There are three establishments here devoted to it, one in Washington, one in Georgetown, and one in Alexandria. They offer some very fine pieces, for this is one of the oldest parts of the United States which, in the early days, had a wealthy population. It is not uncommon to run across a relic of the Washington or Jefferson families, or other famous households of Colonial times.

Last week the Russian Consul General sold his furniture

at auction. It was advertised that all of it had been imported from Paris, and elegant offerings were expected. Although the stuff may have been fine once, it is far from good now. Everything I saw was cracked, broken, and shabby. I suppose all the really good pieces will be shipped along with their owner to Europe.

One of the old Negro women who are occasionally employed about the White House was sitting on a sofa at this sale. The piece was about to be sold. As I examined it, I asked, "Is this a good sofa, Auntie?"

"Yes, suh. Good enough, suh," she replied, "but I reckon it's full of bedbugs."

"How can you tell?" I asked her.

"Oh, I tells by its looks. Most every house in Washington has bedbugs one time or another. We often has 'em visit us at the White House, but we uses a good insect powder and kills 'em. Bedbugs gets on things you sets on as well as things you lays on. If you dusts 'em with powder in February, they doesn't hatch. We fights 'em all the time at the White House and we keeps 'em skase."

One of the strangest auction sales I have ever witnessed here was that of a number of coffins at Duncanson Brothers' auction rooms. The aging politicians were out in force, and Frank Hutton, George Gorham, and a score of others of like fame were among the purchasers. The coffins went quickly, each politician spanning his particular box to see if it would fit his own form, and sneaking away when he found one to suit him. Architect Hill, I noticed, took one of ebony lined with white silk, while Dorsey, of Star Route fame, bought one of mahogany and rosewood.

Washington has many book auctions each winter, at which valuable collections are sold. Such book auctions are always held in the evening, and Supreme Court Justices, Senators, and litterateurs mingle with their crowds. The books are sold by catalogue and the bidding is spirited.

Perhaps the most curious buyer of books here is a wealthy crank whose mind is somewhat disordered, but who understands book values to the last penny. I have often seen him in the auction rooms, a big man with a bullet head, wearing a low derby, pulled down so that it almost hides his eyes. The back of his neck is painted with lampblack and oil, and his round cheeks look as though they were rouged. The sleeves of his sack suit are always too large, and he keeps pulling them down over his unusually small hands. The man's shoulders are padded so that they become almost a deformity, and he wears small shoes made like those of a lady, with the heel near the center of the instep, which gives him a mincing gait.

At all the book auctions this curious figure appears. He carries a book in his hand so that when there is a lull in the bidding, he can turn back to his reading. I could tell you his name, but it will suffice to say he is the son of one of the oldest families of Georgetown, whose mild, harmless insanity is the result of a fall from a horse. His parents left his fortune so tied up that he gets only the income, but this is sufficiently large for him to have assembled one of the finest libraries in Washington.

Sitting in the Willard Hotel lobby last night, waiting for an interview with a Senator, I took note of the odd characters who passed by. First came Colonel George Boudinot, the old Indian lawyer, with his face as bronzed as a copper kettle, hair as black as a raven and as curly as a girl's, and eyes as piercing as an eagle's. He went to the register, glanced over the names to check his Western clients, and then departed. Colonel Boudinot has been the representative of the Indians at the court of their Great White Father for years. He is a striking figure among the curious characters here, and is one whom strangers want to see and to talk to. A man of considerable culture, he speaks English fluently, and is a talented singer. He possesses, however, his race's weakness for strong drink, so that he is not always fit for good society.

Next there came by the gray-haired patriarch who for a long time has represented Jay Gould in Washington. He is a clerical-looking old sinner, this veteran lobbyist, who moves in and out among the members of Congress with all the solemnity of a country parson. No one seems to know much of his early life. He slips around through a crowd like a greased pig at a county fair. But whenever a scheme involving Wall Street is before Congress, he is hard at work lobbying either for or against.

The newspapers are full of the recent visit of a crank to the White House. Many such people present themselves at this shining mansion on Pennsylvania Avenue, and the annals of Washington City are full of their curious stories.

In President Arthur's administration there was one who was convinced that the White House belonged to him. He continually demanded that Arthur move out and let him move in. Once he walked to Washington from his home in the Pennsylvania hills near Pittsburgh, and he arrived to take possession of the President's mansion with boots covered with mud. Informed by the experienced doorman that it would be inconvenient for the President to move just then, he went away muttering that he would come back in a few days, and that meanwhile he would take the matter up with the Attorney General of the United States.

Then there was the troubled woman who came bearing a box filled with old dresses for Mrs. Cleveland. She told the guards she had heard that the President's wife had "nothing fit to wear." It was the more ridiculous in that this woman was three times the size of Mrs. Cleveland, and that her own clothes were shabby and worn.

"I am sure that the President's wife will be grateful, Madam," the guard replied soothingly. And the crank went away satisfied.

A curious crank from Texas turned up at the end of President Arthur's term of office. He was respectable so far as appearances went. Not thirty years old, he wanted to present himself as Arthur's successor.

"Voices from heaven have been urging me to run for the presidency all summer long," he explained. "So a week ago I sold all my sheep, and I closed up my farmhouse, and here I am! The voices assured me that I would become king here and that George Washington himself would cover me with royal gems." Of course there was nothing for this one but to turn him over to the police for shelter, probably in an asylum.

Then not long ago a handsome English woman called at the White House to show the President her "ghost killer." This machine, she declared, would clear out all the haunted houses in the United States. She offered to demonstrate its effectiveness in the Washington jail, where she promised to exorcise the ghost of Garfield's assassin, Charles Guiteau. It was with difficulty that she was convinced that the President was too busy taking care of the living to give thought to these problems of the dead, so she took her case off to Senator Hale.

A daily ritual is observed this year at the White House by an old woman, bent over and poorly clad. Each evening promptly at six o'clock, she arrives. She walks up the curved driveway to the front portico. There she mounts two or three steps, bows her head toward the front door, then hurries away. Sometimes a young girl accompanies her, but usually she is alone.

Often there are several cranks a day among the stream of callers at the President's home. Especially following an inauguration of a new Chief Executive are the numbers large and unruly, and there are many like the men from Pennsylvania and Texas, who imagine they have been called to be the new ruler of the United States. The harmless ones are allowed to go on their way, the more violent are sent to some asylum for the insane.

But the doorkeepers do not dare to consider any crank entirely harmless. In the past twenty-five years two Presidents have been killed by the bullets of crazy assassins. Mr. Blaine, who was a witness to the Garfield assassination, is obsessed with the dangers of permitting such cranks to roam at large here in the nation's capital.

CHAPTER XVIII

Names and Noses in the News

ENERAL BEN BUTLER, the defeated candidate for Governor of Massachusetts, is the best advertised man in the United States. He understands publicity better than P. T. Barnum, and he enlists everyone in the task of making him famous. During his campaign, no name, not even that of the President, appeared oftener in the news.

Gray-haired Dr. C. A. Bartol, one of the severest of Butler's critics, says "Butler prefers notice, however unflattering, to neglect. Silence he would hold a fate of the worst kind."

"It is strange," said a prominent Bostonian the other day, "that the wealthy Ben Butler should have been the poor man's candidate in Massachusetts, but it is so. He is worth millions. He has one of the finest yachts that floats. He owns at Lowell an elegant home filled with art treasures that cost a small fortune. He travels like an aristocrat in a special train which takes him from his home into Boston. He never makes a speech but that his portly form is clothed in a steel-pen coat, in whose buttonhole blooms a rich red rosebud."

No one knows exactly what Ben Butler is worth. He has railroad stock in Virginia, mills in Massachusetts, and real estate everywhere. He does not talk about his personal affairs, and I doubt whether his own family knows the extent of his assets. His house here on Capitol Hill, which cost a furtune, rents for fifteen thousand dollars a year.

Hi, dey tell me dat Ben Butler has shuck his ha'ness sho.
Dey say he's gone a gallopin' and won't come back no mo'.
I reckon he's disappointed—got his belly full o' bile—
Des because ole Masserchusetts won't let him rule er-while.
But Good Lord! Dem long-head Yankees hab waked up, sho's you bo'n,
Dey hab done got sick of Butler a-tootin' of his ho'n.

These are supposed to be the sentiments of a colored man upon hearing of Ben Butler's defeat. Of all the candidates who lost the election, Butler gets the least sympathy. The opinion now is that Butler is politically dead and that the election records of last week are his death sentence. But in this little rhyme, the colored citizen goes on to say:

But I don' belieb de rumor 'bout Butler gwine to quit,
A-mixin' up wid politics and restin' up a bit.
He's lived on 'Publican possums, dished up wid silver spoons,
And now he's had a feast awhile on Democratic coons.
But Masserchusetts done got mad bekase he tried to boss 'em,
And now he's loss his coon, sparerib, and hasn't got his possum.

I'm like the man in the rhyme. I don't believe that Butler is by any means dead, either. Anyone who thinks he will drop into obscurity without a struggle is much mistaken. For the past ten years he has been the most talked-of man in the United States, and in all probability, next year will see him running as the independent, anti-monopolist, anti-capitalist, pro-labor candidate. As such he will take such a vote from the Democrats that they will be defeated by the Republicans. Thus the vengeance of Ben Butler will be satisfied.

John S. Wise, the Republican candidate for the governorship of Virginia, came near being mobbed at Alexandria last night. The outlook is that he will have another duel on his hands before the campaign is over. Wise is a brave fellow. He has fought duels before, though he has never yet killed his man. He has been brave enough, too, to refuse to fight when challenged, as in his nonacceptance of the request of Page McCarty to meet him on the field about a year ago.

The Wise family is accustomed to dueling. Henry A. Wise fought a number of duels, and was second in others, notably the one between Graves and Cilley, which created such excitement some fifty years ago. The blood of John S. Wise also is hot. I am not surprised to hear that he struck with his fist the face of a man who called him a liar not long ago. Although he is now only thirty-nine years old, he was a lieutenant in the Confederate Army. He has a big heart, but his feelings are easily swayed this way or that in a tense moment.

John Wise is his father's son by a second marriage, born at Rio de Janeiro while his father was there as United States Minister under Tyler. On the day of his birth, a dozen different American flags were flown on the Consular Mansion. Henry Wise was determined that there should be no mistake about his son's having been born under the American flag, since he could not be born on American soil. The baby's mother was the daughter of John Sergeant, the Whig candidate for Vice-President in 1832. Henry A. Wise was a gay young widower while Miss Sergeant was in Washington, and it was up in the Capitol dome that he popped the question to her. One of the fruits of their marriage was this present candidate for the Governor of Virginia.

The papers say that Bob Ingersoll will make forty thousand dollars in legal fees out of the Star Route trial alone. The exposure of this great public fraud is one of the scandals of all time. It was discovered as long ago as the administration of President Hayes, yet the case is only now being settled.

The Star Routes were those of the Postal Service over which mail had to be carried by horse or wagon, and which were marked in the Postal Guide with tiny stars to distinguish them from the routes covered by trains or ships. One hundred and thirty-five of these mail routes were involved in the operations of the unscrupulous ring. Among those alleged to have been members were a Second Assistant Postmaster General, Thomas W. Brady, and a former Senator, Stephen W. Dorsey, of Arkansas. Their graft, which was obtained by illegally increasing payments to certain mail contractors, ran into the hundreds of thousands of dollars.

Among the counsel of this great trial, the man who attracts the most attention is Bob Ingersoll. When he rises to speak, the courtroom is quieter than when the judge renders a decision. When not speaking, Ingersoll sits behind a long table, writing, lolling, whispering, or laughing as the mood takes him. Today, he was chewing tobacco vigorously while I watched him, his jaws moving up and down, making their flesh expand and contract like India rubber. Bob Ingersoll likes tobacco, and his bump of reverence is not large enough to make him stop chewing during a court session.

Ingersoll is a peculiar-looking man. His head is as round as a cannon ball, and it is as though the Lord forgot his neck when He put him together. His kindly eyes are blue, his forehead is high, and the top of his head is bald. His small nose is slightly turned upward, and with his full cheeks, his thick lips remind one of those of a mulatto. He looks for all the world like an overgrown boy, and it is not unfair to say that he often acts like one. Sometimes he puts his hands into his pockets when he is speaking, and when he makes a joke, he joins the audience in the laugh it provokes.

It is a whole volume of fun to see Bob Ingersoll laugh. His blue eyes twinkle, his fat face breaks into a broad smile, and his white teeth show. Then the fun seems to go down into his body. He laughs all over, from the fuzzy hair around his bald head to the beefy calves of his fat legs, his big belly shaking until the gold watch chain across it seems to jingle. Bob Ingersoll is not rich but he commands good fees. A friend of his estimates his yearly income at about a hundred thousand a year.

You may see "Infidel Bob" here in Washington almost any day now. He is a New York man by birth, the little town of Dresden, in the northern part of the state, having the honor of his origin. His father was a preacher, so that Bob was duly baptized, actually in a theater where his father was preaching. It may be that this early introduction to the stage has been the cause of his backsliding.

When young Bob was ten years old, his father moved west. He made the boy learn the Westminster catechism by heart, and in due time educated him for the law. Bob Ingersoll first became of national note in the Cincinnati convention when he made his great speech nominating Blaine. His reputation made, he was in demand as a lecturer. He began to utter his infidel sentiments, they attracted attention, and made his lectures pay. His utterances then became more pronounced, and he finally made his reputation and his fortune by denouncing hell and the Bible.

Whether Mrs. Ingersoll endorses the doctrines of her husband or not, I don't know, but whenever he travels, she goes with him, and she is said also to have a great influence over him.

A tall young man with a complexion of the rich color of a ripe chestnut, and limbs as cleanly cut as those of Michelangelo's statue of David, called on President Cleveland the other day. He wanted an appointment to a cadetship at West Point. It was young Hole-in-the-Day, the son of the noted Chippewa chief, and now the king of all the Chippewas. I met him this morning. He is about eighteen years old, is over six feet tall, and has eyes as sharp as those of an eagle.

It was in Washington that the father of Hole-in-the-Day met the woman who became his wife. In 1867 old Hole-in-the-Day came here to see President Johnson. He was made much of by the newspapers, fêted by society, and was everywhere described as the rich Indian king who owned the greater part of the lands of our Northwest.

At his hotel there was a pretty Irish chambermaid who tidied up the chief's room. They two met. They looked. And from their eyes sprang love. Chief Hole-in-the-Day, who had been smiled upon by many of the Washington belles, passed them by and chose the chambermaid. He proposed. She accepted. They were married and she went back to Minnesota an Indian queen. From this marriage came this boy who has inherited his father's name and position.

The old king incurred the anger of some of the tribes by his marriage with a white wife. They suspected him of treacherously giving away some of their lands and they assassinated him. Mrs. Hole-in-the-Day, Sr., still lives. Her son has a true military bearing, walking and looking the king's son that he is. He dresses in American clothes and speaks pure Anglo-Saxon. Governor Ramsay is pushing his case here so he will no doubt receive the appointment he seeks.

Within the next month, Alexander R. Shepherd, better known as "Boss" Shepherd, is expected to return to Washington. The papers are now full of his praise, and a grand celebration is to be given in his honor. Few will remember that when he went away from Washington he was denounced as a jobber and a fraud, and he will return the most fêted and honored man in the capital.

It was Shepherd who transformed Washington from a straggling Southern village, scattered over an immense territory, to the most magnificent city of the world. During his period of great power as head of the Board of Public Works in the short-lived territorial government of the District of Columbia, eighty of the three hundred miles of poor streets were improved, the most populous were paved with wood and concrete, parks were laid out, sewers were dug, and canals were filled in. In all, nearly twenty million dollars were spent in beautifying the nation's capital. To pay this immense sum, Congress appropriated five million dollars in cash, two million dollars were raised with street improvement bonds, and the remainder came from bonds floated at a high interest rate.

At the time he was named Governor of the District of Columbia by President Grant, Alexander R. Shepherd was said to be worth one hundred thousand dollars, which he had made in his business as a plumber. While in office he dealt widely in real estate, and it is said he built over one thousand buildings. He spent ten million dollars in construction and handled much more than this in his land deals. While he was wealthy the people praised him, but in 1876, when he became financially embarrassed, there was none so poor to do him reverence.

Boss Shepherd left Washington for Mexico, saying he would not return until he had made enough money to buy the whole city of Washington. I understand that he has made another fortune there in mining, but it is doubtful that he has enough to carry out his proud boast. The Washington he left was a poorer town than the Washington to which he returns. But if the city could pay him what she owes him for the good he once did her, he might be able to supply the rest.

The office boy has just handed me a paper announcing the death of Mrs. Brewster, the wife of the ex-Attorney General of the United States. She was the handsomest woman of the Cabinet families of President Arthur's administration, and one of the most accomplished hostesses of the capital. Her husband, ugly as he is, is undoubtedly one of the most polished gentlemen Washington society has ever known.

Mrs. Brewster numbered Benjamin Franklin among her ancestors. She was dandled on the knee of good fortune until the death of her father, Robert J. Walker, when, receiving no money from his impoverished estate, and finding herself a young widow with three small children to support, she was obliged to take a position in the Government. It was while she was thus employed—in the Internal Revenue Department of the Treasury, I think it was—that she first met Mr. Brewster. Then practicing law, he had come to the Treasury in connection with a case. As he passed the young widow's desk he overheard her whisper to a neighbor clerk, "Well, that's the ugliest man I ever saw in my life!" To her great embarrassment, Brewster raised his tall white hat as he turned and bowed to her. "Thank you, madam," he said, "I always like to hear a lady say just what she thinks."

This adventure was followed shortly by an introduction and the acquaintance ripened into a sentimental attachment on the part of Mr. Brewster. It is said that, in popping the question, the Attorney General declared "You, madam, are beautiful, and I am hideous. But it will not be the first instance of the mating of beauty and the beast. Though you may never come to love me, I swear that you shall never regret having become my wife." And so the match was made.

Brewster himself was a widower. Curiously, both he and his new bride had been previously married to foreigners, his first wife having been a Prussian, and her first husband an unpleasant Frenchman named Delon. After the marriage, Brewster adopted the three Delon children, and little Benny Brewster, the bright boy who furnished the source of so many stories about Washington children, was the sole fruit of the union.

Mr. Brewster's extreme ugliness is the result of severe burns received as a boy. Here at Washington, perhaps to draw attention away from his face, he has affected the clothes of a generation ago: ruffled shirts, velvet vests, and a tall white silk hat with a nap as long as the fur of a cat. The former

Attorney General likes to surround himself with beautiful things. His office, during the Arthur administration, had the furniture, bric-a-brac and hangings of a king's drawing room. He likes Oriental rugs and handsome antiques, and he has spent forty years assembling his china collection. Some of its plates cost two hundred dollars a dozen; one of the dinner sets, which belonged to Louis Philippe, was decorated with hand-painted landscapes, no single piece costing less than fifty dollars.

Mr. Brewster is proud of his family. The Brewster coat of arms is displayed on everything he owns: his silver, his writing paper, even his nightshirts. The splendid yellow coach which he drove about Washington had his arms emblazoned upon its panels, while the buttons on his servants' liveries were stamped with the same crest.

The nose is the emblem of the soul. It is only a wad of cartilage and flesh, but by it you may read its owner as though he were an open book, and its extent and shape gives the measure of the statesman and the fool. The Greeks added an inch to the human nose and made their marble heroes gods.

Of the great men of the past not one in a score has had a snub nose or a pug, and of the mighty men of Washington today, the proboscises of nine out of ten are enormous. Where will you find a bigger nose than that of James G. Blaine, the great Republican politician? It is the nose of a leader, with all the characteristics of a Roman patrician, the kind of nose which Plato says is sure indication of power. It is a clear signpost of Blaine's personal magnetism and of his intellectual force. It seemed even bigger when he was a boy, and it gave him at college the nickname "Nosy" Blaine.

Many of our Presidents have had big noses. Look at the portraits of George Washington, and Thomas Jefferson! President Arthur has a good-sized nose, while the size of that of Abe Lincoln has become proverbial. John Tyler had an immense proboscis, and Andrew Jackson's was one of the biggest and handsomest noses of all.

Jackson was one of the two Presidents who had their noses pulled while they were in Washington. He was on a Potomac River boat which had stopped at Alexandria, when a man rushed up to him, grabbed his nose, and gave it a terrible yank. "Old Hickory" raised his cane, but his assailant escaped. This nose-puller was a lieutenant who had been dismissed from the Navy and who blamed the President for his trouble.

James K. Polk had his nose pulled when he was Speaker of the House of Representatives. It was expected that he would challenge his attacker but Polk claimed that the man who had tried to pull his nose had not succeeded, so the matter was dropped. It is said that Jackson looked upon Polk as a coward because he did not fight, and that he afterward held for him a secret dislike on this account.

It is in the Supreme Court that you will find the biggest noses of Washington. Justice Fuller has the nose of a Roman, while that of Justice Field might have been modeled in ancient Greece. I can never look at Justice Bradley's nose without thinking of figures. The great mathematician and the great jurist are written all over it; it is so big that it seems to be running away with the face. Justice Harlan has a head which would do for a model of Jove, with a nose like that of a god. It is a nose which sculptors would rave about, and it has that delicate rosy hue of the Justice's ruddy complexion which corresponds in color to the best efforts of that florid artist, Peter Paul Rubens.

In the press gallery this afternoon I took a look at the noses of some of the Senators. What a very handsome beak has Senator George Edmunds of Vermont! It stands out like a great rosy bow between those red cheeks, and there is a striking Roman curve between its tip and its meeting with the forehead. Edmunds' head is as bald at the top as a billiard ball, and from his silvery whiskers up over his crown, his skin is as fair as that of a baby. His nose has this same pale hue. It is charged that at times the Senator takes a bit of old brandy for his stomach's sake, but this has never really discolored his nose and he looks as though he fed on grits and spring water. His is a judicial nose, a legal nose, and when it smells at the law it smells for pay.

As to golden noses, however, there are a dozen in the Senate Chamber which would bring wealth galore if their owners were in the hands of brigands. Senator John Sherman made a trip to Cuba a few years ago, during which he came within an ace of being captured by the banditti and held for ransom. His nose is a strong one, but I hardly suppose he would say it was worth $500,000. Yet had they caught him, and with razor in hand threatened to cut that nose off, I imagine they would have gotten their money.

Consider the nose of Senator Leland Stanford of California! You could put it in a wineglass, but Stanford would not sell it for fifty million dollars. The same is true of the long thin smeller of Senator George Hearst. The noses of these two money-makers are entirely different. Stanford's is fat, with large nostrils. Hearst's is secretive and thin, and is said to be the best nose for mines in the country. It is not, however, the nose of a statesman. It has not the pugnacity or cruelty of the nose that sits above the snow-white collar and the red necktie of Senator John J. Ingalls, of Kansas, and defies the world, the flesh, and the devil. There's a fighting nose for you. That nose might be the nose of a pirate. It might be the nose of a reformer, of a writer, or a poet. It is the nose of an orator and a genius. It is the great and only nose of the great and only Ingalls, and it is a nose which some Senators, I know, would like to pull, but dare not.

Among the hundreds of noses in the House of Representatives you will find all kinds, all sizes, all shapes. Congressman William McKinley has a good nose, inclined to be Roman. It is conservative and thoughtful, and its owner does not like to be told that it looks like the nose of Napoleon. It is broad at the top, has a spectacle bridge between the eyes, and it droops just enough to make the face serious. It is a watchful nose, and it is nose that watches out for McKinley.

I saw a nose last night that must have cost—for its coloring alone—ten thousand dollars. It was fastened above the mouth of one of the most noted diners-out of Washington society, and it shows what men can do in the making of their own noses. The nose of the high-liver is far different from that of the man who lives on oatmeal. This man, whom I shall call only General B, is noted for his love of terrapin and champagne. He has held a high rank in the Army of the United States, and he has one of the biggest heads and the most silvery manes in the capital.

General B's nose is a wonder. It is fat, large, and of a bright blue-red hue. It looks like a rose-colored pincushion, and you can read champagne, chartreuse, and old bourbon in its tiny red veins. It is so prominent, indeed, that it caused its owner a good deal of embarrassment at a fancy-dress ball a year or so ago. At the party the General met a charming young lady who pleased him very much. She wore a lace mask, and she chatted coquettishly with him from behind it. Toward the end of the evening, he asked her to unmask, and he found her as pretty as she was witty.

While he was complimenting her, she cried, "Now it is your turn. I have taken off my mask, I want you to take yours off."

"But, my dear, I am not masked," the General replied. "It is my own natural face which gazes with so much admiration upon yours."

"I don't believe it," the gay young lady laughed. "You are wonderfully made up, but that nose could only be false. Come now, take off that nose!"

The General's face grew redder than ever. His nose turned even bluer in his discomfiture. The evening was ruined before he could persuade the pretty girl that his nose was flesh and blood.

CHAPTER XIX

Fabulous Fortunes

MANY OF THE Senatorial figures of these times were born with silver spoons in their mouths. One, however, is so enormously wealthy that his spoon must have been gold— Leland Stanford of California! There he sits at the very tail end of the Republican back row, that big, fat-shouldered man with a neck almost as thick as Cleveland's and a beard as sandy as that of Brigham Young's.

Stanford is said to be worth seventy-five million dollars, and there he sits reading a newspaper through a pair of rubber-rimmed spectacles, dressed in plain black broadcloth little better than the Sunday suit of day laborers all over these United States. That small black necktie did not cost more than fifty cents. His whole "outfit," as they say in the state from which he comes, would not bring ten dollars if sold to a second-hand-clothing man.

Seventy-five million dollars! It is hard to conceive of such a sum. Invested at 6 per cent—and in California that is a very small percentage indeed—it would bring in $4,500,000 a year, more than $86,000 a week, more than $12,000 a day, and more than $500 an hour. This California Senator could buy out most of his brother lawmakers and still have money to spare. The best of it all is that he has made this fortune himself.

Born near Albany, New York, about sixty years ago, in a poor farmer's family, Leland Stanford worked in the summer and studied in the winter. At the age of twenty-five he had finished his law and was admitted to the bar. He then moved to Wisconsin to practice, and had not a fire burned out his office, he might be there yet.

The fire led him to go to California, where he arrived when the gold fever was at its height. He went into business in Sacramento where he made money rapidly. Entering politics, he was, at the beginning of the late War, elected Governor of California. Leland Stanford organized the Central Pacific Railroad, being the chief force in pushing it to its completion. Since then he has made money continuously, and has invested his wealth in all manner of paying enterprises. He owns ranches, vineyards, railroads, and mines. This Croesus of the Senate stands with Vanderbilt and Jay Gould among the wealthiest men in America. Like Vanderbilt, he is fond of good horses. On his great breeding farm at Palo Alto, where he keeps about a thousand fine steeds, he employs one hundred and fifty hands, and his overseer is paid a salary of $10,000 a year.

All Stanford's wealth, however, has not kept sorrow away. Not long ago he lost his only son, a boy of sixteen, and though Parson Newman was paid, they say, $10,000 to conduct the boy's funeral, his words were not powerful enough to cure the stricken father's grief. Senator Stanford has since endowed a college at Palo Alto with $3,000,000 in honor of his son, and has made a will leaving his immense fortune to the state of California. It is reported that he is an ardent spiritualist, and that he has given a good deal of money to the mediums since his son's death.

"Look at that little, dark-faced man over there! They say he is worth more than one hundred million dollars."

This is the remark I heard yesterday afternoon when I entered the committee room in the Capitol where Jay Gould is being investigated. I followed the direction of a pointing finger, and my eyes rested on Jay Gould, the maker and breaker of railroads, and the most powerful rich man on this hemisphere. The newspapers have published his picture, but none give any idea of the real man. He was the last person in the room whom you would have taken for Jay Gould, for beside the tall, stout Congressman who sat near him, he looked like an insignificant pigmy.

If ex-Governor Curtin could be folded in two like a ruler, he would be almost as tall as Jay Gould. Burns, of Missouri, who sat on the other side of the table has enough flesh to make two men the size of this multimillionaire. Still Gould has more power for good and evil than a hundred Curtins or five hundred Burnses. His income is more than five million dollars a year, or thirteen thousand dollars a day.

Let me tell you how Jay Gould looks as he undergoes the Congressional examination. He has just stated that he is forty-nine years of age, and he sits with a tired look on his face, answering the questions being put to him. He speaks easily in tones as soft as a woman's, and there is nothing ostentatious or aggressive about him. A couple of his detectives sit nearby, and his lawyer is at his back to give advice when it is needed. But Gould himself answers the questions and he exhibits no fear as he reads his denunciation of the railroad strikers with a display of feeling.

Jay Gould has as much right to his millions as any rich man in the country today. Money-making schemes are like executive sessions of the Senate; they are conducted behind closed doors, and as to the morality of the procedures he uses, I have nothing to say.

John W. Mackay, the bonanza millionaire, is in Washington this week. It is said he intends buying property and coming here to live, in which case his wife will preside over his Washington mansion and some of the wonderful entertainments which she has been giving in Paris will probably be repeated. She will display her hundreds of thousands of dollars' worth of jewelry, will give grand receptions and elegant dinners. All Washington will bow down and worship her even as the Israelites fell down before the golden calf in the days of the Pharaohs.

The superiority of the aristocracy of wealth over the aristocracy of birth was never better illustrated. Mrs. Mackay's father, whose name was Hungerford, was years ago a barber's apprentice in the little town of Waterford, New York, while John W. Mackay himself kept a saloon in Louisville. His bar was a counter of pine boards and his liquors were served in glasses as thick as a chemist's mortar. At the time of the gold fever, Mackay went to California, where by hard work and sharp bargaining, he made himself one of the richest of the gold millionaires. Now his wife has been for years one of the most noted of society women, and the most fêted of all Americans abroad. Mackay's stepdaughter has married one of the noblest princes in Italy.

Mrs. Mackay is said to be a woman of great good sense and some accomplishment. Her father had risen to be a major in New Orleans before she was married, and her first husband, a doctor who died while they were living in Nevada, left her in reduced circumstances. Mackay, who heard of the poor widow and her child, raised a subscription among his fellow miners to help her, and it was in presenting the money that he first met her.

In thinking of the rich men of the United States, there comes to my mind again the noted philanthropist W. W. Corcoran, who has never cared for money for money's sake. I cannot better sum up the philosophy of life of this millionaire than by this quotation of the dedication of his collection of autograph letters to his grandchildren. It reads—

To my Grandchildren:

As a private individual, inspired by an appreciation of my relations to my fellow-men, I have, from early youth to old age, endeavored to be just to all and generous to the deserving. Blessed by kind Providence with larger possessions than commonly fall to the lot of man, I have regarded them as a sacred trust for the benefit of knowledge, truth and charity. My reward has been an approving conscience, and the gratifying appreciation of the many good and great men, whose testimonies I have preserved in this volume for you.

Many of the letters in this collection afford melancholy evidence of the instability of human affairs; and a perusal of them will suggest to you the propriety of endeavoring to cultivate a spirit prepared to bear with equanimity the vicissitudes of fortune which may alter the most prosperous condition.

The most valuable bequest I can make you is a good name, and I feel sure you will cherish it, for its price is above rubies.

Your affectionate grandfather,
W. W. Corcoran.

July 1 1878

These are modest words from the man who has had the career of William Wilson Corcoran, and whose good name is certainly of greater value than all his wealth. He has given away three fourths of all he ever made. In sums of over five thousand dollars his benefactions amount to nearly six million dollars. In smaller sums he has distributed another million and a half, and his purse is always open. The people who have gained by his benevolence are numbered by the thousands, while the Corcoran Gallery, which he endowed with two million dollars, has given American art a firm establishment in the capital of our nation.

Another slant on the difficulties of intelligent giving is reflected in a comment which one of the rich men of Congress made to me lately.

"It is wonderful," he said, "how fast a man's fortune grows once he gets to Washington. When I came to Congress I supposed myself, from an inventory of my various possessions, to be worth a certain number of millions of dollars. I had not been here a week before the newspapers began to estimate my pile, and in a single month it had swelled to ten millions more than I had when I arrived. Now, I have made money fast at times, but never so fast as the newspapers make it for me. They publish their exaggerated reports and credit me with being such a generous millionaire that they bring an army of beggars down upon me. I get letters from all parts of the country proposing all sorts of ridiculous schemes."

The multimillionaires of today live like so many princes. Many a king would rejoice in the splendors of their homes. Jay Gould keeps up several different establishments, and the machinery of each moves whether he is in residence or not. James Gordon Bennett, the owner of the New York *Herald,* another of such rich men, proposes to come to this country shortly. He might choose to go to his elegant mansion in New York without a moment's warning. His usual evening banquet would be served to him as smoothly as if he had been living in New York right along. Fires would be burning in every room and his staff of butlers and cooks would be on hand Samuel J. Tilden is still living here at Graystone, but his

New York house is ready for him the moment his fancy turns that way. His whim can install him comfortably there with no more annoyance than the traveling to New York.

Such royal living has not been known since the days of Caligula. The only comfort we poor men can get out of it is the knowledge that half the millionaires have neither the stomachs nor strength to enjoy their fortunes. Tilden, for instance, has to live almost entirely on fruit, he cannot speak above a consumptive whisper, and he dare not walk on the street without a servant by his side to catch him if he should fall. John Kelley is another who never goes out unaccompanied, and all of A. T. Stewart's great fortune did not keep his body from being stolen from its tomb.

After all, there are only twenty-four hours in a day for Jay Gould, just as there are for you and me. Terrapin and champagne cannot tickle his stomach into more friendly response than hog and hominy for the laborer. His children's smiles are not brighter than ours, and his worries are fully as great. His little frame will rest no easier in the Ionic temple mausoleum he has erected in granite in the Woodlawn Cemetery, than will ours in our six feet of earth. With his $13,000 a day and his $5,000,000 a year, at the end of twelve months he has only lived as we have. He has eaten, drunk, and slept. The sun has shone, the seasons have brought their variety, and all balance sheets show just so much happiness and just so much misery. I doubt not that on the whole our balance sheets contain as much pleasure as his.

CHAPTER XX

Inventors and Inventions

THE CAREER of Professor Alexander Graham Bell presents one of the most remarkable Monte Cristo romances in this country of mushroom fortunes. A dozen years ago he was a teacher in a deaf and dumb school, his coat well worn at the seams, and his brain bursting with ideas about sending sounds on electric waves carried on wires. Now his check is good for millions. His clothes are of the finest quality and of the latest cut. In his mansion near Scott Circle, which cost a hundred thousand dollars, the furnishings surpass those of the White House. His pressed brick stable is located on ground worth three dollars a square foot, and it is so constructed that many a public man in Washington would be glad to own it for a residence.

Professor Bell jumped by one leap to the head of the scientists of the country. He is now considered the peer of anyone in this city of great men. As a schoolteacher, he taught the deaf and dumb for a pittance. Now a millionaire philanthropist, he spends thousands in carrying out his pet theories in regard to deaf-mutes.

With all his generosity, he finds it hard to use up his income. His library contains the choicest of finely bound books and his workshop in the top of his palatial home takes in a view of all Washington, with its thousands of telephone wires smothering it like a network. Putting his ear to his receiver, he can hear the working of his thought at New York, Baltimore, and Pittsburgh. In imagination he can see the wires which he originated running through all parts of the earth, bringing cities and country villages together into the closest of family relationships.

"Telephone" Bell is of British origin. An Englishman with the complexion of a Latin, he is between forty and fifty years of age, tall and well rounded. His chin and cheeks are covered with a short curly beard. His head is large and round; his forehead high and broad; his eyes a soft velvety black. He dresses usually in business clothes, is democratic in his manner, and courtly at all times. There is nothing of the snob about him and he bears his good fortune like a gentleman.

Mrs. Bell, who is deaf, is one of the most beautiful and interesting women in Washington. Bell became infatuated with her beauty, and married her. In experimenting on an audiphone, that she might be enabled to hear, he discovered the principle of the telephone. In this way his wife indirectly made his fortune. Mrs. Bell has learned to speak by watching and studying the movements of the lips of others. She can carry on a conversation now as well as you or I, and the only difference is in the sounds of her voice, which are not so nicely modulated as those of one who can hear as well as speak.

Her husband's fortune is not the only one Mrs. Bell has made. Eliphalet Andrews, the portrait painter, owes his start to his picture of her. He had come here from Cincinnati unknown, and he had found but little to do. Mrs. Bell gave him a sitting, and he had the luck and the skill to catch one of her most beautiful expressions. The picture was shown at Corcoran's gallery, where crowds flocked to see it. The unknown Andrews was unknown no longer. Orders poured in so that he now deserves his title, "the Portrait Painter of the Capital."

Contrary to the current reports, Professor Alexander Graham Bell does not believe the time has come when telephone wires should be put underground, though he does think that this will eventually be done. For such an arrangement an entirely new kind of wire and new instruments will be needed.

I hear today that a company has been organized in New York, with a capital of several millions, to manage the Baxter transmitter, invented by Myron L. Baxter of this city. By the aid of this invention, people here at Washington talked recently with people in Cleveland, seven hundred and fifty miles away, and heard each other distinctly. The official of the Western Union Telegraph Company, who was present with the experts at the trial talk with New York, expressed himself satisfied. Words whispered fifteen feet from the transmitter in Washington were distinctly audible in New York.

It is probable that the Bell Telephone Company, joining with Jay Gould and the Western Union, will secure control of this invention and use it in connection with their monopoly combination. Thus they could establish a stock company to which the Western Union Telegraph and the Standard Oil monopolies would rank as nothing. The Western Union has now nearly four hundred thousand miles of wire, the Bell Telephone Company about seventy thousand. By the adoption of this transmitter, they could, in a month, reach every part of the country and Canada by telephone, and create a revolution in the telegraph business. If they do so, telegraph stock will go down

like a shot. A great deal of money is now invested in the telegraph, and it looks to me that it is in a very unsafe position.

Wonderful improvements have recently been made in the
Gatling gun. Dr. Gatling, the inventor, has been here for some
days, illustrating them to the leading men of the War Department. He has shown that the gun can now fire on an average
twelve hundred shots per minute continuously, and that the
latest inventions enable it to be fired at any angle. Before this,
the force of gravity prevented the firing upward or downward
beyond a certain degree, but this has been entirely overcome. A
shot can now be sent perpendicularly into the air, and the gun
can be so aimed as to throw bullets inside a fort or any be-
sieged fortification.

Dr. Richard Jordan Gatling is now sixty-six years old. He
is a tall, broad-shouldered, white-whiskered man with a
friendly face, bright blue eyes, and a pleasant speech. I talked
with him at the Ebbitt House last evening about his gun, and
he told me how he came to invent it.

"I had made several inventions before this, one of which was
the wheat drill, now in use all over the country. I think it was
my study on that which prepared me for the Gatling gun. In
1861 I was living in Indianapolis. The War had broken out,
and the country was all excitement. My house was within a
few blocks of the depot, and I was often present when volun-
teers were departing for the field, also when their dead bodies
were shipped back home for burial. One surprise to me was
that the number of men killed by sickness and disease was more
than those killed by ball or actual battle.

"One day, I remember, nineteen corpses were landed at
the depot; only three had been killed in battle. The thought
then struck me, that if a gun could be invented that would do
the work of a hundred ordinary guns, and yet would require
but a few men to operate it, more of the enemy could be disposed of on the battlefield. The horrors of war would thus be
greatly diminished, for the end of each combat would come

much sooner. In the end, lives would be saved. The thought took such hold of me that I commenced to work on it at once. The result was the Gatling gun. The first ones, which were made in Cincinnati, would fire from a hundred and fifty to two hundred and fifty shots per minute."

"Will there ever come a time, Doctor, when wars will end for good?" I asked.

"I do not think so. Human nature is the same in all ages, and the strong will continue to oppress and rule over the weak as long as time shall last. It is so in nations and with individuals. The mother rules the child until it becomes a man. Then it, growing stronger, dictates to the mother. In this world the weakest must always go to the wall. The strong survive. Improved warfare and better arms may give war greater power. But I doubt whether any invention will make war so terrible that men will refuse to engage in it."

I have spent the last week in looking at the freaks of the Patent Office. In this building, side by side with the greatest inventions of the age, are some of the craziest products of the human brain. Today some mighty Edison patents an idea which lights the world; tomorrow some lunatic offers a plan by which all humanity is supposed to lift itself to heaven by its bootstraps. In looking through the Patent Office, one is surprised at the wisdom and foolishness of man's intellect. The one is as great as the other, and from the foolish point of view it would seem that when an idea of a patent creeps into an inventor's head, common sense flies out of the window.

Take the department of canes and umbrellas. There are thousands of canes of all shapes and sizes, one of which is a cane and spittoon combined. It is patented by Myron L. Baxter, the inventor of the Baxter telephone transmitter, and it states that the tobacco chewer has only to pretend to suck the head of the cane, when he can slip his saliva into it to the extent of half a pint. Thus his lady love or the preacher need know nothing of it. "This cane," Baxter writes, "is of great advantage during the continuance of religious services, lectures or other entertainments." Its top is made into the shape of a dog's head, and the opening for the expectoration is in the mouth of the dog.

Another cane has an eyeglass attached to its head, and a third is so arranged that the drinking man may carry his allowance of whisky inside it and take his nip on the sly. There are cane-umbrellas, sword canes, and pistol canes; and canes which are so jointed that they can be formed into the legs of a stool of such a nature that the pedestrian can sit down and take a rest during a walk.

Some of the greatest patent successes are toys, and there are a dozen toy inventors who have made fortunes during the last twenty years. Among these are Crandall, who got up the "Pigs in Clover" puzzle; Plimpton, the man who invented the roller skate; the inventor of the returning ball, and many others. There are perhaps two thousand toys in this one division of the Patent Office.

One of the latest and craziest curiosities is a doll baby that sucks the bottle. The toy, patented by Rudolph Steiner, of Germany, consists of a doll baby sitting on a pan with a bottle filled with genuine milk on a little table in front of it. A rubber tube connects with a glass pipe which runs into the bottle, and going into the mouth of the doll runs down behind and through the doll into the pan. By means of a syphon which comes out through the doll's head, machinery is set to work by which the doll begins to suck, and the milk flows up into its mouth and out into the pan. No sensible mother would ever think of buying such a toy for her child, as it would be the dirtiest and sloppiest of amusements. Still this man Steiner thought so much of it that he patented it both in Germany and America, and he evidently expects to become rich with it.

The illuminated cat, which was granted a patent in 1884, is not a toy. Instead it has the useful purpose of frightening rats and mice. This cat, of pasteboard and tin, is to be made in a sitting posture, and to be painted over with phosphorous so that it shines in the dark like a cat of fire. Its inventor states that it ought to be perfumed with oil of peppermint, which is obnoxious to rats and mice; and that while it serves to scare the rodents away in the dark, it may be made so as to form a useful parlor ornament in the daytime.

The medical patents are of every description. One of the most ridiculous, referred to in a recent speech in Congress, is a tapeworm trap. Its inventor is a man named Myers, who claims he has had great success in catching tapeworms with it. The trap consists of a little gold capsule about half an inch long and as big around as a lead pencil. At the end of this capsule there is a tiny ring, to which a long silk thread is to be tied. By pulling the capsule apart, you set a spring a good deal like that of the old-fashioned steel-toothed rattrap. You bait it with a bit of cheese, starve yourself and your tapeworm for about three days, then swallow the trap, maintaining all the while a careful hold of the thread attached to it. Your tapeworm, which by this time is very hungry, makes a greedy dash for the cheese and, presto! the jaws of the capsule spring together on his head. You draw him out, hand over hand, then set your trap for the next worm.

In agricultural patents, the inventor's brains have gone wild. The old cannon-plow has been often referred to, by which the farmer unharnesses his horses and then shoots with his plow at the Indians. The lovers' gate, however, is new. This consists of a gate that will swing both ways, and which can be lowered and raised to suit the size of the lovers. On the same principle is the adjustable pulpit desk, which will fit all kinds of preachers. The pulpit desk runs up and down on a pillar by means of a spring, and by pressing a button the preacher can raise it or lower it to his height. It is said that this invention was in use in one of the Western churches, where a very short substitute preacher had been invited to discourse. He had not been told of the peculiar arrangement upon which the Bible was placed in front of him. He was an active little man, who had a way of pounding his pulpit and leaning over and shaking his finger at the congregation. During one of his wildest moments, while in this position, he kicked the button with his knee and the pulpit, which had been set at three feet, straightway sprang up to five, carrying the kicking preacher along with it.

The patents for making women beautiful are numerous. There are face powders by the hundreds, and bust improvers by the score. One of the strangest of these crazy patents is the nose improver, which is said to have made a fortune for its inventor. This consists of a metal shell, formed of two parts, connected by a hinge. The shape of its inside may be the mold of any perfect nose, aquiline, Roman, or retroussé as you prefer, and it does its work at night.

The directions state that the nose should first be well bathed with warm water, then greased with olive oil until it is thoroughly softened. After the improver is fitted upon it, the wearer may go to bed and sleep until morning. At first, the operation may be somewhat painful, but this is soon gone as the soft cartilage of the nose takes on the elegant shape of the improver. At the end of eight weeks, a brand new nose is made. The inventor boasts that it will keep its shape until its owner grows tired of it, when he may buy an improver with a different mold, and appear with another equally beautiful new nose.

A Boston woman has taken out a patent cheek-rounder which will take away the hollowness and gauntness from an old maid's chops, and transform them with the delicious, plump look of sweet sixteen. The invention consists of a spring plate with two prongs to be fastened into the teeth. The prongs, with pads on their ends, reach out on both sides, pushing out the cheeks so that they lose their hollow look and seem round and young again. The same woman has a patent for making the fingers taper elegantly by squeezing them in what she calls her "Finger Compress."

For restaurant keepers who have been troubled as to how to get even with slow eaters, Josephine Dorist, of New York, has taken out a remarkable patent. It is a moving table with stools attached, run by machinery. The diner comes in, takes a seat on a stool, and pays his twenty-five cents for the meal that is set before him. The table then begins to move slowly along, and the man's seat moves with it. By the time he should have finished his meal, it has arrived at the other end of the room. There his dishes drop off over a wheel, and he slides from his stool.

There is an endless chain which provides that the procession of dinners and diners may go on continuously. The inventor states that her table will reduce the number of waiters needed in the restaurant. It avoids delay in serving, and makes impossible undue lingering over a meal on the part of the guest.

CHAPTER XXI

The Washington Monument Is Completed

TODAY the aluminum cap was placed on the top of the Washington Monument, and its exterior is completed. Five hundred and fifty-five feet high, it has an area at the base large enough for two big city houses, but its top, where it kisses the clouds, looks to be no larger than the point of a pin.

At five hundred feet above the ground, the monument has four sides, each thirty-five feet wide. Its area at this point is that of a comfortable six-room house, each room of which might be twelve by sixteen. It would take more than a hundred and twenty-five yards of carpet to cover its floor, and a man with a good elevator might make a pleasant summer residence of a house built up there.

196

This square forms the base of the pyramidal top which rises above its fifty-five feet, with its metallic cap as its terminal. This cap is the largest piece of aluminum ever made. It covers a pyramid nine feet high, which shines like a speck of light up there under the rays of the sun. The capstone weighs almost a ton and a half, but its aluminum cover is just one hundred ounces, one third the weight of a similar cap made of copper. Aluminum does not corrode and it is one of the best of lightning conductors. A wire will be fastened to the lower side of the metal pyramid, and run down into the earth. It will probably be the longest lightning rod yet constructed.

Standing beside the Monument, one is greatly impressed with the mechanical skill required for its building. Its stones are huge blocks, in some cases nine feet long, two feet thick, and three or more feet wide. There are more than eighteen thousand of these, of white marble and weighing several tons each. The ingenuity which can raise such stones hundreds of feet above the ground seems the triumph of mechanical skill, and one is inclined to pat himself on the back because he lives in an age so far advanced in the march of progress. He is inclined to sneer at the works of the past and to think that the massive structure before him will outlast the ages.

A second thought bids him pause. He remembers the saying in regard to the Colosseum at Rome:

> While stands the Colosseum, Rome shall stand;
> When falls the Colosseum, Rome shall fall,
> And when Rome falls, with it shall fall the world.

When the Colosseum was built at the beginning of the Christian era, it had a better chance of lasting than the Washington Monument. It was a far more wonderful feat of architecture. The mechanical skill required in its building was quite as great.

Still the Monument will, while it lasts, be considered one of the wonders of the world. It is now the highest structure on earth, forty-three feet higher than the spires of the Cologne Cathedral, and so tall that the Sphinx could be put on the top of St. Paul's in London and still be more than a hundred feet below its aluminum tip.

The Washington Monument will continue to attract travelers from far and near. To see it best you must approach it with the sun at your back. Otherwise the blinding rays of the sun striking its white surface rebound with a dazzling glare. I do not agree with Mr. Smithmeyer, the architect for the new National Library, who says the Monument has no more beauty than any tall chimney. To me it seems a work of symmetrical and magnificent immensity. No man can view it without being uplifted and inspired with noble thoughts.

The massive scaffolding that still hangs about the head of the Monument looks like a network of straw, and with the naked eye, from a distance, the men working upon it can hardly be seen. The frame of the safety net is visible, but its meshes seem to run together like so much cloth. This safety net was put there to catch the workmen in case they should fall. It has already saved many lives. I do not believe the story of the cat which is said to have jumped from the top of the Monument. It is claimed that she ran around the scaffolding twice, then took a leap off into space. Missing the net, she lighted upon the ground. For a moment, so the story goes, she was stunned by her five-hundred-foot fall, but she soon revived and ran off, with her eight other lives still intact.

Step inside the door at the base of the Monument, throw your head back, and look up through the shaft. For five hundred feet there is darkness, but then at the top you see a few rays of the light that creeps in at the windows there. I was peering up myself the other day when I heard a noise made by one of the workmen. It came down the Monument like the boom of a cannon, and I jumped quickly aside. But nothing fell. However, there was a big hole in the boards at my feet which was made by a crowbar just a week ago. It slipped out of a workman's hand and fell clear to the bottom, going through the boards like a shot.

So far no one has been killed in the construction of this

monument. It is probable that it will be completed without loss of life, but when it is, it will make a splendid place for suicides. If the windows are not barred it may become as famous as the Column Vendome in Paris.

The first third of the Monument, built away back in the fifties, is a different color from the upper two thirds, the stones being much darker. The reason for this is that the work on the building was interrupted shortly before the Civil War began. It was not resumed until more than twenty years later, and then with marble much whiter in color. This is the story of how it all happened.

A memorial stone was the cause of the trouble. When the Monument was begun, late in the forties, stones paying tribute to President Washington were sent from all parts of our country, and from foreign lands, too, to be built into its inner walls. Forty of the stones had been set into the old part of the shaft.

The remainder now lie in a long low shed, still waiting to be put into place. There must be several hundred of them, some large and some small. Many come from the different states of the Union. Nevada's is a cube of gray granite, four feet in diameter, with the name of the state in letters of silver, the strokes of which are an inch wide. Kansas boasts a coat of arms on its block, as do several others.

In looking over these stones, I find that a number have come from various Odd Fellow and Masonic organizations. The Philadelphia and New York Fire Departments have furnished two huge slabs; others are gifts from Methodist and Presbyterian Sunday schools.

The Ladies of Lowell have inscribed on their slab these words—

> Here, industry her greatest tribute pays
> To him whose valor won us prosperous days.

The members of the Dramatic Association of America are represented by a square block of pure white marble, from the center of which rises a medallion of Shakespeare, above whose head is cut the sentence "All Who Live Must Die."

In addition to the stones sent by individual societies which wish to advertise themselves, there are others from persons who would like to make the Monument a national museum. Among these is an Egyptian head of some dark stone, perhaps three inches square, imbedded in a thin tombstone of white marble. The inscription states that the stone head is two or three thousand years old, that it comes from a temple erected to Augustus on the banks of the Nile. As Augustus was born only about sixty years before Christ it is hard to see how this stone could be even two thousand years old, to say nothing of three. Another tribute stone purports to come from Carthage, but the design upon it looks remarkably like the trademark of a patent medicine advertisement and I notice a doctor's name at the bottom.

The foreign stones are the finest. That of the Swiss Confederation is granite, beautifully polished. On its face, which is six feet long and four feet wide, is inscribed in bronze letters "To the memory of Washington." Another sandstone block, twelve by twenty inches, has also been sent from Switzerland. It is inscribed "This block of stone is from the original chapel built to William Tell in 1338, Lake Lucerne, Switzerland, at the spot where he escaped from Gessler." Since that stone arrived, the Historical Society of Switzerland has declared that no such person as William Tell ever existed.

Brazil has presented a beautiful gray marble cube, bearing the imperial coat of arms; China contributes a slab of green stone covered with tea-box characters; and the fine gift from the Sultan of Turkey is a marble slab elaborately carved with an interlaced pattern of blue and gold. The Mormons' tribute is a beehive carved upon stone, with a label that says it came from Deseret, Utah Territory. Above this is the watchword of the Mormon Church, "Holiness in the Lord." But there is no mention of polygamy.

Only the Pope's stone is not here. This gift from the head of the Catholic Church disappeared back in the fifties, at about the time when the Know-Nothing party was at the peak of its strength. This anti-Catholic organization resented the fact that the Pope should have anything at all to do with the great monument, so one night a band of masked men broke into the storehouse where the tribute stones were kept. They smashed the Pope's stone into bits and threw them, it is supposed, into the Potomac River. Dr. Toner, the old gentleman who has done so much for the National Library, told me about it the other day.

"I remember the event well," he said. "The Monument Society had invited all friendly nations to contribute these tribute stones and to carve into them suitable inscriptions. The Pope sent a block of African marble that had been taken from the Temple of Concord. As far as I remember, it was inscribed with the simple words 'Rome to America.' The Know-Nothing excitement was rife at that period of our history, and but little was needed to foment hatred against anything foreign.

"A fanatical minister in Baltimore wrote an appeal to the people of the United States to rebel against placing the Pope's block in the Monument. The result was a religious and political furor which resulted in the stone's being stolen and presumably destroyed."

It was this furor that stopped the work on the Monument. The Civil War came before it was quieted down, and it was not until twenty-three years later that the construction was resumed. It is not strange that the new stonework should be brighter than that which had been already darkened by time and the weather.

The Honorable J. C. G. Kennedy, the grandson of Andrew Ellicott, who laid out the capital, tells me a curious fact in regard to the Washington Monument. When it was begun, its measurements were estimated from a certain old historical landmark, a pyramidal slate shaft, which stood at the very center of the District of Columbia. This shaft contained the exact distances and measurements of the first survey of Washington, as well as other historical data. It was near the White House, in the park which now lies between it and the river.

When the Capitol was being located, a line drawn from a monument at the head of Sixteenth Street through the center of the White House intersected nearby one drawn at right angles from the center of the Capitol site. Here a smaller shaft was put up, a marker of little importance. Orville E. Babcock, Grant's Superintendent of Public Buildings, inadvertently allowed the older marker to be destroyed. The most of his engineering was done on paper, and he did not appreciate the historical value of the center shaft which every previous President had carefully preserved. Mr. Kennedy spoke to him about the marker one day, only to find that it had already been broken to pieces and carried away.

When Col. Thomas Lincoln Casey, who succeeded Babcock, made his examination of the Monument, late in the seventies, very few people knew that the larger true central shaft had ever existed. Casey remeasured the Monument construction from the secondary shaft, a short distance away. He found an extraordinary discrepancy in the projection of the altitude, and supposed that its foundation had sunk into the earth. The truth appears to be that the Monument had not settled, and that the difference lay in mistaking the small remaining shaft from the older and larger one from which the Monument construction had originally been sighted.

In accordance with Casey's new measurements, in all sincerity and according to his light, the expensive work of putting a new foundation under the Monument was undertaken. The country applauded Casey for his accomplishment, and Congress paid the bill. The fact that it may have been entirely unnecessary is startling news indeed.

In a few days now the Washington Monument is to be dedicated. Already the city is filled with the evidence of the approaching event. Photographs and lithographs of the great shaft are in every bookstore, and the advertisements in the newspapers are full of cuts of the Monument. In many store windows pieces of the Monument stone, the waste of the masons, are offered for sale. Some of the fragments are painted in oils with crude pictures of the Monument, with Arlington, which looks at it from the hill on the opposite side of the Potomac, and on the reverse side of the stone, a picture of Mount Vernon. These souvenir stones, which sell for from five cents to a dollar apiece, are offered by the tens of thousands.

Of the elegantly engraved invitations to the Monument dedication, only a few were issued. Each one consists of a card about the size of a cigar box top, on which is a picture of George Washington with the Monument rising behind him. Beautiful female figures representing War and Peace clasp their hands over his head, and a branch of laurel lies at the bottom of Washington's medallion.

An amusing story is going the rounds to the effect that the ghost of Martin Van Buren is jealous of the attention which George Washington received at the dedication of the Washington Monument last week. Uncle Jerry, the old Negro butler who has served at the White House for more than twenty years, is the chief figure in the tale.

It happened on the day of the dedication, when the flags were flying and the cannons were booming in honor of the Father of His Country. The south windows of the big East Room of the White House were crowded with favored visitors. The panes of glass in these windows were shaking with the reverberations from the big guns, when Uncle Jerry came running to find Colonel Dinsmore, the chief usher.

"Cunnel, come quick!" he called. "Fo de Lawd's sake, come quick! Old Master Van Booren done jumped down offen de wall. He jealous of Master Washington. Don't you tell me dey ain't no sperrits hyar in de White House. Jes come look fo yo'self."

It was true. The portrait of President Martin Van Buren,

which for so many years had hung safely on the wall of the White House corridor, had fallen flat on the floor. Was it the vibration caused by the cannon? Or the fact that the cord by which the portrait was hung was worn through? Uncle Jerry is sure it was the ghost of Van Buren, whose face looked redder than ever with his anger at so much more fuss being made about President Washington.

The stroke of lightning which the Washington Monument received a day or two ago shattered its capstone. This accident revives and strengthens the doubt as to whether the tall shaft was not, on the whole, a bad investment. It has cost about $1,300,000, a large amount for a nation to put into an uncertainty. Scientists say that nothing but time can tell whether the Monument will stand. The pyramids, Pompey's Pillar, and the ancient obelisks were planted in the pure dry air of Egypt, and who knows whether they would have endured the rigors and humidity of American centuries?

The marble of which the Washington Monument is built may, fifty years from now, have so changed that it will crumble into powder. One million three hundred thousand dollars is a good deal of money to scatter upon the winds, even when there is a fair prospect that it will continue to point out to posterity that a great man once lived.

Had Washington himself been consulted as to the expenditure I believe he would have disapproved, and have asked that the money, if it must be spent for him, be used in such a way as would not only perpetuate his name but also be of some good to humanity. A million three hundred thousand dollars would have established the National University, which was one of the hobbies of Washington's latter days. It would have founded a great Academy of Art here in the capital. This would have immortalized the name of Washington and perhaps kept his memory alive after the Washington Monument's toppling stones will have been sold for building other structures.

This shining white shaft on the banks of the Potomac is a wonderful feat of masonry, but there is nothing upon it to tell that it commemorates George Washington. No statue of the great man ornaments its base, and should time sweep away this nation as it has those of the past, it may be some day as much of an enigma for antiquarians as the obelisks of Heliopolis or the excavations of Nineveh.

CHAPTER XXII

Reminders of the Civil War

ARTEMUS WARD once said that it would have been five dollars in Jeff Davis's pocket if he had never been born. There is no doubt that it would have been many million times that amount in the pockets of the Southern states if they never had known him. He has been a millstone around the neck of the South ever since it emerged from the War. The speeches he is now delivering are holding the South back in the march of civilization. They lie like a wet cloth on Northern sentiment in favor of Southern progress, and they will keep many a Northern man and many a Northern dollar from going south of Mason and Dixon's line. Jeff Davis cannot appreciate that we are not still in the days of 1860.

Davis thinks this country is going to the devil. He says there is no hope but the restoration of the old ideas. About a year ago he told me that we were dancing on a volcano and that the

Constitution and the system of government of our forefathers
existed only in name.

Jeff's book was one of his greatest failures. Appleton, the
publisher, thought the story of the Civil War written by the
Secessionist would be a great hit. But the first draft, written
by Davis himself, was unfit for publication. It read like a
schoolboy's Fourth of July oration, full of blatant eulogies and
secession sentiments. Appleton then sent a professional writer
to help Davis redraft the manuscript, and the book was published.

Called *The Rise and Fall of the Confederacy,* it comprised
two volumes of, in all, fifteen hundred pages. Still a crude piece
of work, it caused no stir among the reading public, and financially it was a flat failure.

To me one of the most amusing things about this book is
the note at the end of the second volume which states "the
publishers are responsible for the orthography of these volumes." In looking at the spelling I find it to be the same as that
in common use in the United States. The statement, no doubt,
is made by Davis because of the feeling in Richmond at the
time of the War against using even a Yankee dictionary, as
they termed that of Noah Webster. The editor of the Richmond *Examiner* declared he would not permit the Yankees
to dictate his English for him.

To prevent this he bought a copy of the Johnson-Walker
dictionary and ordered his proofreaders to follow its spelling.
If you look at a copy of the *Examiner* from the war years, you
will find such words as *public, rhetoric,* etc., spelled with a *k*
at the end. You will see that *u* is retained in not only such words
as *labor* and *honor,* but also in *terror, horror,* and other words
from which the *u* has long since disappeared in English usage.

In his book, Jeff Davis takes great pains to show that the
doctrine of secession is still alive, but he admits that the War
proved the right to secede impracticable. He states that secession can never again be attempted.

Col. A. H. Markland, who was the head of the Army mail service during the War, is preparing a book of stories and reminiscences illustrating the lighter side of the conflict. He tells little incidents of camp life which the historian forgets to mention. I am permitted to give here a story from this book in advance of its publication. It describes how General Howard once unwittingly compelled General Sherman to take a Seidlitz powder, when what he really wanted was a drink of old bourbon whisky.

When his army was at Goldsboro, North Carolina, General Sherman one day made a visit to the headquarters of General Howard. Feeling the malarial effects of the climate, General Sherman badly wanted a small draught of whisky to drive them away. Now all the officers of the Army knew of General Howard's temperance proclivities and were careful to show respect for them. General Sherman was sure there would be no whisky in Howard's quarters, and so he did not mention his wants, at first. But when Dr. John Moore, the medical officer, came in, General Sherman gave him the wink, and said, "Doctor, have you a Seidlitz powder in your quarters?"

The doctor understood Sherman's signal and replied, "Yes, I'm sure I have. Come along and I'll fix you up."

But General Howard quite innocently interposed, wishing to be helpful, "It's not necessary for you to go all the way to Moore's quarters. I have plenty of Seidlitz powders here, and good ones too. I'll get you one."

Now if there was anything in General Howard's quarters that Sherman did not want, it was a Seidlitz powder. So he said to his host, "Never mind, General. Give yourself no trouble. I will be stopping in the doctor's quarters in a short while."

But Howard was already getting the powder and the two glasses of water. Also, Dr. Moore was a great joker, and he quickly said, "You'd better accept the powder from the general. I'm not sure I have as good a one in my quarters." Howard had his powder already fizzing in the glass, and he smiled happily as he handed it to General Sherman. Rather than offend him by telling the truth, Sherman drank the foaming stuff, to his own disgust, but to the satisfaction of General Howard, and to the amusement of the doctor and the other staff officers present.

I saw General Sherman on the street today. He had a cigar in his mouth, his sandy gray whiskers were closely cut, and his face looked fatter and fuller than for some time. I understand that he is glad his term of office is coming to a close. He has, during his service as Commander of the Army, been one of the busiest men in Washington. His office in the War Department is a big room on the first floor, hung with pictures. Tecumseh usually sits in a chair which turns on a screw, behind a big desk and before a broad window.

The General is pleasant or the reverse as he happens to feel. If his humor is good, there is no more affable man in Washington. If it is bad, he is worse than a snapping turtle. One good thing about Tecumseh is that he makes no distinction among his callers. Senator or department clerk, each gets the same treatment.

General Sheridan took possession of the office of Commander in Chief of the Armies of the United States yesterday.* I found him this morning in the seat so lately occupied by bluff Tecumseh Sherman. Sheridan looks much more like a soldier than Sherman. He is erect, and though short and fat, his appearance is martial and commanding. Dressing better than Sherman, he looks as though he took more care of his personal appearance. He has a large face, a broad, full forehead, and fat, ruddy cheeks. He wears no beard, but his mustache, gray and well trimmed, is decidedly handsome.

As if care had left its marks, his face bears many a wrinkle. It is a pleasant face, with gray eyes, its most striking feature, as small and sharp as a needle. They seem to look right through you, and they always look straight at you when he is talking.

* November 4, 1883.

It is plain that there is a soul behind them. If their owner is angry they can, as a blood-and-thunder novel would say, glare with a look of baleful hate. General Sheridan has broad shoulders and short, heavy legs. He would, I think, seem bigger on horseback than upon foot, and I am sure that as a cavalry commander he made a striking figure.

A story is told of the battle of Chattanooga which illustrates the devil-may-care bravery of Sheridan. He was riding up the mountain at the head of his troops. Under the hot fire of shot and shell, he shouted encouragement to his men, and oaths at the enemy. It was as if he bore a charmed life. Twenty enemy batteries were turned upon him, but he scorned any danger.

At one time he took a canteen of whisky from his side and lifted it to his mouth. "How are you, Mr. Bragg?" he yelled, and he held it out toward the Confederate General's headquarters. Just as he was moving it to his lips, a bullet struck it out of his hand. "That's damned ungenerous," Sheridan shouted, as, unmoved, he rushed on to the battle. His horse was killed under him, and he led the rest of the charge up the mountain on foot.

People who have at times tried to bulldoze Sheridan have usually fared badly. There was the case of the big-headed railroad conductor in 1863. Then Sheridan was at Bridgeport, Alabama, while General Thomas was stationed at Decherd, Tennessee. Sheridan paid a visit to Thomas, bringing him back with him to see his works. The two Generals were riding in a train together, when there was a delay at a station. When Sheridan asked the conductor why they did not get on, the big fellow, some six feet tall, gave a rude answer to the short, stocky officer. Sheridan advised him to be more polite and ordered him to send the train forward.

"I take my orders only from the military superintendent of this road," the conductor replied with insulting indifference. "I—" But Sheridan did not allow him to continue. He struck him two or three times with his fist, and threw him off the train. He ordered the train forward, himself acting as conductor. When the train was on its way once more, he sat down beside General Thomas and resumed their conversation as though nothing unusual had happened.

It was President Tyler who sent Stonewall Jackson to West Point. One of Jackson's old friends told me today the story of his appointment. Tyler had announced that he would appoint ten young men to the Military Academy. Stonewall Jackson, whose real name was, of course, Thomas Jonathan, was a poor boy, living in Lewis County, Virginia. His one ambition was to become a soldier, and when he saw the announcement, he decided that he must go at once to see the President. Having no money to pay his fare to Washington, he decided to walk. When he arrived at the White House his boots were yellow with mud, and his clothes were covered with dust. He was poorly clad, his face was tanned, and his hands were horny from his hard work at home. Standing erect before the President, he said:

"Mr. President, I want to be a soldier. I want above all things to go to West Point."

"Well, who are you? And what are your recommendations?" President Tyler asked him.

"My name is Thomas Jonathan Jackson; I come from Lewis County, Virginia. I did not know that I had to have recommendations, and I don't know whether I could have gotten any if I had known."

"Do you know your Representative in Congress?"

"I don't know whether I do or not," the embarrassed country boy replied. His crestfallen look must have aroused the sympathy of the President, for he continued his questions, drawing the youth out as to his ideas and his ambition. Finally he asked him how he expected to get to West Point if he were appointed.

"I walked here. I can walk there too," was young Jackson's simple reply.

When Jackson had gone, Tyler turned to my informant, who had been present during the interview.

"I like that boy," he said. "He has character. I shall appoint him."

Jackson returned the next day at the hour named, and President Tyler not only gave him the appointment, but furnished him with new clothes and the money for his journey. The friendship which began on that day endured throughout their lives.

General Ben Butler is here again, looking about the same as during the past twenty years. His left eye has the same peculiar twist, and there are no more crow's-feet around it than there were when he was in Congress. I understand that General Butler is about to embark on a new venture that will bring him again into prominence.

Butler is one of those characters who like to be different from the majority of humanity, and he has an appetite for notoriety which nothing will satisfy. His campaigns for various offices, in many of which he knew from the start that he had no chance of success, have cost him large fortunes. On his gubernatorial campaigns Butler spent, so a friend tells me, a hundred thousand dollars apiece, while his outlay during the presidential race of 1884 was so great that he had to mortgage his big stone house on Capitol Hill for ninety thousand. And this was to get the ready money needed to put himself forward as the "People's Candidate."

No one knows exactly whether Ben Butler is rich or poor. Some say he is worth a half dozen millions. Others wonder whether he is worth that many hundreds of thousands. I happen to know that he has mining and other lands scattered here and there all over the country. I can assure any person who holds notes against Butler that he may consider them gilt-edged, for the General makes enough now at his law practice to satisfy the debts of the average man.

Ben Butler is a curious fellow in his animosities, and enough humor shines out of his cocked eye to have made him a Josh Billings or a Sam Cox, if his interests had turned in that direction. Speaking of Cox, everyone remembers how the whole country roared when Butler silenced one of Cox's long speeches in Congress by the words "Shoo fly." I heard last night of a funny little incident in regard to his treatment of John A. Bingham, our late Minister to Japan. Bingham and Butler were in Congress together, and Bingham was delivering one of his most eloquent orations, in which he held his audience spellbound. Judge Pettis of Pennsylvania told me the story.

"I was sitting beside Ben Butler when Bingham finished," he said. "The speech was such a moving one that for a moment the rapt silence that had attended it, held; you could have heard a pin drop any place in the chamber. We were all ready to burst into applause when Ben Butler, cocking that queer eye of his at me, said in a voice loud enough to be heard over half the room, 'I always did like that speech.' "

Yesterday I heard the true version of the Monkey and the Hand Organ story, which has been privately told in Army circles here now and again, but not always correctly. It comes to me from a high Treasury official who had to do with the settlements of General Butler's Civil War accounts. The sums of money were large, and certain items seemed out of all reason. Butler was called to the Treasury to go over his bills with the inspectors.

One New Orleans item objected to was "Banquet, Post Office to St. Charles Hotel."

"Now," said the Treasury official, "it's all right, General Butler, for you to give as many banquets as you please, but I don't see how you can ask Uncle Sam to pay four hundred dollars for a supper which you chose to give the postmaster at New Orleans at the St. Charles Hotel."

"Oh," Butler laughed, "I can explain that item. 'Banquet'

is the name of a street in New Orleans, and that four hundred dollars was spent in making repairs on it between the Post Office and the St. Charles."

After the laughter had subsided, the inspector said, "I have no doubts but that all your accounts are correct—except for this one. If you can explain '$50 for a hand organ and a monkey,' I will pass your account. What possible use could a hand organ and a monkey have for the Government of the United States?"

"I can explain that too." General Butler's eyes twinkled as he told the story. "It was during the hottest time of my campaign in the vicinity of Baltimore. The rebels were close-mouthed and I could get no inside news as to their doings. One day I saw a crowd gathered around a man with a hand organ and a large dancing monkey. I noticed that the organ-grinder looked much like a certain smart Irishman in my own corps.

"That evening I called the Irishman to headquarters. I knew him well, and I was sure I could trust him. I gave him the money to buy the hand organ and the monkey, together with the very clothes which their owner was accustomed to wear. Dressed in these, I sent him out as a spy. With the monkey and the hand organ, he traveled all over the surrounding country, and the information he brought back was invaluable in the campaign. It was worth thousands of dollars to the Union Army. And," General Butler concluded, "you can thus see why it was good business for the United States to pay fifty dollars for a hand organ and a monkey."

In a streetcar the other day I saw a fine-looking, gray-haired, white-whiskered Congressman giving away ten-dollar bills to his fellow travelers. More than this, I was one of those who received them. The giver was the Honorable Otto R. Singleton, of Mississippi, and the bills bore the stamp of the Confederate Government. It stated on their face that that Government would redeem them two years after the signing of the

Treaty of Peace between the United States and the Confederacy.

Like many a noted Southerner, Mr. Singleton had a great deal of Confederate money when the War ended, and a short time before the final crash he had sold a plantation for seventeen thousand dollars in this currency. He has preserved the bills well. They are the same fresh-from-the-bank five-hundred-dollar bills which he received away back in the sixties.

Mr. Singleton is not the only man in Washington who lost a fortune by investing in such Confederate money. I doubt not that out of the score of former Confederate soldiers now sitting in Congress, there are many who have trunks full of this worthless paper.

CHAPTER XXIII

The Death of a Hero

YESTERDAY MORNING the news of the death of General Grant came to me in central Ohio. Today I am here at Mount McGregor, New York, within a few steps of where he lies in his coffin.

All along the road coming east, I saw evidences of the love this country has for its dead hero. In New York City I found Broadway streaming with somber colors, the stores and houses shrouded in black bunting, which in some places were entwined with red, white, and blue. Hawkers were already selling Grant funeral badges; newsboys were crying papers headed with black and containing a thick supplement covering the President-General's life. At Albany, which also was draped with sable, a meeting had just been held in which it was decided that the body should lie in state in the State Capitol. More black

216

was seen at Saratoga, making the summer gaiety there seem almost fantastic in comparison with the mourning.

Here at Mount McGregor, the hotel is covered with black, the little depot is draped. Crape hangs on the door of the Drexel cottage where the General lies, and where sentries are on guard to keep out the thousands of visitors. By the new process of embalming which is being used, almost any length of time may be given to making the elaborate funeral arrangements. To-night's announcement is that it will take place in ten days.

Appropriately, it has been decided that a private ceremony according to the Methodist ritual will be held for the family in the cottage, preceding the grand services planned by the nation. Colonel Fred Grant has selected New York City as the place of burial, where a great tomb is already proposed. A great deal of nonsense is being spread abroad as to the impossibility of Mrs. Grant being buried by her husband's side within it. Why is not stated. Mrs. Grant is surely entitled to as much consideration as Martha Washington, whose marble coffin stands beside that of her husband in the tomb at Mount Vernon.

There have been few cases of conjugal love more constant and deep than that of Grant and his wife. During his long illness, Mrs. Grant has been continuously at the bedside of her husband. Her devotion has been almost phenomenal, and an old friend of his tells me that Grant loved his wife and his family above everything else in life. "The General liked to talk of them as he sat by the campfire," he says, "and Mrs. Grant was with him on the battlefield whenever it was possible."

It was love for his family, the doctors declare, that kept the General alive so long to work for them.

"We have cases in history of men being ill," Dr. Newman, the eminent Methodist minister, said to me this afternoon, "and working during their sickness to keep their families from want. And Grant held on to life in a supreme effort to finish his book so as to provide for his loved ones. He was greatly distressed, not only at the losses of his own family in the failure of the banking partnership with the unscrupulous Ward, but because of those of hundreds of small investors who had had faith in the Grant name. It is said that he has borrowed from the Vanderbilts enough to pay each one of these, and that he has insisted on giving his swords and his battle insignia as security."

General Horace Porter, for nine years with Grant as a member of his Army staff, and as his private secretary in the White House, is here today, ready to accompany Colonel Grant to New York to select a spot for the sepulcher. In response to my questions about the General, he said to me:

"General Grant's life was a series of surprises to those who knew him. His military career was a surprise. So also were those masterly state papers which he wrote during his term in the White House. The greatest surprise of all is his remarkable literary gift which has come to light in the writing of his memoirs. I have read a great part of the manuscript, and I assure you that if one of you correspondents had written some of its descriptions, you would head the news of the day in your paper."

I have spent today gathering material about President Grant's book and his method of writing. It was at the request of the Century Company that he undertook to set down his memoirs. As the work got under way, he grew to enjoy it, and his life was undoubtedly prolonged by his desire to complete the project he had undertaken. As soon as the writing was finished, he relaxed, and four days after he laid down his pen, death came to relieve him of his suffering.

The first parts of Grant's memoirs were written with his own hand. He used a pencil, always the same one until it was worn to a length of two or three inches. Harrison, his body servant, has kept a large number of these pencil stubs as souvenirs of his master. Other parts of the memoirs were taken down by Dawson, one of the leading shorthand writers of Washington. Mr. Dawson tells me that Grant feared death might claim him before he could finish, and that thus he wrote

first of the principal events of his campaigns, filling in the
minor incidents later. He could not write regularly, but when
he did write, the work went swiftly, with few interlineations.
During the nine months, he averaged over one thousand words
a day. Mr. Dawson believes that Grant could have made some
fifteen thousand dollars a month from his writing. Many
publishers have lately approached him, but their requests did
not come until it was too late.

The New York *Herald* makes foolish charges against Mr.
Drexel, in whose cottage the body of the ex-President is lying,
in stating that the bringing of Grant to Mount McGregor
was chiefly to benefit the mountain resort. On the contrary, it
was well known that his death was near, and that it would be
harmful to the summer's program of pleasure here. Long before Mr. Drexel proposed that they should occupy his cottage,
Colonel Fred Grant and his mother had already decided that
Mount McGregor was the best place for the sick General. It is
twelve hundred feet above Saratoga, and the eyes of the dying
President rested on one of the most beautiful scenes in the
United States.

Seated in his cushioned chair of red leather upon the piazza
of the cottage, Grant looked over mile upon mile of rich farm
land. The Hudson River Valley lay, like a patchwork of multi-
colored velvet, dotted with small silvery lakes, a thousand
feet below. Across the valley the gently sloping green hills,
clothed in soft haze, must have turned the sick man's attention
from his affliction. And to the north the richly colored Adi-
rondacks must have brought back to his mind the many mountains over which he had led his armies. Grant could surely
have had no better place to die.

Karl Gerhardt, the sculptor who has made the death mask
of General Grant, is a black-haired, black-eyed, thin-faced
young man of about thirty-two. He began work as a drafts-
man but became interested in modeling on the side. Charles

Dudley Warner and Mark Twain were astonished at the excellence of his studies of his pretty young wife. One was a bust, the other, which he called "The Startled Bather," showed a seminude woman preparing for her bath. It was Mark Twain who made it possible for the young sculptor to go to Europe to study, and thus started him on his career.

Some time ago, Gerhardt began to model a bust of Grant, working from a photograph. Then, with an introduction by Mark Twain, he secured the sitting from the General which was essential for its completion. Later he made the only full-sized statue of Grant ever modeled from life. And now he is the one chosen to take the mask of his face as he lies still in death.

Buck Grant was asked today if he did not think smoking caused the throat cancer which resulted in his father's death. He replied that such a notion is absurd. Cancer might be latent in anyone's system, and might be brought out by a variety of causes.

"In my father's case," he said, "I have little doubt but that the primary cause of the cancer's development in the throat was the eating of a peach. Part of the fuzz stuck in Father's throat, causing an irritation from which the cancer was formed. Then too, my father was in poor health, and the failure of our banking partnership with Ward, with the accusation that he was cognizant of Ward's swindles, all contributed to his physical disturbance and depression. I believe that but for Ward's misconduct, and but for the delay in the passage of the Pension Bill in Congress, my father might be living today."

Mrs. Grant is becoming composed, but she still keeps to her room. The General's remains are in the same state as since their embalmment four days ago, the only change being in the large green wreath of oak leaves which his small granddaughter, Julia, made and placed on his breast.

It has been decided that the General shall be buried in citizen's clothes. Indeed he has no other. The greatest General of our time is without a single insignia of his rank, not an epaulet, not a sword to lay upon his coffin. All his military treasures have been given to the Government, and he is to be buried with his Grand Army badge alone to tell of his military greatness.

Everyone is talking about the bickerings between the Saratoga Post guards and the Brooklyn troop which Colonel Grant has selected. The Saratoga men walk their beat about the cottage with firm steps, like actors on a stage. They can hardly restrain their jealousy of the Regulars who are quartered in V-shaped tents, in front of which there is a stack of muskets, and on whose doors are tacked rosettes of black and white crape. Each soldier wears a band of crape on his sleeve, and the flag on the cupola of the nearby hotel hangs at half mast. A compromise has just lately been reached by which both sets of guards will be used.

Before General Grant died, several photographs were taken as he sat on the piazza. Now these are being sold by the thousands by the photographer who will no doubt make a fortune. The funeral promises to be immense. A telegram from the casket-maker states that one hundred thousand people have already called at his establishment to look at it, and that police had to be ordered out to handle the crowd.

Flowers are pouring in from all parts of the country. The feature of today's tributes is an immense floral pillow as large as a child's mattress, made of immortelles of different colors. It comes from the Meade Post, of Philadelphia, and upon it is a great sword made of yellow flowers, with handle of red. In purple immortelles in the right hand corner are the words "Comrade U. S. Grant," and on each side of the sword are rosettes of thistles, oats, and wheat. A fringe of gray sage runs all around the edge of the pillow, which is said to have cost $750.

The crowds here are great relic hunters and seem eager to

obtain some memento of the dead hero. They want bits of crape from the cottage where he died. They have carried off loads of oak leaves and sticks for making canes. If there were not a strong guard, the cottage would be badly mutilated and the furniture ruined. This afternoon the cottage was opened to visitors, and hundreds of eyes looked through the double glass front of the casket upon the full length of the dead General, lying upon his cushions of cream-colored satin. The head rests on a satin pillow embroidered in raised roses; the body is dressed in citizen's clothes, a black broadcloth, double-breasted frock coat, buttoned over the chest; the feet are covered with slippers, with a pair of white silk socks showing between the slippers and pantaloons.

The fourteenth day since Grant's death dawned in the midst of rain and fog so thick that the cottage could scarcely be seen a hundred feet away. By nine o'clock, however, the sun began to break through, and long before ten the mist lifted and the Hudson Valley lay clear and sparkling in all its beauty beneath the eyes of Mrs. Grant as she stood on the piazza and bade farewell to the scene which has been attended with so much sorrow for her.

The break of day saw the first streams of sight-seers, arriving in wagons and carriages from the surrounding country, by train and omnibus from farther away. The hundreds who filed through the Drexel cottage found the General's body in a good state of preservation in spite of the many days since his death. The only change seemed to be in the darkened hue of his skin.

Clergymen to the number of forty arrived in two omnibuses, while a special train brought General Hancock and his staff and other distinguished guests who were welcomed by Colonel Fred Grant and shown to their seats on the piazza for the funeral ceremonies. At the family services, which took place two days ago, there were present only the family and the minister and his wife.

Today, while the psalms are being read and the prayers are being said, the sound of the cannon's salute is heard at half-hour intervals. The throngs under the trees about the cottage join in the singing of the hymns "My Faith Looks Up to Thee" and "Nearer, My God, to Thee," and crowd closer in their effort to hear the long funeral oration pronounced by Dr. Newman. The divine speaks for a full eighty-five minutes, exalting Grant as no man has ever been exalted since the days of Heliogabalus in old pagan Rome.

The service over, the four portly ministers who have conducted it, with sashes worn across their shoulders, take their places on the cottage piazza. Members of the Brooklyn Post Guard, in their blue uniforms, line up on both sides of the door. General Hancock and his staff step to the head of the columns of infantry and artillery. The military pallbearers come forth with the beautiful casket, two standing at each end and four grasping each of the solid silver rails that run along the sides. They strain under the six hundred pounds of weight until their faces are red. Two trumpets burst forth in a sad, piercing dirge, in time to which the procession marches to the railroad station.

Just in front of the coffin walk the two younger Grant boys, also General Sheridan and Colonel Grant. At an opening in the trees the sun strikes the casket. What a magnificent thing it is as it shines in its royal purple and silver! Little Julia's wreath of shining oak leaves still lies upon it, but the glass lid is covered and the body is shut away from sight.

Behind the coffin march General Hancock and the military guard of honor. And back on the cottage piazza a group of women in mourning dresses and veils are gathered about an old lady whose tears stream down her cheeks. These are the members of the Grant family who are to come to New York on the next train.

At Saratoga the casket is transferred from the black-draped funeral car that has brought it down the mountain to the regular funeral train which is to be used for the remainder of the journey. Imagine an engine, every part of which is painted black. Let its tender be draped with the most somber of bunting, and to it attach nine cars, each of which is artistically draped in soft black ladies' cloth. Imagine pleated crosses of black flannel on the doors, and rosettes and pleats of black between all the windows. Drape the second car more heavily and stretch over its windows an immense American flag. Let the black train be pulled by a black engine emitting volumes of black smoke, at a speed of twenty miles an hour, and you have the Grant funeral train as it went toward Albany today.

There is more to the picture. Draped houses in each village; crowds of men, women, and children on fences; workingmen on freight cars; women with babies; grandfathers with canes—all come out to see the train go by. In Albany a great procession moves, the firing of cannon is heard, and a funeral car in the form of a temple of crape is dragged by six coal-black horses, with net mourning drapery and ostrich feather brushes on their heads.

In the catafalque in the Capitol, which is eighteen feet high, the body of General Grant is being viewed by thousands tonight. The evidences of the love the people have for their dead hero are unequaled in history. It was six o'clock when the public was first admitted. It is now almost morning and the weeping throngs are still passing. At midnight dirges were sung in the Capitol grounds by several choruses, the electric lights that played over the listening crowds giving the scene a weird and solemn appearance. At twelve-thirty tomorrow the train will leave for New York.

Every point along the route of the funeral train to New York was crowded. Cannons boomed here and there, other trains were held back, and flags, draped in crape, waved. At West Point salutes were fired on both sides of the river, cadet bands played mournful tunes, and umbrellas were the only notice which the crowds took of the pouring rain. At the penitentiary at Sing Sing, a guard on the wall presented arms, and the flag waved by the station agent was the same banner of black and white which was waved when President Lincoln's body was carried along this same road twenty years ago.

As the train approached New York, Nature stopped her weeping and cast over the heavens above the city one of the finest rainbows ever to follow a storm. The enormous crowds which greeted the funeral procession on its arrival in the metropolis were only an index of the multitudes which will doubtless turn out for the final ceremonies.

New York is overflowing with strangers tonight. The *Commercial Advertiser* estimates that the funeral visitors will leave twelve million dollars in the tills of the New York businessmen. The crowds of out-of-town visitors number hundreds of thousands, come to witness the greatest pageant ever seen in the United States. Fully two hundred thousand persons have filed past the purple and silver casket in City Hall, and have gazed with tear-filled or curious eyes upon the face of the General who lies in it in state. It has taken nearly five hundred policemen to keep them in order, and more will be on duty along the line of march up Fifth Avenue tomorrow.

Numberless touching stories could have been gathered from the old soldiers and the soldiers' widows and sons who have bent over the coffin glass. Negroes lifted their children so that they might have a glimpse of the man who helped set their people free. The richly dressed and the shabby rubbed elbows as they paid their last respects to the dead hero.

Tonight the silver bars are being polished to remove the tarnishing prints of the thousands of hands that have caressed them today. The glass is being cleansed, and the casket is being made ready for the splendid procession tomorrow. At sunrise, at noon, at sunset, and now at midnight, the chimes of Trinity Church have been ringing. Professor Widdows, Patti's first manager, the man who rang the chimes at the Centennial and at New Orleans, is playing Grant's favorite hymns upon them, the sound merging into "America" to end the solemn concert.

At Riverside all is ready. The seats erected along the Drive have all been sold, those nearest the temporary tomb bringing five dollars apiece. Places on nearby roofs and in windows with a view have also been at a premium. Ground belonging to private persons close by has been rented for lemonade stands, restaurants, and souvenir booths at a cost of ten dollars a foot, or a hundred dollars for the day for a stand ten feet long.

All the world has read of the wonderful parade and the ceremony at Riverside yesterday. New York has never witnessed a more impressive procession than the funeral march of President Grant along Fifth Avenue. Five hours were required for the parade to pass any one spot. Among the thousands who marched were three Presidents of the United States: Hayes, Arthur, and Cleveland. The Northern Generals, Sherman and Sheridan, were among the pallbearers, as were also the Southern Generals, Buckner and Gray. Along the six miles of the line of march, it is estimated, a million sorrowing Americans, both rich and poor, stood to pay tribute to their dead hero.

At about five o'clock the sable-draped funeral carriage, drawn by eight coal-black horses, reached the simple tomb at Riverside, and the coffin was lifted from its black temple on wheels and placed in the vault that had been prepared for it. Historic Riverside seems appropriate as the last resting place of this great American general. Here British cannon roared during the War of Independence, and from here was launched the successful attack of England's General Howe on Fort Washington.

Yesterday's vast crowds bore silent testimony to the affection which the American people feel for Ulysses S. Grant. It remains for time and history to tell just how great a soldier and statesman he was.

CHAPTER XXIV

The Woman's Rights Movement

THE PLACE is Lincoln Hall at Ninth and D Streets, Northwest; the occasion the Woman's Rights National Convention. Let me describe the scene. A large square room seating several thousand people with a stage at one end; an audience rising tier upon tier in amphitheater style from the stage to the rear; and in each of the two side galleries, windows filled with people standing. On the stage are the most noted woman suffragists of the United States, and not a bad-looking lot, either. Miss Susan B. Anthony leads the convention. With dignity she stands proudly before the thousands of ladies and the one hundred men present, while she reads a letter from Elizabeth Cady Stanton.

Susan B. Anthony is of medium height, well formed, and just a little inclined to be stout. She has a grave, sallow face, a high forehead above which her straight iron-gray hair is parted and combed down, half-covering her ears. Miss Anthony has hollow cheeks, a large nose of aquiline mold, blue eyes framed in sunken flesh, a large mouth that droops at the corners, and upon her upper lip, the downy mustache of a seventeen-year-old boy.

The great suffragist speaks well. Standing straight and looking her audience in the eye, she drives home her points with logical arguments. Today she is dressed in a rich black satin, trimmed at the sleeves and throat with old lace. A red velvet bonnet covers her gray hair, a gold breastpin with watch and chain attached shines at her neck, and a pair of gold spectacles rests on the narrow bridge of her nose.

Miss Anthony is now sixty-four years of age, and she stands at the head of the movement for which she has been fighting since she was a young woman. It is thirty-six years since she was converted to the cause of Woman's Rights when, as a young schoolteacher, she attended a convention at Rochester, New York. Her father had reared her with ideas already well in advance of those of the girls in neighboring homes.

A member of the Friends' Society, Daniel Anthony had married out of the faith, taking a Baptist for his wife, but he was far too intelligent and too valuable a member to be read out of the Meeting. Mr. Anthony believed that girls should receive the same educational advantages as their brothers. Although at that time his cotton manufacturing paid well, he made it clear to young Susan that she must be equipped to earn her own living. So she prepared herself for teaching, the only profession then open to one of her sex. When her father's cotton business failed, she, at seventeen years of age, was already taking care of herself, earning by her teaching two dollars a week and her board.

Two years after her conversion, Susan B. Anthony formed an alliance with Elizabeth Cady Stanton, who, like her husband, was an active anti-slavery worker. In London, Mrs. Stanton had met the late Lucretia Mott, who had been denied

her seat at the World Convention on Anti-Slavery because
she was a woman. Out of their indignation at this and other
such instances of unfair discrimination, the Woman's Rights
Movement was born.

In 1848 Mrs. Mott and Mrs. Stanton called a convention
"to discuss the social, civil, and religious condition and rights
of women," at Seneca Falls, where they passed the "Declaration of Sentiments," a new Declaration of Independence for
women. In 1872 Miss Anthony voted in Rochester, New
York, and was fined a hundred dollars by the courts for so doing. She refused to pay. The matter came before Congress.
Ben Butler and Matt Carpenter defended her, with the result
that she neither paid the fine nor went to prison.

The convention of today is one in the long series which have
already been held, and another step in the crusade which these
two women began nearly forty years ago. For more than
thirty years Susan B. Anthony and Cady Stanton have been
the two great leaders of the movement. Susan is the better
thinker, Cady the better writer; hand in hand they make a
powerful team.

After Miss Susan had opened today's meeting, and a prayer
was delivered by the Reverend Florence Kallock, Belva Lockwood was introduced. You ought to see Belva. A slim, tight-
skinned woman on the shady side of middle age, in an elegant
blue-black velvet, trimmed with creamy lace, she looks as
though she had stepped out of an old portrait. Her face is well-
powdered, and her silky gray hair is combed over two rolls at
the sides and tied in a knot behind the crown.

Belva's face is beginning to show wrinkles around the eyes,
but she has a pleasant expression and a distingué air. She
speaks in a loud, grim, nasal tone, chopping her sentences into
five-word sections as she goes along. Miss Lockwood is the
chief woman lawyer in Washington. She is the first woman
ever admitted to practice before the Supreme Court, and I
understand she has plenty to do. Strong and healthy in spite of
her years, she can make ten miles an hour on the tricycle she

rides daily to and from her office. Today she spoke on Woman's Rights, and made a fair showing for the temperance work done by her associates.

The next speaker was the offspring of a noble sire. She was the daughter of Cassius M. Clay, and the present president of the American Woman's Suffrage Association. Miss Clay is tall and very thin, well dressed, and, like the other speakers, wears a bonnet and flowers. Her argument, which was good, was delivered with a decided Kentucky accent. She reported that her state was going forward with courage. Kentucky husbands, she said, do much to impede progress although they are chivalric in other matters; they even threaten their wives with divorce if they listen to Susan B. Anthony's lectures or read Woman's Rights papers. At this I noticed Miss Anthony clench her fists. A dark frown came over the face of Phoebe Cousins. And a woman in the rear of the hall cried out "For shame!"

Harriette R. Shattuck, from Massachusetts, who next made a report, is dumpy and short. She wore a wool dress of an olive green, with yellow ancestral lace, a lightning-bug breastpin, and a dove-colored hat with a red bird of paradise perched on its top. She has beautiful black hair, full round cheeks, and sparkling black eyes. Young and decidedly pretty, she also is brainy and her discourse sparkled with figures and facts. She said a canvass of 814 women in Massachusetts showed 405 in favor of women's voting, 166 were indifferent, and 160 refused to tell. Only 44 declared they were opposed.

A tall, lean woman with a homely face and slate-pencil bangs was presented by Miss Anthony as May Seymour Howell, the great reformer of the New York legislature. She was dressed in brocaded silk, with a profusion of flowers and jewelry, and her bracelets jingled as she sawed the air to make the most eloquent speech of the evening. She delivered it in campmeeting style, and opened by saying, as she drew herself up proudly, "I am one of the few women in the United States who have voted!"

The audience gazed at her in admiration, and she went on, "I want to tell you just how it felt." She then described her emotions, comparing them to a bride's feelings at the altar, or those of a Christian woman at the Communion table. Ridiculous as this was, she told it so well that the audience wept, and there was a full bolt of linen in the handkerchiefs used to wipe away the flowing tears.

A Western editor who has no sympathy for the cause of Woman's Rights, in describing this convention, makes the following statement:

"Several noted platform women were there. They were either old maids or married women who are not happy at home. There was not a woman on the platform who has a happy family of husband and children."

To this Miss Anthony has replied, giving a list of the suffrage leaders, together with the numbers of their children. She writes:

I will begin with the oldest—

Lucretia Mott, 5 daughters, 1 son	6
Elizabeth Cady Stanton, 5 sons, 2 daughters	7
Martha C. Wright, 2 sons, 3 daughters	5
Antoinette Brown Blackwell	5
Lucy Stone, 1 daughter	1
Harriet Robinson, 3 daughters	3
Mary A. Livermore, 2 daughters	2
Lillie Devereaux Blake, 2 daughters	2
Matilda Joslyn Gage, 1 son, 3 daughters	4
Belva A. Lockwood, 2 daughters	2
Elizabeth Boynton Harbert, 1 son, 2 daughters	3
Helen Ekin Starrett, 8 (or 9) children	8

Of the older pioneer suffragists, Susan B. Anthony is the only one who has never been a wife. Of the earlier of the younger speakers, Phoebe Cousins is the only one not married. Hence you see how utterly false is the charge of the enemy, both as to wifehood and motherhood, against the leaders in our movement.

One of the most curious Washington followers in the train of Susan B. Anthony and Elizabeth Cady Stanton is short-haired Dr. Mary Walker. This woman, who served as a surgeon during the War, always dresses in the finest broadcloth Prince Albert coat. Her legs are encased in well-cut pantaloons; she wears a nicely laundered shirt, and a necktie. And she looks just like a little, ugly, withered boy dressed in a man's clothes. There is nothing either striking or intellectual in her features. Her brown-black hair hangs in soapy locks down to her neck beneath her tall hat for dress parade or her derby for more ordinary occasions. I suppose Mary Walker thinks she is doing great things to advance Woman's Rights by wearing a man's clothing, but I fear she does more harm than good.

Miss Anthony is again at the Riggs House.* She tells me she expects to have considerable agitation this year in Congress.

"Twenty-five Senators," Miss Anthony says, "have told us that they are not opposed to our movement. I do not perceive the ridicule of the past in their present-day attitude. We are making progress, especially in the South. There, men invariably say that women in their section want nothing to do with Woman's Rights. They know less about the opinions of their women than they did about the desire of the Negroes for liberty. A niece of Jeff Davis, a high-school teacher in New Orleans and herself an advocate of Woman's Rights, reports that there are four hundred female teachers there to eight male teachers. Yet the Governor will not appoint women to places on the school boards. There is growing sentiment against such discrimination. The day will come when the South will be as eager for the rights of women as is the Territory of Wyoming."

* January, 1886.

Those who are accustomed to laugh in their sleeves when woman's suffrage is mentioned, may not find the subject so amusing in another decade or two. Anyone who mixes with many people can testify that there is growing sentiment in favor of the arguments of these woman's suffrage leaders. The question has even been raised as to whether, when at last they have obtained the vote, women ought not to have seats in the halls of Congress. I have lately gathered some expressions from public figures as to what the effect would be "If Women Came to Congress." I give you a few of their replies.

From Susan B. Anthony: "When women come to Congress, both the men and the women will be put on their best behavior—morally, intellectually, socially—because the sexes together always inspire one another to be and do their best. The huge cuspidors at every seat will be banished; the heating registers will no longer emit the fumes of burned tobacco juice; the two Houses and the corridors will cease to be filled with tobacco smoke thick enough to be cut with a knife; the desks will not be used as foot benches. Decency and good order will be observed in the discussions, the proprieties of civilized society will obtain, and justice—not bargain and sale—will decide legislation. May the good time come soon!"

Clara Barton, the founder of the Red Cross, writes me at length:

"It would seem that a glance backward would be helpful in this attempt at forecasting the future. What has been the result of mixed assemblages of men and women; in the miner's camp and in all pioneer life? Did the advent of women there demoralize? Did it impair the atmosphere, morally, religiously, socially, or economically? Did it retard progress?

"If women had not gone, what would have been the result?

"The churches—were they better without women? Has their presence there been demoralizing? Have they bred discord? Have they readily entered into iniquitous and tricky plans? Have they been easily bought and sold? Are they costly elements in the churches? Would the churches like to dispense with their presence?

"If women had not gone, what would have been the result?

"Schools—have women students demoralized such schools, colleges, and universities as have admitted them? Has the standard been lowered and the curriculum made easier to suit their inferior capacities and to enable them to keep abreast of their male classmates?

"This would be the more correct testimony in this matter. The experience is comparatively new and has been fraught with difficulties. We are willing to submit it to twenty years' trial and then decide the results.

"Where women are members of conventions, do they disturb or lower the tone of thought and action? We have no way of judging the future but by the past, and judging by the past, what are we to expect if women should come to Congress?"

And then there is this tabulation from Elizabeth Cady Stanton:

1. It would result in justice, liberty, and equality for women.
2. It would lighten the burdens of men.
3. It would improve the manners of the statesmen at the Capitol and in society at large in the city.
4. It would give us the united thought of man and woman on all the vital questions of the hour, introducing the moral element into the discussion of questions now viewed only from a material standpoint. And thus it would promote the welfare of the nation and the stability of the Republic.

Isabella Beecher Hooker, the peculiar sister of Henry Ward Beecher and Harriet Beecher Stowe, author of *Uncle Tom's Cabin*, answers my question in the words of Tennyson:

> And so these twain upon the skirts of Time
> Sit side by side, full summed in all their powers,
> Dispensing harvest, sowing the To-Be,
> Self-reverent each and reverencing each,

Distinct in individualities.
But like each other, e'en as those who love,
Then comes the statelier Eden back to men;
Then reign the world's great bridals, chaste and calm,
Then springs the crowning race of human kind.

Mrs. Hooker has been an active advocate of Woman's Rights, but her oratory is inclined to wildness, and she does not get along too well with the other promoters of the Cause. She has long been regarded as a crank, and she herself once retorted to an accuser, "Yes, I am a lunatic. Everybody with more than the pro rata share of brains is a lunatic."

Cassius Marcellus Clay, ex-Minister to Russia, writes thus: "My views with regard to woman's suffrage are well known. If women came to Congress, you ask, what would be the result? Well, the demoralization of men and women resulting from the employment of women clerks in Washington is a known fact. And the 'result' of this further so-called advance would be a quickening of the *descensus Averno*."

A different view is held by Thomas Dun English, author of *Ben Bolt* and ex-member of the New Jersey legislature: "The question involves a groundless speculation. The women of this country as a mass do not desire to become members of Congress; with few exceptions they do not even desire to vote, nor to perform military service—these two public duties naturally being attached to each other. But if such conditions were changed—if with the elective franchise, representative duties were imposed upon women—from my experience in legislature, I should say the result would be the deterioration of Congress and the moral degradation of such of the gentler sex as become members."

Senator John J. Ingalls, of Kansas, is more moderate in his thinking. He writes: "It would depend on the kind of women they were. If they were disciplined parliamentarians, philosophic thinkers, trained debaters, students of history, acquainted with political economy, accomplished in oratory, and exempt from all the incidents of maternity, the result might be beneficent."

It is Michigan's Congressman J. C. Burrows who has no chance of being wrong in his answer to my query about the effect of women in Congress. He replies simply, "The Lord only knows!"

CHAPTER XXV

Our Colored Citizens

SPRING is now fairly begun in Washington, and today is comfortable without a fire and with open windows. The buds on the trees are swelling, the crocuses are in blossom, and the first of the wild flowers are peeping through the leaves. Men are going to business without their overcoats, and women are decking themselves in their bright dresses.

Some complaints of malaria are made by the whites, but the Negroes are happy. In the sunny spots along the streets, or wherever the sun beats hottest, they may be seen lolling and basking in its burning rays. At no other time have I noticed so much the magnitude of the colored population of the capital. They seem to be everywhere now, in the White House, on the streetcars, and in the fashionable hotels, as well as on the streets, in the alleys, and under the roofs of the thousand and one shanties which they inhabit here.

There are sixty thousand colored people in the District of Columbia, numbering among them rich and poor, educated and uneducated, patrician and plebeian. The social laws prevail in the Negro population of Washington, as they do among their foolish brethren of paler color. They have their castes of society, and the lower scramble for the higher grades, as among the whites.

Quite a number of these Negroes are wealthy, Senator Blanche K. Bruce and Fred Douglass, the famous colored Recorder of Deeds, probably leading the list. Many are educated, and the professors of Howard University here will rank with the average college man throughout the nation.

The majority, however, are poor. It is natural that this should be so. They are the servants of the capital, and their wages are, I think, lower than those of servants in other cities of the Union. The women are household servants; the men are coachmen, footmen, cooks, waiters, and peddlers. Many are hucksters on a small scale. The fish peddler and the soft-shell crab man who come daily past my window are Negroes who carry their stock in trade in their hands. The rag men are legion, all with the complexion of Ham. The catering business of the capital is chiefly conducted by colored men, some of whom make a good deal of money.

My own caterer owns an elegant three-story brick and carries on his cooking operations in the basement, while he uses the upper stories for his family. His house is on Iowa Circle in one of the most aristocratic sections of the city. I am told he is worth a great deal of money and that he has made it all from his catering. He certainly might well be rich. He supplies over one hundred persons with two meals a day, charges them each twenty-five dollars a month, and twenty-five hundred dollars a month is a pretty good business for anyone.

Many of the Negroes of Washington dress well. On a Sunday afternoon they are the most elegant folk on the street. Have you not noticed that a finely dressed Negro can outshine a finely dressed white man? Well, it is true. His dark skin shows off the clothes better, and he wears them with more of an air. The Washington Negro likes bright colors and elegant apparel. The young ladies of the colored elite wear their rabbitskin cloaks with the skin side outward, the white fur showing in striking contrast to their ebony faces. Also seen often is the young Negro dude who wears a plug hat and carries a cane, just like his white brother.

A good many of the older Washington Negroes were formerly slaves, and guides point out a spot not far from the Capitol where auctions were held for buying and selling them. Some citizens of the capital are still violent seccessionists who consider it a disgrace that the colored race should have any representation at all in the Administration.

Our colored citizens here have skins of all shades from the chocolate brown of the pure African to the light café-au-lait of the octoroon. Many of these last have the best of Southern white blood in their veins, and I see daily on the streets colored girls far more beautiful than the average damsel of Caucasian descent. Some of them sell their beauty in the market of human flesh which still prevails all over the world, and the thousands who make up the demimonde of Washington include among their numbers colored girls more luscious than any women ever painted by Peter Paul Rubens.

The education of the Negroes in Washington is carried on in separate schools. There is full attendance and I am told that many of the children learn quickly.

The colored churches are the equals of those where the whites worship, several having each more than one thousand members. In the fashionable part of town here is one Catholic church whose Negro choir is famous. There are black saints in the niches, and the congregation is made up of the colored aristocracy. The members attend in plug hats and kid gloves, some of the ladies wearing dresses that would not disgrace a White House reception. The music in this church is so famous that many strangers include a service in their sight-seeing program.

The rector of one colored Episcopal church is a graduate of Trinity College and a preacher of real ability. Then there are two colored Presbyterian churches, but the numbers in their congregations are comparatively small. The rank and file of our colored citizens worship in the many churches of the Methodist and Baptist faiths.

A curious custom among the Negroes of Washington is their membership in burial societies whose main purpose is to assure proper ceremony at their funerals. Perhaps it is because his days on earth are spent in drabness, that the average colored man desires to leave it in a burst of elegance and display. He appears to be able to contemplate death with more equanimity and even satisfaction if he can be assured that a long line of mourners in gala attire will parade behind his coffin to the strains of a band. So he joins one or more of these burial societies whose high-sounding names are truly impressive.

There are The Sons and Daughters of Gethsemane, The Most Devoted Brethren and Sisters of the Star of Bethlehem, The Ancient and Honorable Order of the Galilean Fisherman, and many more quite as euphonious. The annual dues pay for the elaborate funeral regalia and for the ritual of the lodge meetings, which are held regularly. Their burial society payments always come first, before doctor bills or collection plates, for each member knows that a lapse will result in spoiling the big time he visualizes for his funeral.

Almost any Sunday you can see the handsomely draped hearse and the gaily dressed parade of one of these colored funerals. The brass band blares forth. The members of the deceased's society or societies, dressed in gold lace and white plumed hats, step out importantly as they march down the center of the broad avenues. The entire membership is there, for failure to appear means a large fine, and no excuse except illness or work will prevail. Because it is the time when most Negroes are free to march and to watch, Sunday is the favorite funeral day. Often the departed is kept from his final resting place longer than is actually practicable in order that he may have the prestige of a full Sunday procession.

Yesterday was the anniversary of the emancipation of the slaves in the District of Columbia, and the Negroes of the capital, without exception, took a holiday. From fifty to sixty thousand dark-faced men and women, boys and girls, came out into the drizzling rain.

A happier crowd I have never seen. Laughing eyes and grinning mouths were met at every step, and colors the most gaudy and dresses the most fantastic prevailed among the masses. A long procession to the music of several bands marched through the principal streets, attracting great crowds of sight-seers. It was indeed a sight. Every colored man who could afford it had a cab for the occasion. The various societies among the colored population came out in uniform. Colored infantry, colored cadets, and little tots tramped through the slush as happy as though the spring sky was smiling, instead of frowning upon them.

The different trades were well represented. One wagon was labeled the "Oyster Shuckers," and in it, as the procession moved along, Negro men opened oysters which they handed out to the bystanders. Another wagon was devoted to the brick-makers, who were seen molding bricks. Still others were occupied by carpenters and members of other trades.

In one wagon drawn by four horses sat a Negro beauty clad in bright scarlet robes, representing the Goddess of Freedom. In another stood the Goddess of Liberty; and those that followed bore gorgeously dressed dark-skinned girls, chosen by the various city wards, each headed by the favorite who had been selected as queen for the event.

I saw the striking figure of Fred Douglass at the White House last Saturday. The Negro statesman was dressed in black broadcloth, with a tall hat covering his bushy white hair, and a pair of cream-colored kids upon his hands. For the first time during Cleveland's administration, he was calling at the White House to pay his respects to the President under whom he is acting as an officer.

Douglass walked politely up to Colonel Dinsmore, told him that he had come to see the President, and that he had delayed making his visit in order that the President might not interpret his action as a bid for the retention of office. Colonel Dinsmore informed him that the President had refused to see any callers on Saturday except those having previously arranged engagements with him. Mr. Douglass, saying that he had done his duty in making the call, walked away, a dignified and impressive figure.

Fred Douglass is one of the most striking-looking men in public life today. He has coarse hair, as white as new-washed wool, which stands out in a bush from his big head. He has an open, solemn face full of character. His black eyes look out from heavy overhanging eyebrows, and his mouth is firm and decisive. In speaking he uses as good language as any white man, and his words are so chosen that they often bear quoting. Mr. Douglass was sitting in his office when I called to see him yesterday, and he began at once to talk of the elections and the Civil Rights Bill.

"I have just been reading your interview with Senator Sherman," he said, "in which he makes such a noble stand on the late decision of the Supreme Court. Sherman is a statesman, courageous, farseeing, and of impeccable honesty. If he were elected, he would see that the laws were enforced by both North and South, and that equal rights under the law were given to all people, whatever their politics or color."

"Mr. Douglass, you had much to do with getting for your race the privileges they now possess under this Civil Rights Bill," I said.

"Yes," replied this distinguished man of color. "I remember well our struggles of a decade or so ago. It was in 1866 that the idea of universal suffrage was first brought before the people. Andrew Johnson was so opposed to it that he would not discuss it for a long time. I was a member of the colored delegation that called on him in the White House that year, and mentioned universal suffrage and equality under the law.

"President Johnson would hardly let us open our mouths. He scornfully declared that what he had always meant by making the Negro free was making him free to labor, and that giving civil equality to the blacks would initiate a war of the races. He spoke for perhaps fifteen minutes, and then he dismissed us without an opportunity for a reply. After we left we talked the matter over. Knowing the President would have his speech published, we prepared our reply, which we sent over the country by the Associated Press. This first called the attention of the people of the United States to our view of the case. And the result was the ultimate passage of the Fifteenth Amendment to the Constitution."

So now Fred Douglass is married. January has united with May. Sixty-six marries forty-six, and the black teams with the white. Mr. Douglass has often told me that he believes the solution of the race question lies in the amalgamation of the Negro with the white, but he never intimated that he intended to give the country a practical exemplification of his views. Mrs. Douglass is a white lady with a slender form, a pretty face, and dark eyes and hair. She is, I am told, a graduate of Cornell University, and for some time before her marriage she had been employed as a copyist for Mr. Douglass in the office of the Recorder of Deeds.

One of the richest colored men in Washington, Fred Douglass is worth about one hundred thousand dollars. His present income is nearly, if not quite, seven thousand dollars a year, so you see he will have enough to maintain his white wife in a white way. Immediately after their marriage, the Negro leader took his bride to Uniontown, a part of Washington where, about three miles from the Capitol, on a hill overlooking the Potomac, he has one of the pleasantest homes in the city. Strangely enough it is the old Manor House of Van

Hook, the Negro hater, who owned in times past much land about Washington, and who used to insert in every deed he gave to buyers of his lands the stipulation that no colored man should be allowed to purchase house or lot in his neighborhood. Today in this man's own house, surrounded by all the comforts of the white man, by books and magazines, and now married to an educated white lady, lives the most famous Negro of the day. Truly the world does change.

I understand that the President is enraged over the objections which the District Democrats are raising to his appointment of Mr. Matthews, also a colored man, to the place of Fred Douglass as Recorder of Deeds. One Senator tells me that the President has even indulged in profanity.

"The District Democrats," says the President, "do not appreciate that the colored people of the United States are worth a great deal more to the Democratic party, with their tens of thousands of votes, than the office-seeking white element here which has no vote at all. I gave them the Marshal of the District, though Garfield and Arthur had appointed to that place men from away. They are the most ungrateful set I have found among all the ungrateful groups which come to the White House. I have appointed Matthews and I want him confirmed."

There is little doubt but that Matthews will eventually be confirmed. The Republican Senators will have to vote for him, or else put themselves on record as against the colored man. I understand that Matthews is able, and that his Democratic loyalty goes back many years. Cleveland, who met him in Albany, has a high regard for this man.

Four distinguished visitors sat in the Senate galleries at the same time yesterday. They were Lily Langtry, the Fat Boy from the Dime Museum, colored Senator Bruce and a little man with a monstrous head which for $150 cash in hand he has willed to a medical college in this city. The Fat Boy looked out of little piglike eyes at the great men below while he made sleepy remarks to a very lean woman beside him. Langtry had not been in her seat five minutes before chivalrous Senator Bayard, of Delaware, left the Senate floor and seated himself beside her. He pointed out the big guns of the Senate to her, then took her to lunch and acted as her guide about the Capitol.

Senator Bruce sat in the gallery beside his beautiful wife. The colored Senator is very careful of his wife. I understand he never lets her go alone into the galleries of Congress, or in fact into any place where some white vixen might have the chance to insult her. I suppose he brought her today to hear the discussion of the civil rights question.

Mrs. Bruce is not so pretty, perhaps, as Mrs. Langtry, but still she is good looking, and I'll warrant you she thinks more in an hour than Langtry does in a year. She has Caucasian features, large, beautiful eyes, a somewhat brunette complexion, and long, slightly waved hair. Her form is slender and shapely, and she dresses in elegant taste. She is well educated and said to be an intellectual.

The features of her husband are more African, and their small son, Roscoe Conkling Bruce, takes after his father. Senator Bruce has a well-built figure, broad shoulders, and a large head. His complexion is café-au-lait, and his slightly curly hair is well brushed. He dresses well, and he is as intelligent and polite a gentleman as you will find in Washington.

Now about forty-five years of age, Senator Bruce was born a slave in Virginia, at about the same time that a son was born to his master and mistress. It may well be that the two were half brothers. At any rate they were brought up together, Bruce serving his master's legitimate son as a kind of whipping boy. They were taught together and if the white boy did not know his lessons, his half brother of another color got the punishment. Blanche K. Bruce took naturally to study while the other did not.

The result was that he managed to get a good education,

and when the Civil War made him free, he was a strong young fellow of twenty-four, better equipped than most of his race for battling with the world. He was at this time in Missouri, but in 1859 he went to Mississippi, where he had once been a slave. With money he had saved, he became a planter there. At once he showed qualities of leadership, was made sheriff, and served so well that he even received a number of white Bourbon votes. Elected to the State Senate, he acted as Sergeant at Arms, and in 1875 he was sent to represent that state in the Congress of the United States. How well he did there is a matter of history.

As Register of the Treasury Bruce is well liked. He has saved money since he came to Washington, and he owns a comfortable brick house on Ninth Street where he lives in good style.

CHAPTER XXVI

Prescriptions for Long Life

OCTOGENARIANS and septuagenarians flourish here in Washington like the flowers that bloom in the spring, and in most of them the blossoms of their old age are more beautiful than were the blossoms of their youth. The oldest statesmen of our country are the jolliest. A man who is seventy can afford to be witty, and he who has lived to be eighty and still feels well enough to enjoy life ought to laugh and be merry all the day long.

It is now several years since I began to collect opinions from famous men as to longevity. I have interviewed them about their habits of working and playing, of eating and sleeping. I have asked as to their use or abuse of intoxicants and stimulants, and whether they consider marriage an aid in keeping young. Each man has his own prescription, and the views I have assembled are as wide apart as the poles.

247

A number of octogenarians attribute their vigor to fresh air, or to the daily habit of taking very cold baths. Some take walks at daybreak, and a good many have faith in the healthful effect of a drink of whisky just before dinner. They smoke from one to twenty cigars a day, and though a number consider tobacco a filthy weed, they do not give it up.

The Honorable Cassius M. Clay, the great abolitionist and diplomat, has sent one of the most interesting replies to my query. Now nearing eighty, he seems to be endowed with perpetual youth. He writes from Whitehall, Kentucky:

"Some curious statisticians aver that the average life of animals is five times the age of maturity. Taking that age in man to be twenty, he should live one hundred years. The Jewish savants said truly 'The fathers have eaten sour grapes, and the children's teeth are on edge.' But fortunately for me I have had excellent health throughout my life, and I attribute it to inheritance, to exercise, and to open-air living."

Mr. Clay expatiates upon the value of moderation in diet and exercise, and nine hours of sleep each night. He advocates a comfortable climate where changes are not too sudden or severe. And for avoiding baldness he bans the use of all hair lotions and other such cosmetics.

"I attribute the present propensity to baldness to malpractice," he writes. "N. P. Willis, the poet, who is noted for his fine head of hair, always bathed his head and hair with cold water. The natural oil of the skin gave vigor and gloss to his profuse locks. I followed his practice and I have as much hair as when I was a boy. I never use cosmetics. Dandruff is the outer cuticle of the scalp, reinforced by invisible perspiration which hardens in the air. It is an indication of a healthy scalp. I use only water, the hairbrush, and the fine-tooth comb."

To my query as to spirituous liquors, tobacco, and tea and coffee, Mr. Clay says:

"I favor their moderate use, but oppose prohibition which would make us a nation of sneaks, and which has been a potent factor in causing women to put on the breeches and ride astride of the war horses of politics. I am, however, in accord with King James, who once said—

> " 'Tobacco is a nasty weed,
>   Right from hell they brought the seed.
>   It fouls the mouth and soils the clothes
>   And makes a chimney of the nose.' "

Mr. Clay believes that marriage leads to longer life, but he prescribes a marriage in which there is "unity of rule," namely with the husband at the head of the household. "What is the upshot of this woman suffrage rebellion against God and Nature?" he asks. "It brings the home, the family, and indeed civilization, into darkness and chaos."

Harvey A. Watterson, one of the brightest members of Congress fifty years ago, is today as young in his thoughts and his actions as he was when President Harrison's grandfather was in the White House. He writes me in part:

"One thing which has contributed to my long life is the fact that whenever I have stubbed my toe, I have not spent my energy mourning over it, but have gone on, thanking God that I did not break my head. Men have been known to fret themselves to death but I shall not die from worry."

Judge McArthur, formerly of the Supreme Court of the District of Columbia, at seventy-seven, does not look older than the average man of sixty. His chief prescription for good health is hot-air baths.

"I keep myself in good condition by taking one of these every week," he explains. "Turkish baths are beneficial, but my favorite is an alcohol hot-air bath. The vapor that comes from burning alcohol is even better than ordinary steam. When I am away from home, I keep my pores open with red-hot water baths, but in my own bathroom I like my alcohol vapor. I put a gill of alcohol in a little iron cup which I place under a chair. When I have undressed, I set the alcohol afire, sit down above it, and throw a large blanket about myself and my chair. In a few minutes I begin to perspire. Water streams from my pores, my skin breathes once more, and I am clean. When the alcohol is burned out, I jump into a tepid bath, rub myself dry, and feel like a new man."

In her answer, Susan B. Anthony, now well past seventy, quotes Phillips Brooks, who once said: "To be at work, to do things for the world, to turn the currents of things about us to our will, to make our existence a positive element, even though it be no bigger than a grain of sand in the great system where we dwell—this alone is to live. Long-lived people who keep up their work to the last are the people who have found out this secret, namely that congenial work is the joy of life."

To my question as to how Miss Anthony has kept her remarkable health and working power past three score and ten years, she replies:

"A human being is born to think, to will, to enjoy a liberty bounded only by respect for the equal liberty of others. To think one's self into such a realm of perfect freedom of thought, and to possess and enjoy such liberty of social action is to tread the natural path of human development. As machinery lasts longer if it be kept in action, so a body and soul in active exercise escapes the corroding rust of physical and mental laziness which prematurely cuts off so many women's lives. If I am able to travel and lecture at past seventy, it is because I have always worked and loved work."

On marriage, Susan B. Anthony feels somewhat differently than the Honorable Cassius M. Clay. "If it be a marriage," she writes, "with a husband who highly respects his wife's individuality, who treats her in all particulars as he himself would want to be treated, were he a woman of fine spirit and independent thought, I should say that such a marriage is conducive to longevity and is an ideal human relation."

Of the same age as Susan B. Anthony and of equal vitality is Mrs. Louisa Drew. For the past sixty-odd years she has been delighting audiences here and in Europe with her genius. Her portrayal of Mrs. Malaprop has laughed more fat on the bones of the people of the United States than the humors of

Bill Nye or Josh Billings. For thirty years she was manager of a theater, and her letter to me shows that she has always been comparatively free from ill health. She writes:

"I have always lived generously, and have enjoyed life. Many sorrows have come to me in my later life, but they have not crushed my spirit. I married early, at the age of sixteen, but I should not advise so early a marriage in most cases. I know of no way of preserving health, intellectual or physical, except through the exercise of the faculties. I have been so singularly blessed with good health that I am scarcely a proper subject for your purpose."

One of the great men of the Episcopal Church today is Bishop Thomas M. Clark, who graduated at Yale when Andrew Jackson was still in his first presidential term. He was made Bishop of Rhode Island some forty years ago, he has published several books, and now, at about eighty years of age, he can do more work than most of the young clergy about him.

"I attribute my health," writes Bishop Clark, "and my longevity chiefly to the inheritance which has been transmitted to me from my ancestors. I am descended on my mother's side from the Reverend Jonathan Wheelwright, one of the earliest of the Boston ministers, who was banished from the Massachusetts colony for heresy about the year 1640. He lived to an extreme old age, as have most of his posterity, my own grandfather having been ninety-three years old before he ever had to send for a physician.

"As to my own personal habits," Bishop Clark continues, "I smoked tobacco faithfully for fifty years, then some time ago I gave it up altogether because I did not care to be a slave to any habit. I have not been a total abstainer in the use of liquor except for certain limited periods when I thought that the welfare of others required it. I have been accustomed to sleep as other people do without giving it thought. A scrupulous regard for sanitary rules and special attention to bodily health have never interested me very much. I have, in fact, no consciousness of old age, and but for the impediment in walking I should consider myself as young as I ever was. I know, of course, that the end must be near, but it does not really seem any nearer to me than it did fifty years ago."

George Bancroft, the famous historian, is working at an age long after most literary men have passed away. Now nearing ninety, he still takes his daily horseback ride into the surrounding country. Mr. Bancroft is a great outdoor man, and when I asked him about his prescription for longevity, he replied, "I spend about three hours a day in the saddle, go to bed early, and get up early. I find I can do my best literary work in the morning." It is a heart-warming sight to see this old man mounted upon his Kentucky riding horse, going forth with all the zest of youth, his groom following behind him.

CHAPTER XXVII

Amusements and Festivities

THE POPULATION of Washington is more like that of Paris or Vienna than of the usual American city. The people are more interested in amusement than in work, and a celebration of any kind is sure of a large attendance. Theaters here are always well patronized, races draw large crowds, while the most ordinary of circuses brings tens of thousands out to the show grounds.

On the last day of last February* the old National Theater, lying within three blocks of the White House, was a mass of smoking ruins. This week, only seven months later, a magnificent new structure stands in its place, and on Monday night the new National was thrown open to the public. Rhea was the star and *Lady Ashley* the play. All fashionable Washington was there. The beaux appeared in their claw-hammer coats, the

* 1885.

belles were attired in evening dress. President Cleveland, however, was absent and the only member of the Cabinet present was Secretary Lamar, who occupied a box at the left of the stage.

This new theater is the talk of the town, the verdict being that it is one of the coziest, prettiest, and best appointed houses of the country. It is a wide five-storied building of Philadelphia brick, with interior arrangements of such a kind that a full view of the stage may be had from any part of the house. This is the seventh opening of the National Theater. Though burned down time and again, it has risen as promptly from the ashes as the heroes who have died upon its stage have jumped up and come before the curtain to receive the applause of the audience.

John McCullough made his debut on the National stage as Hamlet and in February, 1884, he played his last role here as Richard III. He was then moody and preoccupied, he repeated himself over and over in conversation, and it was from here that the rumor that he was failing went out to the public.

I saw him one evening in the Willard Hotel, where I presented my card and asked for an interview. He did not look at the card, but said, "My time is valuable. What do you want? I charge a dollar a word."

"All right," I said.

"Are you studying for the stage?" he asked.

"No."

"Have you written a play?"

"No."

"Autograph?"

"No, indeed."

"Life insurance? Book agent?"

"No!!"

He gave up. "Well, what?"

"Newspaper," I said. "*Cleveland Leader.* See card. Health. Cleveland anxious. Favorite actor. Much interested."

"Oh," replied Mr. McCullough with a smile. "Health much better. Quite well. Tell Cleveland. Washington good town. Here all week. Next Cincinnati. Now must go. Previous engagement. Sorry. Goodby."

Washington is a good theater town, for most of our Presidents have been fond of the play. George Washington had a box reserved for him in the new Chestnut Street Theater in Philadelphia, and he frequently took his family to see the Grand Circus. He attended the theater so often indeed that the newspapers of the time criticized him severely for his lightmindedness. Whenever he entered the playhouse, the band always struck up the "President's March," to whose tune "Hail Columbia" was afterward written.

Jefferson acquired his liking for actors and acting when he was in France. His tastes were varied, embracing everything from a Shakespearean tragedy to a circus side show. In his diary you may find entries stating that he paid eleven cents for seeing a twenty-one-months-old lion, five cents for seeing an elephant, and twenty-five cents for looking at Caleb Philipps, a dwarf. To this item is appended the note, "He weighs thirty pounds now, and when born, he weighed with the clothes he had on, three pounds."

Madison, Monroe, and John Quincy Adams were all theater-goers, and during the last years of his life, Adams took part in quite a discussion concerning the character of Hamlet. Jackson often went to the theater, as did Van Buren and other Presidents before Lincoln.

The theater was President Lincoln's chief recreation; he was often present in a closed box at Ford's when the people did not know it. He frequently took his little son, Tad, with him and the child would sometimes venture behind the scenes. On one such occasion when there were a number of characters upon the stage, the actors dressed Tad up and led him to the footlights. The President thought there was something familiar about this child actor. Then he recognized his son and burst into such a hearty laugh that the audience heard it, and clapped until Lincoln stood up in his box and bowed to them.

President Arthur used always to come late into the presidential box, but the moment he appeared, the orchestra struck up "Hail to the Chief," so that the entire audience might applaud. Cleveland is reported to be fond of the theater, but I do not think he has seen a play since he has been in the White House. He is said to enjoy comedies and farces and to like a minstrel troupe or comic opera better than grand opera or an oratorio.

The "Jersey Lily," Mrs. Langtry, has been at Ford's Theater the first three days of this week. I saw her in what she calls her favorite role, that of Kate Broadcastle in Goldsmith's *She Stoops to Conquer*. Lily Langtry is certainly a beautiful woman, but by no means as extraordinary as her managers pretend. Many an American girl excels her, and her even white teeth, her peachy cheeks, her violet eyes have their matches in the belles of Baltimore, Cleveland, or Washington.

Her acting is undoubtedly second-rate, though Mr. Schwab, her manager, says she is steadily improving. I do not think she will ever make a great actress, for though she may have the ambition she has not the brains or the talent. I suppose she knows this and is making her hay while the sun shines. A few wrinkles in her rosy cheeks and a touch of age in fattening or withering her plump form will transport her into the oblivion of quiet life off the stage.

The presence of Ned Thorne, the actor, who is playing here with Nat Goodwin in *The Black Flag*, has called to mind some amusing stories of his past in the capital. One was told me today which I have not yet seen in print.

Ned was living in Washington some years ago when the Owl's Club was in its infancy. One day he was seeing his wife off for New York, and as she kissed him good-by she said, "Be a good boy, Ned. I will pray for you tonight."

"Well, if you do," Ned replied, "pray that I get a hand with four aces, for I am playing poker at the Owl's Club."

Contrary to his usual bad luck at cards, that evening he won right along. After playing far into the night with excellent cards, he looked at the hand dealt him and made a large bet, exclaiming, "My little woman is on her knees sure enough!" He had drawn four aces, and of course he took the pile. He now declares himself a firm believer in the efficacy of prayer.

I rode downtown in a streetcar yesterday with Minnie Maddern, who is playing here this week in *Frogg's Ferry*, *The Storm Child*, and other plays of that sort. Her hair of tawny gold formed a strange contrast with her long eyelashes and eyebrows, made jet black by the use of the eye pencil. Her face is white as milk, and her eyes blue as the summer sky, but for me her painted eyes destroyed the beauty of the picture.

Minnie's red hair is a large part of her stage capital. Like that of Kate Claxton, it does much to set off features which, beneath a black topknot, would hardly pass muster. Red hair has for ages been typical of beautiful women. All Titian's beauties are redheads, and the ideal painter's model of the past had the creamy complexion and red gold hair which Minnie Maddern has today.

Wrestling is a favorite sport with many of our public men. Ex-Senator Roscoe Conkling is, it seems, an excellent wrestler, who prides himself on his muscular development. While he was in the Senate, he had a gymnasium set up in the big brick house on Fourteenth Street where he used to board. Every day he went through an exhaustive series of exercises, especially those for the use of the punching bag and the boxing gloves. One day, the story goes, Matt Carpenter took dinner

with him, and after the two statesmen had finished their post-
prandial cigars, Conkling asked Senator Carpenter if he would
like to see his gymnasium.

In the room filled with dumbbells and horizontal bars, Conkling performed a few athletic feats. Then he asked Carpenter if
he would like to try a round at boxing. Senator Carpenter
threw off his coat, put on the gloves, and the two began to
strike and to parry. Senator Conkling soon proved himself to
be the better man and gave his friend a thorough drubbing. In
ten minutes he had exhausted him. Carpenter laughed as he
drew off the gloves, but in his soul he resolved that he would
have his revenge.

His opportunity came when a noted professional boxer
came to town. I think it was Jem Mace whom Carpenter
paid to go with him to see Conkling. Mace was introduced as a
constituent, and shortly adroitly turned the conversation to
gymnastics. Again the party adjourned to the gymnasium
where Conkling smilingly asked Carpenter if he did not want
another round. Senator Carpenter replied that he had had
enough, but that perhaps his constituent would like to box.
Conkling gladly assented, secure in his prowess. Well, Mace
knocked the lordly Roscoe out on the first round. He pounded
him as though it was a real fight. He mopped the floor with
him from one end of the room to the other, while Carpenter
stood by and laughed. When he went away with his "country
constituent" his Senatorial brother seemed far less exuberant
in his adieus than he had been in his welcome.

Do statesmen play cards? To this question the answer is
yes. The President himself is quoted as having his favorite
game. Garfield was fond of euchre and whist, and there are a
score of men now in the United States Senate who understand
the most subtle intricacies of poker.

"Poker Bob" Schenck still lives in Washington, and the
title he got from the little pamphlet published in England while
he was American Minister there, still sticks to him. Actually

it is an undeserved title, which Mr. Schenck owes to the lack of consideration of an English duchess rather than to any excessive card-playing habits.

Mr. Schenck met this lady at one of the Court receptions, and their conversation somehow turned to card playing. He described to her the way poker is played in such a way that she became intensely interested. She begged him to write out for her a set of directions for playing the great American card game. This Mr. Schenck did, and the duchess thus learned from him how to play poker.

As the game's fascination wove its toils about her, she wanted her friends also to take up her new fad. For convenience she had Mr. Schenck's letter printed in a pamphlet which she distributed among her friends at Court. A malicious scribbler who saw it telegraphed to the American newspapers that our Minister in London had published a book on poker playing. The newspapers here made no investigation. They dubbed him "Poker Bob" and the name stuck.

I strolled into the White House today. It looks forlorn and dreary, for the family are away. The carpets are up and the rooms are as bare as though the house had a "For Rent" sign on it. The stately Negro who tends the door walks about in his shirt sleeves, and a party of curious sight-seers are the only living beings visible.

The billiard room at the White House looks as empty as any of the others. It will doubtless surprise some of our rigid moralists to hear that the President's mansion has a billiard room. It has, however, and it is one of the most popular places in the Executive Mansion. Grant, who was a good player, used the tables a great deal. Garfield, I understand, also was fond of billiards, and new equipment was bought during his occupancy.

The billiard room of the White House is almost as old as the mansion itself. The fact that the Presidents played billiards was first discovered by the puritanical objectors in the last days of Madison's administration. At this time it was disclosed how the first billiard table came there, and what it had cost. Duff Green of the Washington *Telegraph* wrote that he knew from a firsthand source that the table had been bought by John Adams, that it had been secondhand, and that Adams himself had paid fifty dollars for it.

But why should our Presidents not play billiards? It is exercise and recreation, and when you remove it from its usual unsavory surroundings, it is as innocent as shinny or leapfrog.

Next Thursday is Thanksgiving, for which great preparations are going on in the kitchens of our statesmen in Washington. Many of the prominent men will journey to their home states to eat dinner with their families, but those who own houses in the capital, and have their wives and children with them, will do their feasting here. The market men are busy laying in vast stocks for their stalls. There will be at least one hundred thousand dollars spent in Washington on Thanksgiving turkeys. The mincemeat in the markets could not all be packed into a freight car, and the oysters will be counted out by the thousands.

During the past week I have consulted a number of our leading ladies about recipes for Thanksgiving dishes. Every Washington hostess has some new ideas to offer, the result of her own personal experience.

Mrs. Justice Field tells me she has received a number of angry letters from temperance women because she once advised that a Thanksgiving turkey be fed on English walnuts and sherry a few days before it was killed. She says the bird likes this diet and that it makes the meat delicious and tender.

The terrapin season is now in full swing, and some of the finest diamondbacks ever known are now for sale here. They are bringing higher prices than ever, a great number for the Thanksgiving tables of the rich bringing from fifty to sixty dollars a dozen. Almost any kind of genuine terrapin is worth two and a half dollars, the average price paid here now being thirty-six dollars a dozen. The gourmets of Washington and Baltimore consume more terrapin than those of any two other cities of the land, and the demand is always greater than the supply. The number caught in one year at three dollars apiece figures up to be a total of two and a quarter million dollars. This is a large amount to pay for turtles, which in the Bible, you will remember, are condemned as unclean and inedible.

There are perhaps a thousand men fishing for terrapin upon Chesapeake Bay. The turtles roost in coves and along the shores. They are captured in nets, and it is by no means an easy task to make a good haul. Terrapin are only good when put into the pot alive, and so they must be carefully handled until they are brought onto some statesman's table.

I know few Senators who are not fond of terrapin. Secretary Bayard, who has gained more fame for his terrapin cookery than for his statesmanship, is the proprietor of a large terrapin farm on the Chesapeake Bay. There are several such farms in Maryland. One, in Calvert County, has a small salt water lake, surrounded by a board fence to keep out the muskrats and the foxes. The sandy hatcheries are protected by boards in such a way that the females cannot escape, and the young terrapin remain in this nursery until they are about one year old. Six inches is the best size for a tender terrapin, larger ones being coarse in both flavor and texture.

The Indians of this region were fond of terrapin too. It is said that the original name of this delicacy was "torrepine," taken from the name of an Indian tribe which made a treaty of peace with Governor Philip Calvert at the mouth of the Susquehanna River in 1661.

When Reverdy Johnson was sent as Minister to England, he took a number of terrapin with him for the big dinners which he proposed to give in London. He took along also the famous Negro cook, Wormley, who later established one of the big hotels of Washington, and who left a fortune of one hundred thousand dollars, all made out of pleasing other men's stomachs. Everyone in London talked about these terrapin dinners of the American Minister. They contributed largely, no doubt, to the success of his diplomatic mission. Since that time there has been a regular demand for terrapin in the London market, and a number of diplomats are having the toothsome reptiles shipped to them across the Atlantic.

From lobbyist Sam Ward, greatest of Washington gourmets, comes this famous receipt for the preparation of diamondbacks for the table:

HOW TO COOK THE TOOTHSOME TERRAPIN AS IT OUGHT TO BE

Immerse the live terrapin in spring water, boil'ng hot, for five minutes, to loosen the skin. The skin is then removed with a knife, thoroughly polished to free it from any foreign substance with a piece of chamois leather. Then replace the terrapin in the boiling water, the temperature of which should be regulated by a thermometer. When the claws become so soft as to pinch into a pulp by a moderate pressure between the thumb and forefinger, it is sufficiently boiled. Take it out and remove the bottom shell first, as the convexity of the upper shell catches the rich and savory juices which distinguish the terrapin from the mud turtle and the slider. Cut off the head and claws, and carefully remove the gall and sandbag. A little of the gall does not impair the flavor of the terrapin, but the sandbag requires the skillful touch of a surgeon, the heart of a lion, the eye of an eagle, and the hand of a lady. Cut up the remainder into pieces about half an inch in length. Be careful to preserve all the juice. Put in a chafing dish, and add a dressing of fine flour, the yolk of eggs boiled so hard they are mushy, quantum sufficit of butter fresh from the dairy, salt to taste, red pepper, a large wineglass of very old Madeira (to each terrapin) and a small quantity of rich cream. The dish, like everything else fit to eat, except Roman punch and Stilton cheese, should be served smoking hot. Some persons have been known to season with spices, but this, like the rank perfume which exhales from the handkerchiefs of underbred people, is apt to arouse suspicion.

Washington is having its first spell of good sleighing in years. Pennsylvania Avenue is alive every afternoon with sleighs of all kinds, and their occupants, the ladies in sealskin sacques and the men in fur overcoats, are a strange sight in this Southern city. The dignitaries are out daily. There is many a double sleigh with its coachman in livery, and sleighing parties are all the go. Southern belles of this administration are having their first sleigh rides. Everything imaginable that can be made into a sleigh has been utilized, and the combinations of some of the rigs are as wonderful as the most absurd inventions in the Patent Office.

I heard the other day a story of how Senator and Mrs. Hearst expect to spend Christmas in their home state of California. Instead of holly and poinsettia, the California Senator's wife will decorate her tables with roses, camellias, and heliotrope, also with the luscious fruits of her Western state, including clusters of grapes a foot and a half in length. Her terrapin, brought from Maryland, will be kept in an artificial lake until needed.

But in addition there will be frogs' legs, roast mountain sheep, and turkey. Mrs. Hearst speaks especially of her last course, which will be fresh strawberries in cream, new figs, watermelons, berries, persimmons, pineapples, and oranges. The most astonishing feature of the Hearst family's last Christmas was the snow with which they covered their lawn in honor of a visitor from Vermont. Great quantities of ice were crushed and sprinkled upon it so thickly that the green grass was hidden from sight. However, the ice soon melted and, as Mrs. Hearst explained, this is not a frequent accompaniment of Christmas dinners in California.

The Christmas Clubs of Washington today celebrated the festival of Santa Claus by providing dinner for over two thousand small guests from the poorer sections of the city. This idea, which has had such signal success, was originated by a number of kindhearted young people from some of the most prominent families of the capital. Miss Nellie Arthur was president of the first club, her successors being Miss Nellie Vilas, Miss Pauline Whitney, and other young ladies of the Northwest.

Four enormous dinners were held this year, one at the National Rifles Armory, one in East Washington, one in Georgetown, and one, given by the Colored Christmas Club, in the Metropolitan Church. Mrs. Cleveland was among those who looked in on the long tables there, crowded with hungry colored children. Their dark eyes fairly stuck out of their heads at the sight of the tempting turkeys and other delicious food. The First Lady, with the badge of the Christmas Club gleaming white on her fur-trimmed garnet coat, helped distribute the toys and candy from the sparkling Christmas tree. She laughed as heartily as the children at the Punch and Judy Show that took place after dinner.

The Lenten season has passed. Washington is festive with crocuses and forsythia. Already the trees are showing green, and there are blossoms in the parks. The buds are bursting on the shrubbery of the gardens, and the gloomiest of statesmen are beginning to smile. The sky is as blue as the Lord ever painted it, with His warm sun shining down on the black asphalt streets. Men are going about without overcoats and ladies have put away their sealskin wraps.

President Cleveland gave the biggest reception of the year on Monday last when the children of Washington appeared to roll their Easter eggs on the White House lawns. They came by the thousands, of all ages and colors. Little pickaninnies of three, four, and five trotted in with baskets of colored eggs on their arms, and the small sons and daughters of Senators and Generals, of department clerks and store clerks, pushed one another about in the friendliest and most democratic way possible.

Children are the one touch of Nature that makes the whole

world kin, and happiness on Easter Monday in Washington is not gauged by the color of their skin nor the quality of their clothes. While the President and Mrs. Cleveland were walking about through the crowds, I saw a small colored boy hold two eggs out to Mr. Cleveland and ask him to "pick eggs" with him. Mrs. Cleveland stopped to chat with the first one, then another happy tot, while the White House dog, Hector, scampered here and there eating every broken hard-boiled egg he could find. It was only when he had grown sick from gulping down too many that he fled for seclusion in the basement of the White House.

Phew, how those eggs smelled! The odor infested the air three squares away from the White House. It tickled the nostrils of General Sheridan while he walked from the Metropolitan Club to his office. It made Dan Lamont put his handkerchief to his nose, but the President seemed to enjoy it. In fact, after one has been a half hour in the grounds of the White House he no longer notices it. It is not that the eggs are bad, but let me assure you that thousands of good eggs, boiled hard, give off an odor almost as pronounced.

What a fine playground the White House back garden is! As big as a farmer's meadow, it has trees as old as the century, and there are gently sloping hills, up and down which the youngsters scampered last Monday, rolling their eggs. One game was putting an egg at the bottom of a small hill, then rolling another egg from the top in an effort to hit it.

"Picking eggs," the favorite game of the older children, especially the boys, is a childish form of gambling. I saw the small sons of two Congressmen tapping their eggs on one another, the one whose eggshell broke first, looking sad and disconsolate, while the winner, whose egg had the harder shell, grinned as he put his friend's cracked egg into his pocket. For some time I watched a group of shabbily clad boys who got eggs wherever they could and gobbled them up until their mouths were ringed with yellow.

President Cleveland contented himself without the kissing

of small tots that might have been expected of him. He waved at the little ones, threw kisses in return for their affectionate greetings, and gave them many a pleasant word. Had he begun to kiss the children of his friends, he would have had to continue in true democratic style, and in the end he would have had as much egg on his face as his small, beaming guests.

President Arthur always walked through the White House grounds on Easter Monday, while Nellie Arthur played among the crowds. I saw Colonel Lamont's children there this Easter, also little Phil Sheridan. In President Lincoln's day Tad was noted as the best egg-roller of all, and the small members of the households of Grant and Hayes have laughed and shouted there as loudly as any of the visitors.

This egg-rolling has taken place in the White House grounds every Easter Monday for nearly thirty years. A Washington paper of 1860 speaks of its being already the custom. In earlier years the children used to gather on the grassy slopes near the Capitol, but their sliding down the terraces spoiled the grass, so Congress had to forbid it. Their disappointment was so keen that they were invited to the White House, where they have come each year in increasing numbers. The crowd there on Monday last is estimated at from four to five thousand children.

CHAPTER XXVIII

The Fourth Estate

THERE ARE two Congresses in Washington. One sits on the floor of the House and the Senate; the other has its seats in the galleries. One makes its speeches to the members of the two lawmaking bodies; the other talks to the nation. One sits but a few months in the year; the other is in session all the time, weekdays and Sunday, year in and year out. The latter criticizes the former and praises or condones its actions. It has much to say of the future of great men. It makes and unmakes Presidents, Cabinet officers, and Congressmen. It has the eyes of a hawk, the energy of perpetual motion, brains sharpened by years of discipline, and the good fortune to be responsible to no ring of men for re-election.

This second Congress is the Congress of the Press. When some of its members speak this morning over the electric telegraph, they will this afternoon reach more than a million readers in all the cities of the nation. There is not one of them but has a daily audience larger than any preacher, any lecturer, or any political speaker has ever had in the United States, or, I might say, in the world.

The press galleries of Congress are situated directly over the head of the presiding officers, facing the bodies on the floor below. That of the House occupies nearly the whole of one side of the wall above Speaker Carlisle's chair, and from it the correspondents can look directly into the eyes of the members who speak. In these galleries, fitted out with much gilding and carving, the seats rise tier above tier; and in front of each row is a long benchlike desk into which ink bottles are fitted much like those of a country school.

About one hundred correspondents are now entitled to seats in this gallery. Most are young men between twenty-five and thirty-five years of age, but there are some whose locks have grown gray in the service, and several, like W. B. Shaw and Ben Perley Poore, have lived history here for the past thirty years or more. They come from every state in the Union, and there is not a country village into which some of their writings do not go.

There are no ladies in this gallery, although Washington has some bright female correspondents. Instead the press ladies have seats in the galleries reserved for members' families. This year, Mrs. Snead, whose nom de plume is "Mrs. Grundy," has been favored with one of the seats reserved for the use of the Speaker's family.

Directly back of the press gallery is a writing room, large, airy, and well lighted, and furnished with a long table, running down its center. At one side of this room are the telegraph offices, devoted entirely to the correspondents, where electric clicking is continuous.

Not many years ago a correspondent, who was also an expert telegrapher, saved himself the trouble of running after news by sitting and listening to the telegrams which the other correspondents sent out. He could tell from the clicking sounds just what the other men had unearthed, and many a good story he got thus until the trick was discovered, and the telegraph instruments were for the time removed to another part of the building. The lazy correspondent then climbed to the top of the Capitol, where by putting his wet fingers on the telegraph wire he could also tell what news was being sent out. Today such dishonest reporting would cause his ostracism among his colleagues.

Admission to the press galleries at the Capitol is given to bona fide newspapermen on their signing a statement that they "are not and will not become agents for the prosecution of any claim or other legislation pending before Congress, while occupying a seat in the gallery," and that "they are not employed by the Government in any of the Departments in Washington."

Cases have been known in which correspondents have operated as lobbyists and have used their papers to advance their schemes, but such cases are rare. There is a man connected with the gallery today—at least his name is included in the Congressional Directory—who is charged with having had something to do with the Credit Mobilier scandal, and who is suspected of being an agent of Jay Gould and of John Roach, the big shipbuilder.

Years ago another correspondent was given fifteen thousand dollars with which to bribe other members of the press. In the investigation afterward held, he swore he had used this money to buy a house for himself and it could not be proved otherwise. The correspondents, however, are far more honest than the average Congressman, and had I a questionable proposition to make, I would rather make it to one of the members of the Congress below, than to a journalist in the galleries above.

Ben Perley Poore is the oldest newspaper correspondent in Washington today. Now sixty-three years old, he came here when most of us who write Washington gossip were in swaddling clothes. He still edits the *Congressional Record,* and is the clerk of the Senate Committee on Printing. He is now preparing a book dealing with his recollections of public men and matters over the past half century. I can assure you it will be interesting.

It is astonishing how many Washington correspondents have become famous. There is hardly a leading newspaperman in the country who has not served here. James Gordon Bennett, who founded the New York *Herald* wrote the first gossipy letters ever sent out from Washington. Carl Schurz, who has just refused a present of a hundred thousand dollars, wrote Washington letters for the New York *Tribune,* and Whitelaw Reid, now the *Tribune*'s editor, was at one time employed in Washington. Villard, the railroad millionaire who recently failed, was a Washington news gatherer, and Mark Twain began his eastern career by writing letters from Washington for the *Alta-Californian.*

Horace Greeley used to come often to the capital to write, and during his three months in Congress he kept up a continuous correspondence for the *Tribune.* The anecdotes about Greeley's remarkable powers of digestion, which have lately been going the rounds of the press, recall one of Parton's stories. Greeley was greatly interested in the *Log Cabin,* his campaign paper that supported William Henry Harrison for President. During the period just before the election, he could think and talk of nothing else. One night he was invited to a friend's house for supper. The hour came. All were present. But Greeley did not appear. After waiting a reasonable time the rest of the party sat down to their meal. A half hour after they had finished, in came Mr. Greeley. Making no apologies for being late, the famous journalist at once began to talk about the campaign. His hostess tried to ask if he had had his tea, but he brushed the question away and went on with his flow of words. She then brought in a large cake basket, holding perhaps a half-peck of doughnuts, rich and buttery. She handed them to Mr. Greeley thinking he would take one or two, then pass them on. But he set the dish down mechanically upon his knees. He picked up a doughnut and munched it as he talked.

Then he picked up another, and another, and another. He kept on eating and talking until the entire half-peck was consumed. As he finished the last doughnut, his hostess took the empty basket away. On the principle, I suppose, that cheese is good for the digestion, she next set down a big plate of cheese in its place.

Mr. Greeley's torrent of words never stopped. Block after block of cheese went into his mouth, and before he had finished his story a second plate was emptied. This also was quietly removed, and the person who described this scene to me was sure that Greeley, neither on that evening nor afterward, was ever aware that he had eaten anything at all.

Cleveland's official organ is *The Washington Post,* which is edited by Stilson Hutchins. The *Post* is a blanket folio with eight columns to the page, and twice this size on Sunday. Enterprising and spicy, it pays a good deal for Sunday letters, having among its contributors Joseph Hatton, the noted London novelist, Joaquin Miller, the poet of the Sierras, as well as many others.

Mr. Hutchins is still a young man, and he is undoubtedly a power with Mr. Cleveland. He started life as a printer's boy in New Hampshire some forty years ago, and in due time drifted west. In St. Louis he bought out the *St. Louis Post* and made money on the venture. After a period when he served in the Missouri Legislature he came to Washington, where he has added materially to his fortune and where he owns a fine house on Massachusetts Avenue.

The Washington Post will now make more money than ever. The advertisers here will patronize it because it is the court paper. The thousands of clerks who want to keep on good terms with the Administration will subscribe to it, reading it ostentatiously in their offices to hide their actual Republican sympathies.

Washington is a city of toadies, always cheering for the party on top. Clerks, citizens, and businessmen, all are the same, and to such an extent that some of the merchants think advertising in the anti-Administration papers hurts rather than helps their trade. *The Evening Star,* for this reason I suppose, seems to be hedging toward Cleveland though during the campaign it was avowedly for Blaine.

One of the most remarkable public characters in Washington lives on Newspaper Row. This individual goes from one office to the other every night and holds conferences with the various correspondents. He is acquainted with Senators and Representatives, and he often is present at intimate dinners of the newspapermen. Still, he is less than a foot tall, and like the wild man in the circus, he has hair all over his person. In fact, he is a little Scotch terrier and his name is Fidge.

Fidge is about the size of the ordinary white poodle, and he has the brightest of bright eyes shining out of a bushy face. He is said to be the cleverest dog in the United States. Senator Henry W. Blair of New Hampshire calls him "Socrates." He says he believes Fidge has the soul of some great man of the past, which in the course of its transmigration is now inhabiting the little dog. Blair sometimes sits for hours in the newspaper office of the St. Paul *Globe* experimenting with this dog's remarkable intelligence.

The other day I heard the distinguished Senator address the animal with these words:

"Fidge, I am sure that in the aeons of the past you were some great man. Perhaps you were Plato, and spouted philosophy as some Senators talk on education. Or perhaps you were a noble Roman, and the same mind that voices your bark today may have conceived the orations of Caesar. Would that you could tell me who you once were! Speak to me, Fidge! Speak Greek or Latin and I'll try to understand you."

No one has yet heard Fidge actually speak, but his owner, Correspondent Frye, insists that he understands and responds to more than three hundred words. Fidge goes on errands at commands given in an ordinary conversational tone of voice.

"Go upstairs, Fidge," Mrs. Frye said one day. "Go into my room and bring down my pocketbook from the bedside table." No motion was made, and the dog must have understood some of the words, for he trotted off upstairs and returned with the pocketbook.

"Go find your master in Willard's Hotel. Give him this note, Fidge." This is a frequent command given the little terrier by his master's wife. And Fidge takes off straight for the hotel, finds the correspondent, and lays the note at his feet.

Not long ago, Mr. Frye was not well, and he gave the dog a quarter wrapped inside a note. "Take this to the drugstore, Fidge," he commanded. "Give it to Dr. Brown himself. Dr. Brown!" He spoke the man's name twice. Ten minutes later the dog was back with a Seidlitz powder, and also the change from the quarter.

Congressman Stahlnecker, of New York, is one of Fidge's greatest admirers. He and Fidge often drink a glass of beer together at the Willard Bar. Fidge laps his beer out of his own glass, and he is so tidy about it that no one makes any objection.

Fidge is affected by drinking just as a human toper is. A glass of wine or two glasses of beer will turn his head. He will then act as foolish as any human drunkard. Without being told, he will dance on his hind legs, will jump up on chairs and bark, and will show off the rest of his tricks.

But it is seldom that Correspondent Frye allows this to happen. He depends too much on his canine friend. "Who would bring me my morning paper while I still am in bed?" he asked me, as we talked about Fidge and his cups. "Fidge even knows that I prefer the *Sun* to the *Tribune*. Only once has he made a mistake and brought the latter newspaper. I looked at him sternly and asked him what he meant by bringing me such a sheet. With his tail between his legs, he slunk away with it, and returned with the *Sun,* his tail waving proudly. He never made that mistake again.

"And then I depend on Fidge to take letters to the post office," the correspondent continued. "At one end of the counter there is a small swinging door, against which Fidge pushes his paw. Inside, he takes the letter to a little old clerk who cancels the stamps. I have never yet lost a letter, and Fidge has carried columns upon columns for my newspaper to the post office for me."

It is not surprising to me that the manager of Forepaugh's Circus has offered Frye a thousand dollars for this clever dog. Nor am I surprised that Frye has firmly refused the offer.

CHAPTER XXIX

Lobbyists, Smugglers, and Repentant Thieves

THE PAN ELECTRIC TELEPHONE scandal is the sensation of Washington. In this case, which is being tried before the Secretary of the Interior, Lamar, the claimants declared that Alexander Graham Bell did not invent the telephone, but stole his idea from others. He is even charged with having been in collusion with Patent Office officials.

Bell's legal expense in defense of his patents has already amounted to a fortune. In his library there are volumes upon volumes of printed testimony, containing arguments for and against his right to the title of inventor of the telephone. In the Drawbaugh case, which was settled in Bell's favor not long ago, five hundred and fifty witnesses were examined; months and years were consumed in taking their testimony. Drawbaugh's own testimony filled three large printed volumes of eight hundred pages each, while that of Bell filled four. The trial itself lasted for weeks.

This Pan Electric case, involving the Secretary of the Interior, the Attorney General, a Railroad Commissioner, an Assistant Commissioner of Patents, and numerous Congressmen and Senators, outranks all other scandalous cases of corruption of our public men, and all other attempts of unscrupulous lobbyists to influence Congressional legislation. There are such blots on the pages of our history from the very beginning of our Government. Members of every Congress from Washington's administration to that of Cleveland have been charged with corruption. Many persons have been investigated, and some have been found to be actually implicated in deeds which should have sent them to the penitentiary.

The Yazoo fraudulent land claims were perhaps the biggest swindle of early times. These had to do with lands which the state of Georgia sold to favored speculators for almost nothing. One transaction provided for payment at about one and two-thirds cents an acre. The bill passed but the following Legislature declared the sale illegal, and the Speaker of the Georgia House threw the act into a bonfire made for the purpose in front of the State House. Claims were compromised at twenty-five cents an acre. There is no doubt but that much lobbying was done and that many a legislator's vote was bought.

The Ohio Purchase was similar. In 1787 the Government gave five million acres of land to the Ohio Company, made up of New England men who lobbied the bill through Congress. Some of the greatest men of the day, including Alexander Hamilton, were involved in this speculation. When, later, Congress began its investigation, the parties involved were too highly placed to be touched, so the matter was dropped.

It is even stated that the location of the nation's capital was lobbied through Congress by George Washington among others, although it is not charged that he paid actual money for votes. But it has been pointed out that his own property,

Mount Vernon, and that of his wife, where Arlington now is, stood to benefit greatly from this choice of location.

The Pacific Mail Steamship Bill, which gave a subsidy of $500,000 a year to the Pacific Steamship Company, was another case of Congressional corruption, involving an immense lobby and the expenditure of $800,000. A single ex-Congressman is said to have received $300,000 of this, the other half million being divided among the other lobbyists. The investigating committee could not prove that any member of Congress had received money, but it will indeed be a cold day at Washington when $800,000 is spent to influence legislation and some members of Congress do not get a large share of it.

The Star Route trial, which has proved a failure, has again demonstrated that no jury of Washingtonians will ever condemn stealing from the Government. Washington City deems the United States Treasury its legitimate prey, and it would laugh at the man who would not steal from it if he could.

One might go on ad infinitum in recording examples of corruption in the past, but he could not cite one equal to this Pan Electric scheme which, based on the selling of millions of dollars of valueless stock, tries to grab the rights to a successful invention and makes high officers of the Government into the most accomplished of burglars. Everyone is curious about the men involved. We hear of nothing but the Rogerses, father and son.

The father, who has engineered the selling of the stock, has had a checkered career. He is well educated, was an Episcopal clergyman who became converted to Catholicism, and wished to become a priest. The Catholic Church, being a good judge of character, would have none of him. After the War, his sympathies still being with the South, he wrote a secessionist drama entitled, I think, *Mrs. Surratt,* which lauded the woman who was hanged on the charge of being involved in the plot to assassinate Lincoln.

This drama old Mr. Rogers had on his hands when his son Harry, the inventor of this new telephone, became connected with the Government as electrician at the Capitol. There he constructed his first telephone, which he patented under the name "Secret Telephone," and which later he sold to the Pan Electric for about $60,000.

While the Pan Electric scheme was under way, his backers thought it wise that young Rogers should remain as electrician of the Capitol. Rogers told Attorney General Garland that salary was of no consideration, but that his being there would advertise the company and permit him to experiment at government expense. Garland, it is charged, counseled him to keep the place and to turn the salary in to the company. Nice advice, if it is true, coming from the Attorney General of the United States!

The Honorable Casey Young, ex-member of Congress from Tennessee, has been grand manager of the scheme. He is confident that his Pan Electric telephone is going to be a huge success, and he tries to convince the public that its inventor is being persecuted by Bell. Robert Vance, the Assistant Commissioner of Patents, another figure in this Pan Electric gallery, was the one who first introduced the bill in its favor into the last House.

Attorney General Garland is not rich. I suppose that out in the wilds of Arkansas, where the code of public morals is not the most advanced, his actions in this business would be looked on as smart rather than as unscrupulous. From his education, I can easily imagine that Garland might have gone into this scheme without a full appreciation of the ethics of his actions. Take a Western frontier town, where the practice of law is chiefly bleeding Eastern capitalists for the defense of their land claims! If a man succeeds, no one asks how he obtained his success. The frontier lawyer's conscience becomes flexible. He continually excuses himself and whips the devil around the stump. Soon he has no conscience left, and when he gets into public office he does things he would never have done with a different background. I am told that Cleveland understands

Garland, and that he leaves little of importance for him to decide.

Scandals such as the Pan Electric have given the people of the United States an exaggerated idea of the extent of the lobbying in Washington. Congressmen do not often sell their votes for actual money, and much of the lobbying here is legitimate and honorable. A man who seeks to influence legislation by convincing Congressmen of the best way to vote, by arguments only, is also called a lobbyist. During the agitation about the wool tariff this year, many prominent men in that business were here lobbying, among them little Dave Harpster, of northern Ohio. No one would ever think of accusing Farmer Dave of anything shady, and the large part of the Washington lobbyists are just as honorable as he. Of the hundreds of pension lobbyists, national bank lobbyists, tariff lobbyists, steamship lobbyists, mail contract lobbyists, etc., nine-tenths are sound businessmen who would not think of trying to buy votes in Congress.

There are a number of state claims lobbyists, and there are office-seeking lobbyists innumerable. The representative of Collis P. Huntington is paid by the millionaire twenty-five thousand dollars a year. Huntington often comes from New York to help him. You may have read last winter how one of the Senators refused to come out into the lobby to meet this great railroad king. The newspaperman who represents the Pennsylvania Railroad gets a cool ten thousand dollars every year. At present the laws against lobbying are strong enough to send anyone who breaks them to the penitentiary; for a Congressman they impose a like penance, and in addition bar such a one from ever after holding public office.

Sam Ward, king of the Washington lobbyists, died this week in Italy, aged seventy-one. It is five years since he has done any work here in Washington, but his name is still spoken and old politicians will tell stories by the hour of his marvelous dinners and his princely manners. For sixteen years his house was the favorite resort of statesmen, diplomats, and politicians; even the President now and then sat down at his table.

Ward spent money like water. No delicacy was too costly, no wine too rare for his guests. He did not deal with small projects; instead, the measures he was connected with ran into the hundreds of thousands of dollars. For his first work he received twelve thousand dollars for entertaining alone, and he was so successful that for later jobs, which he helped to do in Congress, he was able to ask what he pleased. A gentleman for whom Ward engineered a bill of large dimensions told me about it last night.

"Samuel Ward never asked a man about a measure in which he was interested at his dinner table," he said. "As a matter of fact I do not think the proposal for service ever came from him in the first instance. But he treated his friends so well that they were always anxious to do something for him, and usually asked how they could help.

"Ward was a curious-looking fellow. Short and stout, he had a noble head, twinkling eyes, and a snow-white imperial beard which gave him the appearance of a French count. Always dressed in the best of clothes and the whitest of linen, he habitually wore a rose in his buttonhole and diamond studs in his shirt. Wherever he went he stood out above the crowd as a distinguished character. He was finely educated, could speak half a dozen languages, and he so delighted in the study of the classics that he carried a pocket edition of some Latin or Greek author so that he could read while he waited for members of Congress."

Sam Ward's history reads like a romance. He was born in the city of New York while the War of 1812 was raging. His father was one of the richest bankers then in Wall Street. Sam's tutors included George Bancroft, the historian, and he went to Columbia College, where he began, on the side, an investigation of the science of gastronomy. While he studied hard, he lived well, acquiring the reputation for giving the best dinners among the students. When he later was sent to Europe for more study, he delved into the mysteries of French cuisine. There is a story that he even spent several months assisting the chef in the kitchen of a certain French epicurean.

When he returned to America Sam Ward married a daughter of William B. Astor, a partner in his father's bank. Ward always spent more money than he made, and the financial crash about ten years later brought him to bankruptcy. It was at the time of the California gold fever, and there Sam Ward was in turn auctioneer and merchant, accumulating a large fortune. A fire wiped him out, and we next find him among the Piute Indians, playing the role of a chief.

Savage cooking apparently did not agree with Ward, and he again returned to Wall Street. Here he made enough money to live well and for the next ten years he led a roving life in Mexico and South America. In 1865 he came to Washington with five thousand dollars in his pocket, and from that time until Garfield's death he was one of the best livers and most courted characters of the capital. In 1881 he went back to Wall Street, where his fortunate speculations enabled him to keep up an extravagant establishment. Two years ago, when a particularly successful coup had netted him a half million dollars, he departed for Europe. Sam Ward belonged to the higher class of lobbyists. His operations were on a grand scale and he dealt only with prominent men. He really had influence, and he did not stoop to petty means to gain his ends.

"Officers of the U.S. Navy are the greatest smugglers in America," a leading Treasury official told me yesterday. "Go into their homes here in Washington and you will find them filled with objets d'art, fine pictures, bronzes, and Turkish rugs which have been picked up in foreign countries and smuggled past the Customs House. Their cellars are stocked with choice wines which they have brought home in the same way, and the fine cigars they smoke cost only half price when they come in, as they often do, on our naval vessels from Cuba. It used to be, and not long ago either, that certain Navy officers made a business of selling such cigars to their friends.

"A curious case of smuggling cigars happened not long ago. A merchant vessel was sent by the Navy to Havana to bring back some sailors who had been shipwrecked. While there, these men got hold of a lot of cigars which they bought in such quantity that they stacked them up in a great pile on the deck. Over this pile, almost as big as a cord of wood, they threw an old sail cloth. When the customs officers asked if they had any dutiable goods, they pointed to the pile and said with a laugh, 'Oh, we've got some cigars here.' The customs officers thought they were being guyed, and did not look under the canvas.

"Twenty years ago," the Treasury officer went on, "the S.S. *Trenton* landed a wagonload of boxes and trunks at Fortress Monroe, near Norfolk. A customs officer who watched, unseen by the Navy officers, suspected that these contained dutiable goods. He saw them loaded on a wagon and rushed off to the express office at Newport News. He got there first, however, and seized the boxes and trunks, which were addressed to Navy officers in Washington and New York. Fees for duty amounting to five hundred dollars had to be paid before they were allowed to go on their way."

Mr. Clark, the Chief of the Merchant Marine, in a report on the subject of transferring his branch of the service to the Navy Department in 1883, speaks also of smuggling by naval officers. He says that in five years naval officers smuggled in over seven hundred thousand dollars' worth of goods, at their own appraisement, and that he personally knew of fifty who were engaged in such practice. He reports that during this time, forty-two different packages were seized at the express offices where they were being shipped beyond the reach of the customs. Some of these packages were addressed to the officers, others to their families, and still others to friends. One package, containing two hundred and eighty-eight pairs of kid gloves was addressed to a merchant in New York City.

"There is no doubt," my informant concluded "but that the smuggling still goes on. It was not long ago that five hundred Turkish rugs were landed at New London, Connecticut. They were listed at the officers' valuations as worth twelve and eighteen dollars apiece, but were worth many times those sums."

The Conscience Fund of the Treasury now amounts to more than a quarter of a million dollars. Every week and nearly every day, Treasurer Huston receives one or more envelopes containing money from persons who do not sign their names. The amounts sent range all the way from two cents to hundreds of dollars, and the majority of the anonymous senders state that the money rightfully belongs to the United States. Some of the signatures are "Conscience"; scores affix the word "Restitution" in a disguised hand; a few have no signature. Some are like the following, which was written on a half page of foolscap, enclosing a hundred-dollar bill, and bearing in the middle of the paper these words:

> From one who wishes to observe hereafter the commandment "Thou shalt not steal."

This was all. There was not even a dash in the way of a signature. Another letter enclosing $12.50 read thus:

> One with a troubled conscience sends $12.50 which he stole from the Government. He is sorry for his fault and he will send the rest later on.

Another, from Chicago, contained $25 and its sender wrote:

> Mr. Treasurer: Please accept this from one making his peace with God, and appropriate it to the use of the Government. It belongs to the U.S.
>
> Restitution

The Government began its Conscience Fund in 1811, during which year $250 was received at the Treasury. From that time on there was a large increase, money being refunded by conscience-stricken paymasters and smugglers. In 1867, $12,000 was sent in; in 1868 there came $29,000; and the amounts continue to be received at the rate of thousands each year.

I spent some time today looking over the great files of such letters, and I find many of them full of pathos. Behind each one there is a story of crime, little or big. The largest amount from one man received to this date was $5,000. It came in the cheapest of Manila envelopes, in Treasury notes of $1,000 and under, wrapped in a quarter sheet of dirty note paper upon which was written:

Hon. Hugh McCulloch— The enclosed is money that rightfully belongs to the United States, though the world would say I came honestly by it. I count, however, a clear conscience of more value than money can represent or express.

Some of the letters from Army officers are interesting, and they show that soldiers, too, have consciences. Here is one that was received at the close of the War:

Troy, N.Y., 1867— Inclosed find $112 which I was paid for a horse lost in the service of the United States, but which was lost partly through my fault. I have never felt fully satisfied when thinking of this affair. I shall ever hereafter feel better in mind to have refunded this amount to the Government. I find the way of religion and the straight path best.

Yours truly,
Restitution

There are hundreds of such letters. Those received from customs evaders are quite as numerous. Ladies who have smuggled jewelry, gloves, and Paris dresses past the officers on the piers at New York on their return from Europe, become stricken with remorse and send money to the Treasurer of the United States. There is "unpaid duty on kid gloves" amounting to $5.50; $500 from Chicago "for extra tariff duties unlawfully evaded"; $270 in gold from a Baltimore hardware importer who says he "is anxious to deal fairly with all men, and to be at peace with God and Country."

CHAPTER XXX

The King Is Dead, Long Live the King

CHESTER A. ARTHUR is now lying at the point of death in New York, and not one man in a thousand in Washington is paying any attention to his condition. A few years ago the nation went wild if he had the colic; when he had a bilious attack on his Florida trip, the papers were full of editorials about it.

Arthur's illness is largely due to his life in the White House. He lived too high, exercised too little, and kept too late hours. He did not breakfast much before ten o'clock, and his dinner did not begin until nine or ten in the evening. He often sat at the table until after midnight, where, though he was not a glutton, he consumed fine wines and terrapin and other rich food. Steward Crump, who also served under Garfield and Hayes, did not enjoy Arthur's administration, for the last dishes were often not washed until the wee small hours of the

285

morning. President Arthur rode horseback for a time, but in spite of his doctor's advice he discontinued this, and grew heavier and heavier from lack of exercise. The fact that a man as stout as he was put on forty pounds was entirely against the prospects of good health. Arthur ought to be now just in his prime, for he is only fifty-six years of age.

The most painful contrasts in American history are found in the lives and deaths of our Presidents. The American people are as fickle as monarchists. They worship the up and ignore the down. It is always a case of "The King is dead, long live the King." The President of the United States has more power than the Queen of England; the ex-President is worse off than the ordinary citizen. We exalt a man to the throne for four or perhaps eight years. We expect him to entertain like a prince, to administer our affairs like a statesman. At the end of his term, we tear his robes from his back, cut off his salary, and cast him out upon the world. Yet we expect that he will live in such a way as to maintain the respect due the position he has left.

When he was in the White House, President Arthur was fawned upon by both political parties. Congressmen and Senators bowed before him. Supreme Court Judges frequented his council chamber and Admirals and Generals respected his commands. Millionaires speculated upon his slightest words. A hundred thousand officeholders felt themselves held in the palm of his hand. The fair and the great of American society delighted to do him honor.

Then came the fourth of March, 1885, and with it Grover Cleveland. President Arthur was out; his army of followers vanished. The toadies twisted their limber tongues to sing a Democrat's praises, and Arthur retired to New York and obscurity. He came to the White House possessed of $100,000; he left it, I am told, worth less than $75,000. His respect for the dignity of his position was too great to permit him to go back to the law, and there was no suitable occupation for him. Like many of his predecessors, his life since he left the

White House has been an unhappy one, and I doubt not this
has had much to do with his illness.

It is a disgrace to America that she has no pension or annuity
for her Presidents after their retirement from office. The election to the White House unfits a man for ordinary business,
and it is to the interest of the nation that he be exempted from
it when he retires. A pension of $5,000 would be sufficient to
enable an ex-President to live without discredit, in ease. The
expenditure would be far more creditable than adding each
year proofs of the old adage that republics are ungrateful.

We Americans are curious people. We want our statesman
to make no money in politics. If he does amass a fortune, our
newspapers publish pictures of his palatial residence and under
them put the question, "How can this man build such a house
on $5,000 a year?" If the statesman engages in speculation, we
straightway cry "jobbery and corruption," and if he does not
spend all his salary we charge him with stinginess and parsi-
mony.

Had Blaine not been worth a dollar, there is little doubt
but that he would have been elected President. Most of our
Presidents have been poor men. George Washington was perhaps the wealthiest, and Rutherford B. Hayes will rank next.
Martin Van Buren had saved a fortune when he came to the
White House, and Harrison's enemies in his campaign claimed
he never ate with anything but a gold spoon. Fillmore retired
to Buffalo, where the rise in real-estate values left him enough
at the close of his term to keep him comfortable for the rest of
his life.

But many of our other Presidents left the White House in
straitened circumstances. At the age of sixty-six, after
twenty-six years in continuous public service, John Adams
retired to his little estate at Quincy, Massachusetts, with barely
enough to give him the necessities of life on a farm. The only
thing he had from the United States was the privilege of sending his letters without postage.

Thomas Jefferson had to borrow nearly $10,000 from a Richmond bank to pay some of his debts before he left Washington, and the history of the last seventeen years of his life was one of almost continuous financial embarrassment. In requesting this loan he declared:

"My nights will be almost sleepless, as nothing could be more distressing to me than to leave debts here in Washington unpaid, if indeed I should be permitted to depart with them unpaid, of which I am by no means certain."

In spite of this loan, he owed $20,000, and a few years later, in order to relieve his necessities, he was forced to sell his library, which he had been sixty years in gathering. In 1819 and 1820, hard times came to this country, and Jefferson, an old man, lost $20,000 more through a note he had endorsed for a friend. There were no purchasers for his lands, so at his request, the Virginia Legislature passed an act permitting him to dispose of Monticello by lottery. The publicity in connection with this lottery brought in so many subscriptions for his relief that the idea was abandoned.

Jefferson received the money gratefully. "Not one penny of it has been wrung from the taxpayers," he said proudly. "It is a pure, unsolicited offering of love." He died at eighty-three, thinking his estate would support his children, but with continued hard times the sale of his property merely paid off his debts. Jefferson's only surviving granddaughter, Mrs. Septimia Meikleham, lives in poverty in Georgetown, and Congress has refused to help her.

President Madison's widow, the peerless Dolly, was for a time, dependent upon the bread and meat brought her by an old servant, but her last days were made easier when Congress bought for $30,000 her husband's manuscript notes of the Constitutional Convention.

Monroe died in poverty in New York, from whence it was twenty-seven years before his body could be removed to Richmond. John Quincy Adams must have received over a half million dollars in Government salaries, and he is one of the few

Presidents who again took up public life after he left the White House. After a year of retirement, he entered the Lower House of Congress, where he served sixteen years, dying here in 1848.

Andrew Jackson returned from his second term with $90 in his pockets, to find his farm going to ruin, and himself so deeply in debt that he had to sell a portion of his lands. Through the debts of his adopted son, he was forced to borrow $10,000 from Frank Blair, and at his death he was still deeply in debt. By act of the Tennessee Legislature, his heirs hold only a life interest in the Hermitage. President Tyler supplied much of the money for running the White House out of his own pocket, for Congress would not pay even the salary of his secretary. Although moderately wealthy while in Washington, Tyler left but little for his children. It was due to Congress that Abraham Lincoln's family was provided for, and the financial distress of General Grant was humiliating to the nation as well as to himself. Truly, as Sidney Smith used to say, "There is nothing so expensive as glory."

The following advertisement is from yesterday's newspaper:

FOR SALE— Seven autograph letters of General George Washington; never published; very valuable and historical; also suit of clothes worn at the first inauguration; all of the above are perfect and thoroughly authenticated. Addrss "Nearest Relative," this office.

So the nearest relative of George Washington wants to sell the suit of clothes in which the great hero appeared at his first inauguration! What a commentary on the idea that the descendants of great men inherit the abilities of their ancestors! The descendants of nearly every one of the Presidents are in poor circumstances today.

I called today on Mrs. Septimia Meikleham, the only surviving granddaughter of Thomas Jefferson, to whom Congress has just refused a pension of five thousand dollars a year. Taking a car at the Patent Office, I rode up F Street to the Ebbitt

House, switched around Fourteenth to H, then along Connecticut Avenue, the fashionable new street of the capital. Passing the great mansion of the British Minister at N Street, the car line sweeps around Dupont Circle, then crosses the bridge into old Georgetown. There the streetcar horses are changed, and a new driver takes you uphill and down until at the end of the line, facing the big Georgetown Convent, he drops you almost into the country.

Within a stone's throw of the convent, I found Mrs. Meikleham's house, an old-fashioned two-story frame, with a porch looking west. Going through a gate that sagged on its hinges, I crossed the lawn, mounted the steps, and rang the bell. A gray-haired woman servant led me into the parlor. While I waited, I looked with envy at the antique treasures with which the room was crowded. Some of the pieces are out of Monticello, others have come from houses of other great men of the past. Two wide-armed mahogany chairs that were used by Louis XVI were presented to Mrs. Meikleham by her uncle, Gouverneur Morris. Just beside the fireplace hangs an embroidered bag, the clasp of which was a present from Dolly Madison, who gave Septimia her first lessons in needlework in the White House.

Mrs. Meikleham is a tall, well-formed woman with a fine, open face, bright blue eyes, and rosy cheeks, looking fifty rather than her seventy years. Her auburn hair, the same color as her grandfather's, and as yet not heavily mixed with gray, is combed down behind her ears in the old style of the past. As I looked at her I thought her one of the handsomest old ladies I had ever seen. Her costume corresponded with the refinement of her face and her surroundings. A black cassimere dress, simply made, was finished at the neck with a white kerchief, tucked in at the bosom, and a pretty lace cap was worn atop her auburn hair.

Mrs. Meikleham talked freely about her Congressional bill. She was hurt and disappointed by the action of Congress. Not that she felt so on the basis of a refused plea for charity. She had not asked for the appropriation on that ground, she said. She was quite willing to take her chances of survival with the rest of suffering humanity, but she thought a slight had been cast on the name of Jefferson, to whom she referred as the civil "Father of his Country," just as Washington was the military "Father." She felt that a gift from the people of the United States to one of Jefferson's descendants was due in gratitude for what the nation had received from him.

It would be a good idea for the United States to have a National Mausoleum like Westminster Abbey, in which Presidents could be buried and statues there erected. At present some of our Presidents have neither slab nor monument to mark their graves. General Harrison's body rests in a brick vault on the top of a little hill fifteen miles west of Cincinnati. A big flat stone lies upon its top but there is no inscription, and the only beauty about the grave is that of the pine trees that surround it with their perpetual green.

John Tyler's body lies in the Hollywood Cemetery at Richmond, Virginia, without stone or bust to mark its resting place. Ten yards away is President Monroe's grave, but he was not buried there until the centennial anniversary of his birth. Monroe waited twenty-seven years for an appropriate tomb. At last now he rests in a vault over which is a large granite sarcophagus with an inscription testifying that it was erected "as an evidence of the affection of Virginia for her good and honored son."

Van Buren's grave, notwithstanding his wealth, is now bleak and bare, without flower or shrub, at Kinderhook, N.Y., and a year or two ago the little granite shaft which stood over the remains of Thomas Jefferson at Monticello had been mutilated and its inscription destroyed by relic hunters. His tomb's gates were rusty and it had the appearance of a ruin.

George Washington has been twice entombed. Mount

Vernon is now his resting place, and the sarcophagus in which he is buried is in a brick vault overlooking the Potomac, marked with but the one word "Washington."

The two Adamses are buried in the Unitarian Church at Quincy, Massachusetts. When John Adams died, his son, then President, obtained a deed to a burial lot, fourteen feet square, in the cellar of this church. Upon this he built a granite tomb for himself and his father. Here lie the two Presidents and their wives, while on the walls of the church above are long inscriptions commemorative of their lives and worth.

There have been a number of stories published about the graves of President Tyler. Some say he was first buried in Washington, and that afterward his body was moved from place to place. The truth is that he was never buried in the ground at all, but was brought immediately to his father's old farm in Kentucky, where his body was placed in a vault. It has lain there ever since, and there is a gray granite monument surmounted by a marble statue of the General nearby.

Frank Pierce has a monument of Italian marble at Concord, New Hampshire. Strange to say the name upon it is Francis Pierce, instead of Franklin Pierce, as he was known throughout the country. Like the monument of Millard Fillmore at Buffalo, it is simple in the extreme. James Buchanan lies in a vault in the Lancaster Cemetery, where his life is chronicled in the dates of his birth and death and the fact that he was the fifteenth President of the United States.

Twenty-three lines are required for the inscription on Polk's tombstone, which lies in Nashville, twelve miles away from that of Andrew Jackson, a much greater man whose record is summed up in three. Jackson's body lies in his garden at the Hermitage beside that of his wife, his monument bearing these words: "General Andrew Jackson, born March 15, 1767; died June 8, 1845."

Congress is not so parsimonious when it comes to funeral provisions for its own members. It is estimated that the cost of

Senator Miller's funeral will be more than $7,000. A committee of Congress had to be sent West with the remains. The ceremonies at the Capitol cost a great deal of money, and if many more Congressional deaths occur, there will be no trouble in finding out what to do with the surplus in the Treasury.

There is no doubt but that great extravagance has existed for years in this matter of Congressional funerals. It is a delicate subject to handle, but it is one, it seems to me, of which people should be informed. When a Congressman dies in Washington, he is buried in the richest style. The pallbearers and other dignitaries connected with the ceremonies must each wear silk scarfs which cost $9 and more apiece, and though a dozen funerals occur during the same season, you will not hear of the same scarf being used more than once. The pallbearers must also have gloves at $2.50, and the undertaker's bill seldom runs less than $500, while the casket in which the dead Congressman's corpse reposes is an expense to the Government of at least $400 more. So there are few funerals of Congressmen which cost Uncle Sam less than $1,000.

If a member of Congress is buried away from the capital, a committee of both Houses, consisting of ten or more members, is sent along to accompany his body to its last resting place. This committee often takes a special car, and shameful to relate, it frequently makes its funeral march into a procession of Bacchus. Its baggage is largely made up of wines and liquors. Champagne flows like water, and the bills for meals are the heaviest items of the expense account.

I glanced through a volume or two of the accounts of the Clerk of the House yesterday where I found such funeral expenses scattered throughout the Miscellaneous items. The Clerk does not lump each account with its details together on one page, but distributes the items so that the real size of the bill is not at first sight so apparent.

Take, for example, the funeral of the Honorable Thomas Allen, who was recently buried at Pittsfield, Massachusetts. This is not more than a day's ride from Washington, yet the transportation charges were $829. A single lunch for the party was $122. Among the items were a porter's fee of $5 and another of $3.50 for a hat which a messenger lost on the train.

It is curious to discover that the Government also pays the funeral expenses of such of the ordinary employees of the Capitol as are overtaken by death. One laborer who received a salary of $840 a year was buried at a cost of $380, while another of the same grade took $463 out of Uncle Sam's pocket by dying.

In the case of both Congressmen and employees, it is customary to vote the heirs of the deceased an amount equal to the remainder of the salary for the Congress in which they were serving. The widow of Representative Rankin, for instance, will receive somewhere between five and ten thousand dollars for the rest of her husband's term, as a gift from Congress out of the pockets of the taxpayers.

There seems to be no reason why the people should pay the funeral expenses of one of their servants in Congress, any more than they should pay those of an officer who dies while serving them in another branch of the Government. The average Congressman has an eye to the main chance, and I do not doubt but that this little custom of giving his heirs the remainder of his salary draws many dollars away from the life insurance companies.

Grover Cleveland's is a different case of "The King is dead, long live the King!" Although his is only a political death, to the nation he might as well be sleeping now inside his tomb. In a few days his name will have dropped out of the letters of the Washington correspondents. No stories of his doings will be told over the teacups. All attention will be centered on his successor, Benjamin Harrison. Already in the newspaper columns, compliments for a White House bride are giving place to descriptions of White House grandchildren.

Mr. and Mrs. Cleveland are packing to leave the White

House. Both the President and the First Lady have taken the results of last November's election with good sportsmanship. Entertainments and gaieties are apparently to be kept up until the very last, and in recent days, perhaps because her responsibilities seem lighter, Mrs. Cleveland has even indulged in dancing the waltz at public parties. I watched her the other night, turning and twirling in the arms of an elderly Senator with a fat stomach and a bald head. When their gay dance was over, the Senator was mopping his forehead, wheezing and puffing, and I wondered whether indeed he did not find waltzing with a healthy young woman, fond of the dance, more difficult than conducting a strenuous debate on the floor of the Senate.

The ladies tell me that Mrs. Cleveland is accepting all invitations to social affairs, so that she shall miss none of the pleasures of her position in her last few days as First Lady. It is likely that, even in New York, she will miss Washington, and it is sure that Washington will miss her. Everyone in Washington speaks well of the President's young wife. She has steadily risen in the respect and affections of all, in spite of the bad start incident to her husband's arrangements for her wedding, with his dodging out the back door and hiding up in the mountains. Frances Folsom Cleveland has won great admiration by her conduct in the White House. She is apparently unspoiled by the praises which have been heaped upon her, and she has retained to the end her simplicity and her charm, her good sense and her dignity.

When President Cleveland steps down from the throne, he will carry with him the esteem and respect of all classes of people. In spite of his so-called reforms, he has made a good President, and his critics have grown fewer and fewer in the four years he has been in the White House. Even the Republicans feel real affection for him. As one Army officer of that political faith said not long ago, "Grover Cleveland is the most popular person today in the United States—with the exception of Mrs. Cleveland."

CHAPTER XXXI

Ben Harrison's Era

I SAW PRESIDENT HARRISON walking with a friend on Connecticut Avenue last Sunday. He wore a plain black overcoat, buttoned tightly around his rotund form, a pair of brown kid gloves, a tall hat, and a shining black silk tie. He chatted with a companion as they walked, and there was nothing remarkable about his appearance or the notice taken of him by the other promenaders.

President Harrison, in his daily habits, is showing himself more democratic than any of his predecessors of the past decade. He sees no reason why his change of address from Indianapolis to Washington should limit his moving about as freely as in the past. He does not insist upon going about alone, but often chooses the busiest streets of the city for his promenades. I have seen him enter a store to make a purchase just like any shopper, and he has even been known to drink a glass of soda water at the counter here, as he used to in the drug-store back home.

President Harrison's grandfather was one of the most noted walkers among the past Presidents. He did his own marketing, getting up early and trotting out, often without an overcoat to protect his slender old frame, to get chops and steaks for his White House breakfast. Of late years the etiquette of presidential life has rapidly changed. The President grows bigger as his office grows older, and his activity is now wrapped around with red tape from beginning to end.

Ben Harrison was seven years old when his grandfather, William Henry, was elected President in his famous Hard Cider and Log Cabin campaign. Ben is not so tall as Harrison the First, and his face is more square. The President's hair is still brown, his beard full and sandy, his eyes blue and his forehead high and broad. Although he is reputed to be cold and indifferent, I have found him genial and pleasant, cordial and free in expressing his opinions, but decided in his refusal to allow me to publish them.

The new President and his family are now nicely settled in the White House, which is filled to overflowing with his daughter's family and his wife's relatives. Old Dr. Scott, the ninety-year-old father of Mrs. Harrison, has taken up his residence there; Mrs. McKee, the Harrisons' daughter who has come from her home in Indianapolis to help her mother with her social obligations, has her two small children with her; and Russell Harrison and his wife, the son and daughter-in-law from Montana, are frequent visitors. Helping Mrs. Harrison with the renovation of the White House are her elder sister, Mrs. Scott Lord, and her widowed daughter, Mrs. Dimmick. It is no wonder that Mrs. Harrison finds the Executive Mansion too small.

The Harrison household is run on the most methodical lines. The President himself is a meticulous man, whose desk is kept clear of confusion and litter. He complains that during his first weeks in the White House, constant interruptions have broken into his normal routine, and he is now seeking relief from the streams of callers and office seekers who are besieging him. President Harrison does not seem able to stand the grind of unceasing labor as well as his predecessor, nor to have Arthur's facility of unloading minor responsibilities upon the shoulders of his helpers.

One of the White House secretaries tells me that the business of the Executive has increased greatly since the days of Lincoln and Grant.

"Up until the time of President Hayes," he says, "hardly a scrap of paper was kept here to show what a President did or why he did it. Now we keep a record of everything, and we make a point of answering every letter. Notes are kept of the contents of all important letters received, and by our records here, in case of an appointment, we can tell just why and upon whose recommendation the appointment was made. If the appointee turns out badly, the President is relieved of the blame which is placed upon those who asked for his appointment."

President Harrison and his family usually have prayers before breakfast, which is served at about nine o'clock. Baby McKee's high chair is pulled close to his grandfather, whose affection for his small namesake is the talk of the nation. This pretty little fellow and his place in the affections of the President have been so much commented upon in the press that word has gone out to let up lest the people of this country should come to believe the tales about this child's having more influence than the members of the Cabinet.

Toys have been pouring into the White House for Benny McKee and his baby sister, Mary Lodge. His pony and cart and his favorite French mechanical dog have lately been put aside for a miniature tennis set with which he plays, with a pretty, tasseled silk tennis cap on his head, often with his grandfather a fascinated watcher. The most popular picture of Baby McKee shows him in a natty yachting cap that was specially made for him.

When the Harrisons first moved into the White House, this child had not yet learned to walk well. He still often crawled about like a crab. Many a visitor in the President's study has felt a warm little arm around his leg in the midst of his interview. One day during a conference when Benny's presence was not noticed, a roll of important papers disappeared. A frantic search was made by the President's secretary, who could not hold back a cry when he pulled the window draperies aside and found Baby McKee stirring the contents of a huge spittoon with the precious roll. Grandpa for once lost his patience with his darling child, and sent him off with his nurse, while the secretary was set to clean the brown stains off the documents.

All the Presbyterian ministers will sleep better at night now that the President has announced his choice of a place of worship. Mr. Harrison has taken a pew in the Church of the Covenant, the new Presbyterian church on the southeast corner of Connecticut Avenue and N Street in the very heart of the fashionable Northwest section of the city.

The delay in making this announcement was caused, so Dr. Scott tells me, by the joking remark of a visitor from Indiana, a friend of the President, who stated that General Harrison intended to choose no particular church, that he would go to first this one, then that one, in order to evade the curious crowds that always throng a so-called presidential church.

"I wrote to the General," said the President's father-in-law. "I told him such a course would cause criticism. I explained he could not possibly get rid of the tufthunters, and I mentioned the fact that I myself hold a pew in the Church of the Covenant."

There was no truth in the story from Indiana, but so much was made of it in the newspapers that the President put off his selection until his return to Washington.

Heaped high on the desk in a second floor room in the White House are letters from all parts of the country, asking for scraps of Mrs. Harrison's inaugural gown, written by women who are making crazy quilts. Whether they really expect her to cut up this historic costume, they do not say. Mrs. Harrison has already sent out a bushel of scraps from her ordinary gowns, those she wore to church and to parties when her husband was Senator. But the demand for this particular dress silk is so great that the weavers may be asked to produce enough more to satisfy the quiltmakers.

It does not seem to me advisable to give these women the idea that their every request will be granted. Already they are asking for locks of Mrs. Harrison's pretty brown hair. If such requests multiply and are granted, our First Lady will be shorn like that Woman's Rights crank, Dr. Mary Walker. No, there is a limit. The place for these letters is Mrs. Harrison's silk-lined waste basket.

Mrs. Harrison dresses in quiet taste. No Worth labels are found in her gowns or her jackets. All her clothes have been made either in New York or here in Washington, and she likes to do her own shopping. A milliner on a side street is today crying her eyes out because she failed to recognize the First Lady when she stepped into her store yesterday afternoon. Busy with another customer, the hatmaker paid little attention to the modestly dressed elderly lady. Mrs. Harrison stood for some time, patiently looking at the various hats, and then departed quietly. It was only from another customer who passed her on entering that the milliner learned what an opportunity she had missed.

A class of French instruction, in which many fashionable ladies are enrolled, is being held at the White House under the tutelage of a well-known French professor. This is only one of the many cultural interests of the First Lady, who is also an accomplished artist. Her most cherished project just now is a class in china painting, for which she has invited to come to Washington an expert Polish teacher from Indianapolis. With Mrs. Harrison presenting so much of her own handiwork to church bazaars and her friends, the craze for painting china has revived, and twenty-five enthusiastic ladies are already wielding their brushes upon delicate white porcelain under the direction of this gentleman. The class includes the daughters of the Vice-President, ladies of several Cabinet families, and leaders of Washington society. Their finished work is baked in Mrs. Harrison's own kiln, which she brought here from Indianapolis and which is set up in the home of Mrs. John Wight, at Kendall Green.

A certain closet at the White House is now filled with un-painted porcelain dishes, awaiting Mrs. Harrison's expert brush. Vases and platters, and many other odd pieces have been sent her by Washington ladies with the request that she decorate them, after which they will become prized heirlooms in their families. Many a baby whose parents have named him for the President has received a milk set painted by Mrs. Harrison with cunning Kate Greenaway children.

Another of her specialties is tiles that can be used as pot rests at breakfast or teatime, upon which she scatters flowers or leaves, shepherdesses or milkmaids. Lately, I am told, this accomplished Lady of the White House has decorated also candlesticks, cheese covers, crackerboxes, and flowerpot saucers, as well as milk pitchers and chocolate jugs. Invariably there will be found somewhere in her designs a tiny four-leafed clover, which serves not only to wish good luck to her friends, but as her signature.

Of all his grandmother's work, Baby McKee likes best his porcelain bathtub, which is painted with pink magnolia blossoms. Young Benny is so fond of the beautiful flowers on its sides that he can hardly sit still in the water. When he leans out to kiss them and the tub upsets, flooding the carpet, he thinks it a fine sport.

The present Mistress of the White House is about the best housekeeper that Pennsylvania Avenue mansion has yet known. Early in her occupancy she made a survey of the sanitary arrangements of the White House, which has long been said to be damp and unhealthy, and the plumbing repairs were soon begun.

There is nothing fancy about Mrs. Harrison's methods; she has none of the pretense or affectation of Washington hostesses who ape the embassies' foreign customs and cooking. The President likes the plain dishes of Dolly Johnson, the colored cook he engaged from Kentucky, better than the complicated French menus of her predecessor, Madame Pelouard. In her way Dolly Johnson, too, is an artist. With a Virginia girl named Mary to help her, she can produce a state dinner with as succulent meats and as delicate pastries as delight the patrons of Delmonico's. Both Dolly and Mary wear kerchiefs and aprons, but no caps, for livery is not tolerated in the White House.

The stories that Mrs. Harrison spends half her time in the kitchen, actually taking part in the preparation of food, are absurd, but she knows about every detail of the household, and her servants adore her. No dusty corner in the big mansion escapes her eyes, and each item of the day's menu is discussed with the steward who does the ordering and who supervises the domestic staff.

At the request of Mrs. Harrison, the President has ordered an inventory of the furniture of the Executive Mansion. Even the old bits stored away in the attic are to be listed, for Mrs. Harrison is anxious that pieces which have historic value or connection with presidential families of the past, shall be preserved. Formerly the White House steward made the decisions as to what was needed and what was not needed, and many valuable treasures have found their way out of the White House and into the auction rooms or the possession of private buyers. The source of each article is now being traced so that both its intrinsic and historical value may be determined.

One of the most interesting items that Mrs. Harrison has discovered is the gold-bordered mirror-lake that came to the White House from Paris during the administration of James

Monroe. This splendid centerpiece of gilded bronze covers thirteen and a half feet of the length of the banquet table, and the gay figures about it show dancing bacchants and bacchantes. This used to be a feature of all state table decorations, but somehow, during the reign of one of Monroe's successors, it was relegated to the storerooms.

Mrs. Harrison is concerned over the condition of the house provided for the Chief Executive and his family. She says it is far too small and too inconvenient, and she thinks something should be done about it. Her own family is not the largest which the mansion has housed, yet so much space on the second floor is now requisitioned for the Executive Offices that she is seriously inconvenienced.

"I should like to see the family of the President properly provided for," Mrs. Harrison recently said. "And while I am here I hope to be able to have the present building put into good condition. Very few people understand to what straits the President's family have been put at time for lack of accommodation. Really, there are only five sleeping apartments and there is little privacy."

Several plans have been advanced in response to the statements of Mrs. Harrison. Colonel John M. Wilson, Commissioner of Public Buildings and Grounds, recommends an office building to be erected west of the White House for the use of the President. Senator Morrill is in favor of the enlargement of the present mansion, and points to his bill for this purpose which has twice passed the Senate but which has been rejected by the House. His suggestion provides for an addition to the south.

Senator Ingalls wishes to add another story, while others have suggested an entirely separate and private dwelling house for the First Family, leaving the White House for business and official entertaining. Mrs. Harrison's own preference is for throwing out two wings. She is eager that the project be advanced rapidly so that her successor may be more comfortable than she is. She declares herself pleased with her conferences with Senators and Representatives about the White House improvements. They have assured her that they will cooperate in her laudable effort to make the White House a home, worthy of the dignity and importance of the Chief Executive of this great Republic.

Almost any afternoon you can see Benjamin Harrison driving along the streets of Washington. His turnouts are not showy, but Albert Hawkins, the Negro coachman who has had charge of the presidential stables for a quarter century, says that this President has the finest horses that have ever occupied the stalls there. There are four family horses, all Kentucky thoroughbreds, whose names are Abdullah, Billy, Lexington, and John. Three other office horses are used for delivering messages and packages to the various departments. The President's landau, with its dark green body and silver lamps, is the neatest carriage on Pennsylvania Avenue. The harness is elegant, with silver mountings, but there are no initials, no monograms and no crests. Everything about the Harrison vehicles is simple, strong, and elegant.

The President himself prefers to drive in his mail buggy, without coachman or footman. His hands hold the reins confidently, and the horses are managed with skill. Sometimes it is Mrs. Harrison, or his wife's niece, Mrs. Dimmick, who sits beside him. Often when Mrs. McKee is at the White House, she is her father's companion on his daily airing. President Harrison seldom rides alone. Usually he keeps this hour for relaxation from the affairs of state, but if there is some pressing question about which he wishes a particularly confidential talk with a Cabinet member, a messenger is sent to invite him to accompany his Chief. A presidential invitation being in the nature of a command, the two jog away toward the suburbs, deep in talk.

Last night in Willard's Hotel I had a chat with W. S. Holman, member of Congress from the President's home state of Indiana. We spent a half hour discussing the character of Benjamin Harrison, and how he is regarded by the people of Washington now that he has been in office nearly two years. Congressman Holman is experienced in politics, especially Indiana politics, for he has represented that state in Congress for more than twenty years.

"The trouble with Ben Harrison is that he is too reserved, and he has too few close friends," Judge Holman said. "Not many public men have more ardent admirers among those who know them well than the General does. Everyone respects Harrison's ability and integrity, but how many are there who have a feeling of really close friendship for him? Even in the Cabinet there is little intimacy. The President keeps his advisers at a distance, and his relations with most of them are strictly official. Often I have heard a Cabinet official say he wished someone would find out for him whether the President was pleased with the way he was handling his department; he did not know himself."

"But of course Harrison must have his 'kitchen cabinet,'" I objected. "What about Postmaster General Wanamaker? And his old Army comrade, Don Ransdell, Marshal of the District of Columbia? And his campaign manager, General Clarkson?"

"Those men are close, yes," Judge Holman agreed. "But you can count them on the fingers of one hand. And as for the general public, Harrison's dignified reserve has not aroused any great warmth or enthusiasm. The President's oldest and closest friend back home in Indianapolis is John C. New." He feels it is too bad more people do not know what a good fellow Ben Harrison really is. 'I have often gone camping with him,' Mr. New told me. 'When he's on a fishing trip, Ben takes his drink of whisky in the morning, just like anyone else. He chews tobacco from a plug he carries in his hip pocket, spits on his worm for luck, and cusses when the fish gets away.'"

In my talk with Judge Holman, I asked him whether he thought the prosperity of this present era would last. He did not seem to be too happy about conditions, particularly in his own Midwestern part of the United States.

"We're bound to have some retrenchment in government spending," he declared. "Uncle Sam is becoming a spendthrift, and his pocketbook is now open to everyone for everything. Our people have become too extravagant, and our federal taxes must be cut down. The land grants to the railroads, and the opening up of the West have taken vast amounts of capital away from the East. Farms in the Central United States have dropped thirty per cent in value in recent years."

There is no question, however, about land values here in the capital. Washington grows like a green bay tree, and it promises to double its size within the next twenty years. In 1800 this town's people numbered about 3,000; in 1810 it contained 8,200; in 1850 some 40,000; in 1860, 61,000; and in 1870, 109,000. A census taken in 1885 showed it had more than 200,000 people.*

I heard recently of a boardinghouse keeper who was offered $64,000 for a house that she had bought twenty years ago for $4,000, and there is a Negro woman on F Street whose $5,000 property recently sold for $80,000.

Brokers have grown rich off these increases in real-estate values in the fashionable Northwest and the busy downtown sections of Washington. Henry Clay's old home off Thirteenth Street is now replaced by modern Gothic stores and office buildings. The John Quincy Adams mansion on I Street is still a boardinghouse, but offices are all around and it is now sandwiched in between a grocery store and a milliner's shop, while a physician uses its parlors as his office. Fourteenth Street promises to be the great business artery of the Northwest, and land along the Boundary,† which crosses it, is worth a dollar a square foot. In the vicinity of Blaine's new house on Dupont Circle, where five years ago you could hardly give

* In 1958 the Bureau of the Census counted 825,000 people.
† Now Florida Avenue.

land away, the prices have risen from three to five dollars a foot.

Down on the Potomac Flats a number of dredges are turning what were once marshes into good solid ground. Already many acres have been redeemed, and there is the prospect that five years from now these malarial marshes, which reach from the White House to the banks of the Potomac River, will form one of the finest parks of the capital.

Just now the workers on the Flats are creating a disturbance about the hunters who shoot reedbirds and ortolans on the redeemed ground. They say the shots endanger their lives, and they ask that the city put a stop to hunting there. Reedbirds, by the way, are one of the delicacies of Washington. They are now at their fattest and tenderest. You may buy them by the bushel in the markets here at seventy-five cents a dozen. But it takes six to make one mouthful, for the Potomac reedbird of the largest size is hardly bigger than your first two fingers. Ortolans are worth the same amount, but you may eat blackbirds—and they do eat them here—for forty cents a dozen.

The fact that Washington laborers expect soon to begin work on the eight-hour-a-day plan has put up the price of building, and has caused a break in the construction boom. But the eighthour rule can hardly prevail for any length of time, so the stoppage is only temporary. In the meantime Washington real estate steadily increases in value, and the city grows like Jonah's gourd.

General James W. Denver, the man for whom Colorado's capital city is named, is a strong believer in the future growth of Washington and in its elements of prosperity. "People outside Washington," he recently said to me, "cannot understand why this city is so prosperous. They say the town has no manufactures, and no commerce on its waterfront. They can't see what it is that makes the city grow so fast. As a matter of fact,

Washington has the greatest industry in the United States, with the best-paid employees. The Government payrolls run into a total of millions of dollars a month.

"There is the money factory of the Treasury, whose three thousand workers receive an average of about a thousand dollars a year. There are the Interior Department, which has a like number of workers, the State Department, the War Department, and the Pension Office, to name only a few of the governmental institutions here.

"Then there is Congress itself, with its more than four hundred members getting five-thousand-dollar salaries and spending even more here every year on the average; also the thousand-odd people who throng the Capitol lobbies, hoping to get something. Lastly, there are the nabobs who come here from all parts of the country to make this their winter residence and to spend in Washington the income from their immense fortunes. Millions of dollars are put each year into Washington's social functions alone.

"And besides," added General Denver, "the transient element brings money into the city. Each inauguration attracts one hundred thousand visitors at least, and it is a mighty close calculator who can pass through the capital and spend less than twenty dollars. Washington thus makes two million dollars out of every change in the Administration. In addition there are the conventions, week after week, year in and year out. Today it is the dentists, tomorrow the undertakers, and the day after the scientists.

"Yes"—the General shook his head with conviction— "Washington, with its low taxation, will be the Mecca of the capitalist for years to come. It has, I believe, the best elements of growth of any city of its size in America."

INDEX

309

ABOUT THE AUTHOR

The thirty dollars a week Carp was first paid by the *Cleveland Leader* for his daily Washington columns went farther in the eighties than it would today, but even the better salary he earned as head of the Washington Bureau of the American Press Association did not go quite far enough to support a wife and small son. It was his work with the 300 papers of the Press Association that gave Carp his idea of forming his own independent syndicate, and turned his eyes to the broader horizons of world-wide correspondence.

In 1888, Frank G. Carpenter embarked with his young wife and his clumsy Caligraph typewriter upon the first of his many writing journeys around the world. The familiar name "Carp" disappeared, and during the next thirty-two years, articles by Frank G. Carpenter were read in American homes on 1600 consecutive Sundays, a record for free-lance writers perhaps even today. By-products of this constant travel for his syndicate were the *Carpenter's Geographical Readers,* which humanized the teaching of geography in our elementary schools. From these little gray-green books, millions of American children gained their first realization that faraway cities were not just round dots on a map, and that people in other parts of the world, even with their different ways of living, were a good deal like themselves.

Carp's lifetime of writing is perhaps best summed up in this tribute, written at the time of his death (1924) by his fellow-correspondents in Washington's Gridiron Club:

> Frank G. Carpenter shed a resplendent light in American journalism. Frail of body, unconquerable of spirit, daring in adventure, and with a consuming zest for travel, to wander afar was his pastime. . . . With his flowing pen he pictured the story of lands near and remote. His contributions to the press of America, his volumes of journeys, his geographical textbooks, made his name familiar to his countrymen from ocean to ocean. . . . Necessity was not the stimulus of his untiring toil. It was his inherent love of labor and effort, his

insatiable ambition to be up and doing. In distant China, fighting, he fell. Ranking among the most gifted of its members, the Gridiron Club may well affirm, with pride and affection, the memory which endureth.

ABOUT THE EDITOR

The richest inheritance Frances Carpenter had from her father was a love of travel and a desire to write as he did about ways of living in other lands. After her graduation from Smith College, she served as her father's secretary on many of his journalistic journeys. The first three of Frances Carpenter's many books in the field of elementary geography were planned under his guidance. The others, basic geographies as well as supplementary texts, followed *Carpenter's Geographical Readers* in classrooms throughout the United States. Much of the background for her books of folk tales from far countries came from her trips with her father.

In private life, Frances Carpenter is Mrs. W. Chapin Huntington, mother of two grown daughters who were born in Paris when her late husband was Commercial Attaché at the American Embassy there. She lives in Washington, where she was born, and where she has made her home most of her life.

DATE DUE

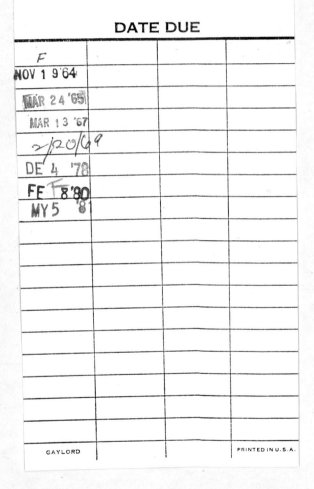

F			
NOV 1 9 '64			
MAR 2 4 '65			
MAR 1 3 '67			
2/20/69			
DE 4 '78			
FE 8 '80			
MY 5 8			
GAYLORD			PRINTED IN U.S.A.